HOW TO CLEAN PRACTICALLY ANYTHING

HOW TO CLEAN PRACTICALLY ANYTHING

REVISED EDITION

Monte Florman, Marjorie Florman, and

the Editors of Consumer Reports Books

CONSUMERS UNION

MOUNT VERNON, NEW YORK

Design by Lydia Link
Second printing, June 1990
Manufactured in the United States of America

Library of Congress Cataloging-in-Publication Data

Florman, Monte.
  How to clean practically anything/Monte Florman, Marjorie Florman, and the editors of
Consumer Reports Books.—Rev. ed.
    p. cm.
  Includes test reports, brand-name ratings, and recommendations originally prepared for
publication in Consumer reports magazine.
  Includes index.
  ISBN 0-89043-284-8
  ISBN 0-89043-344-5 (hc.)
  1. House cleaning. 2. Cleaning. I. Florman, Marjorie. II. Consumer Reports Books. III.
Consumer reports. IV. Title.
TX324.F46 1989
648'.5—dc20   89-33052
                                                                                          CIP

How to Clean Practically Anything (revised edition) is a Consumer Reports Book published by Consumers Union, the nonprofit organization that publishes *Consumer Reports*, the monthly magazine of test reports, product Ratings, and buying guidance. Established in 1936, Consumers Union is chartered under the Not-For-Profit Corporation Law of the State of New York.

The purposes of Consumers Union, as stated in its charter, are to provide consumers with information and counsel on consumer goods and services, to give information on all matters relating to the expenditure of the family income, and to initiate and to cooperate with individual and group efforts seeking to create and maintain decent living standards.

Consumers Union derives its income solely from the sale of *Consumer Reports* and other publications. In addition, expenses of occasional public service efforts may be met, in part, by nonrestrictive, noncommercial contributions, grants, and fees. Consumers Union accepts no advertising or product samples and is not beholden in any way to any commercial interest. Its Ratings and reports are solely for the use of the readers of its publications. Neither the Ratings nor the reports nor any Consumers Union publications, including this book, may be used in advertising or for any commercial purpose. Consumers Union will take all steps open to it to prevent such uses of its materials, its name, or the name of *Consumer Reports*.

Our special thanks to the following staff members for their review of the contents of this book:

Thomas Deutsch
A. Larry Seligson
David H. Tallman
Steven Taub

Contents

How this book can help you

In recent years, Americans have spent more than $5.4 billion annually on soaps and detergents. In addition, each year the public has spent approximately $1.7 billion on laundry supplies such as bleaches and fabric softeners, $2 billion on other cleaners, cleansers, and cleaning supplies, and another $3 million for waxes and polishes. Add to that $8 billion a year for washing machines, dryers, dishwashers, food disposals, and air-treatment appliances—excluding vacuum cleaners and related appliances—and the total is greater than the gross national product of some emerging nations.

If the advertising copy is to be believed, more is better: more detergents, polishes, and paper products. Appliance manufacturers promote more control settings, cycles, and gadgets that add to the appliance's price, and the hidden potential for trouble. Every extra feature contributes mechanical complication that can lead to future service problems.

Unfortunately, the public has little control over how many brands, sizes, features, colors, package variations, and other unimportant differences there are within a manufacturer's line or between one manufacturer and another. But by using *How to Clean Practically Anything*, consumers can make informed decisions that can help them get better value for their dollars and at the same time make a wise choice when they invest in a washing machine, dishwasher, or other high-ticket appliance.

In 1986, Consumer Reports Books published the first edition of *How to Clean Practically Anything*. The book featured test reports and brand-name Ratings and recommendations that were originally prepared for publication in *Consumer Reports* magazine and carefully reviewed and revised for the book. The same methods were used to prepare this revised edition of *How to Clean Practically Anything*, which updates the prior edition and presents a great deal of new product data.

How to Clean Practically Anything brings perspective to the marketplace by separating the good products from the not-so-good products. It is intended to provide a reference source that will save time, money, and effort, and help you get the best value when buying and using cleaning appliances, supplies, and accessories. In addition, *How to Clean Practically Anything* gives you practical advice on how to shop for and buy cleaning products and on the most effective ways to use them in your home. There are tips and shortcuts to help make cleaning more efficient. And if you're dealing with an emergency or difficult stain, you can check Stains and Spots on Fabrics (page 191) or Tips on How to Clean Practically Anything (page 201) for information and cleaning procedures.

How to use this book

In addition to the general advice and information about what the various products will and will not do, you'll find detailed test findings in Ratings charts. Ratings of individual brands and models are based on Consumers Union's (CU's) laboratory tests, controlled-use tests, and/or expert judgments. Although the Ratings are not an infallible guide, they do offer comparative buying information that can greatly increase the likelihood that you will receive value for your money.

Although you may be tempted to buy whatever brand appears at the top of the Ratings order, it is best to begin by reading the full product or appliance report. Then read the section that precedes the Ratings and the notes and footnotes. In those sections you will find the features, qualities, or deficiencies shared by the products in the test group.

The introduction to the Ratings tells you the basis on which the order of the Ratings was decided. When products are listed in order of estimated quality, CU judged the brand or appliance listed first to be best, the next listed second best, and so on. Sometimes, when the differences among the products were judged small and of little practical significance, products are listed alphabetically or by price. These small differences occasionally show in a subgroup of products within the Ratings. These subgroups are bracketed and also listed alphabetically or in price order. Each Ratings chart includes the month and year in which the test group appeared in *Consumer Reports*.

Check-rated models (✓) are high in quality and appreciably superior to other products tested. Best Buy Ratings are given to products that rate high and are also relatively low-priced.

Prices.   The prices for cleaning products are what was paid, or an average of what was paid, in the store by CU shoppers. It's unusual for such products to carry "list" prices, which are established and published by the manufacturer. Therefore, the price you pay will almost certainly be different, possibly substantially different, from the Ratings' price.

Appliances generally do carry list prices. They are often a fiction that enables retailers to appear to be offering a bargain by advertising prices discounted from the "list." Even so, list prices are still a useful relative guide when you are comparing prices of competing models.

Product and model changes.   Manufacturers frequently change the packaging and formulations of disposable cleaning products. Perhaps the "new" version will be more eye-catching or smell better and compete better with its rivals.

You should take advantage of sales and specials as they occur in your neighborhood. (The savings on specials offered several miles away from where you usually shop may be offset by the driving costs to get there.) When you encounter a sale, consider giving up some quality in favor of price. You may find the lesser product suits your needs, and you can always buy another brand—perhaps a better one—during the next sale. Manufacturers spend millions of dollars to encourage brand loyalty; a wise consumer ignores the sometimes transparent blandishments of a manufacturer and cultivates brand disloyalty, trading off price and quality to get value in the long run.

Cleaning appliances are marketed quite differently from disposable cleaning products. Manufacturers commonly introduce "new" models once a year, and sometimes even more frequently. The objectives are to match competition; to boost sales by offering new styles, colors, or features; and sometimes to incorporate technological changes. As a practical matter, however, retailers carry over the older models until their inventories run out. It may take months, even years, for all of the old merchandise to disappear from warehouse stocks. This slow evolution tends to keep models in the Ratings more available than might be expected.

On the other hand, the particular brand and model you select from the Ratings chart may be either out of stock or superseded by a later version when you try to buy it. The Ratings should still prove useful to help you decide what features and performance characteristics are the more important ones, and which are simply frivolous or may actually detract from a product's usefulness.

We hope *How to Clean Practically Anything* will steer you toward safe, practical, and inexpensive home cleaning products. Keep it in a handy place, thumb through it, and use it as a reference to cope with stubborn cleaning problems and narrow down choices toward purchasing products that work for you.

Cleaning the house

Outside obligations can impose significant time constraints on keeping a home at a satisfactory degree of cleanliness, let alone an ideal one. Many people may find that frequent, systematic light cleaning has advantages over periodic upheaval. For one thing, the concept of "continuous processing" applied to cleaning chores is far easier on household surfaces. It minimizes the need for abrasive cleaning and forceful scrubbing—both cause unnecessary wear and tear on wall, floor, and furniture finishes. Some may find it easier and less onerous to do a chore or two a day, rather than let tasks accumulate and become daunting.

Scheduling

A plan for continuous-process house care should start with a list of all tasks to be done during the year. These should be grouped under headings, by work to be done daily, weekly, monthly, semiannually, and annually. It may be possible to budget your time so that weekly chores are spread out over seven days. If responsibilities keep householders busy or away from home weekdays, weekly cleaning may have to accumulate until the weekend. But within limits of available time, it's a good idea to spread out household tasks as much as possible.

Not everyone feels it's necessary to live in a perfectly pristine home. What you clean and how often you do it depends on your personal preferences and tolerances. The following schedule is meant as a guideline to show how a home can be kept quite clean with well-defined cleaning tasks that are done regularly. The schedule can be modified to suit your own schedule and needs.

As much as possible, divide responsibility among all family members. Make certain everyone knows who does what task and when.

Daily. Dishes should be done and kitchen counters wiped. Clean the kitchen sink and wipe the range surfaces (including a microwave oven) after each use. You can try making pickup second nature. As you leave a room, put things away and straighten up; see if there is anything that needs to be taken where you're going. A neat house looks clean.

Once a week. Dust furniture and shelves; brush or vacuum upholstered furniture. Vacuum rugs and floors, moving furniture to clean under and behind it. Damp mop the kitchen floor. Empty wastebaskets. Wash bathroom basins, fixtures, and floors. Dust radiators, woodwork, pictures, mirrors, and lighting fixtures and bulbs. Wipe windowsills and brush shades and blinds. Clean kitchen range burners. Wipe the refrigerator and kitchen cabinet fronts. Polish bright metal surfaces.

Monthly. Do one or more of the following special jobs in several rooms on the same day: Brush curtains and draperies. Wipe wood trim and, where needed, walls and around doorknobs. Wash windows. Scrub the kitchen floor. Polish wood furniture and clean upholstered furniture as necessary, paying special attention under cushions to crevices between the back and the cushion support. To prolong their life, turn mattresses over, end to end and side to side, which will help equalize wear. In hot weather, clean air-conditioner filters according to the manufacturer's recommendations.

Seasonally or semiannually. Take inventory and get rid of items in closets and drawers that are no longer useful. (The more clutter, the harder it is to clean.)

Rearrange clothes closets by season, hanging clothes by type for easy access. Weed out unused clothing that can be contributed to appropriate agencies. Pack winter and summer clothing where it will remain clean and free from moth damage until needed again. (Dry-cleaning establishments may offer free storage for items that are given to them for cleaning.)

Wash mattress covers. Wash curtains and draperies, or have them dry cleaned. Dust the radiant coils behind or underneath the refrigerator.

Annually.   Have the furnace cleaned and tuned in late spring or early fall. A central air-conditioning system and room air conditioners should be checked out before hot weather sets in. Shampoo rugs as needed, or have it done professionally. Put power and hand gardening tools in good order, oiled and greased, before storing them for the winter. The same applies to snow removal equipment in the spring.

Equipment and storage

Arrange storage places conveniently and logically. If everything is kept in its place, it will be easier for you to work and you won't waste time looking for something when you need it. If you live in a two- or three-story dwelling, it could be worth the double investment of having supplies, including vacuum cleaners, on the same level where they are used. Keep special bathroom cleaning equipment and supplies in or near the bathroom, if space permits.

Put cleaning equipment away as clean and dry as possible, so that it's ready for the next use. Be sure that any enclosure where cleaning materials are kept has ventilation holes in the door to allow volatile materials to evaporate from cloths, sponges, and mops. Brooms and brushes should not rest on their bristles. Hang them to prevent premature wear, deformation, and loss of usefulness. Since cleaning products are hazardous, cleaning-closet shelves should be high enough to keep all cleaning supplies out of young children's reach.

Avoid cluttering a cleaning closet with rarely used supplies and equipment, but lay in a supply of paper vacuum-cleaner dust bags. Use the brand that is recommended for your particular vacuum; off-brand bags may not work well. You may also want to stock spare sponge-mop refills, as well as a package or two of hand sponges.

Good dust cloths can be made from cast-off soft cotton garments and bedding. (Although they are costlier to use, less effective than cloth, and harsh on some surfaces, some people find paper towels convenient.) Cloths will hold dust better if they are pretreated. A simple method is to put a cloth into a screw-cap glass jar that has been coated on the inside with furniture polish. Put about two teaspoons of liquid polish into a container and turn it until a thin layer of polish covers the inside surface. Let the cloth stand in the jar a day or two.

Another solution

House cleaning takes up time and effort. One obvious way to escape from it, although the solution can be expensive, is to employ a qualified, reliable, and courteous home-cleaning service. Some people use a professional service once or twice a year; others employ a cleaning person once a week or every two weeks or so. If you decide to use professional help, ask for referrals from reliable neighbors and friends. If that fails, check the *Yellow Pages* under House Cleaning. Always ask for and check references before hiring a cleaning service or person.

Dishes

DISHWASHER DETERGENTS

Liquid dishwasher detergents appeared on store shelves two years ago. Now, all the big-name detergents—*Electrasol, Cascade, Palmolive*, and *Sunlight*—come in liquid form. Liquid detergents are supposed to solve the problems associated with powders. They supposedly do not cake up in the box or in the dishwasher's dispenser cup, or deposit grit on the dishes. Unfortunately they are not as good at dishwashing as powdered detergents and they are less convenient than they may at first seem.

Unlike dishwashing liquids sold for washing dishes by hand, "liquid" dishwasher detergents aren't really liquid. If they were, they would wash out of the dispenser cup before the dishwasher had finished the first cycle. The products are actually gels containing fine, powdered clay and other suspended solids that make them thick enough to stay in the dispenser cup when you close the dishwasher door. Despite that innovation in form, the new liquids closely resemble the old powders in substance. All dish-

1

washer detergents use chemical surfactant to loosen dirt and disperse fats. Other substances, called builders (usually phosphates), soften the water to help the surfactants work. Most products also contain bleach to break down proteins, remove stains, and keep dishes free of film and water spots.

Dishwasher detergents may also include specialized ingredients to protect metal utensils, colored decorations on china, and the metal parts in the dishwasher as well. Many contain perfume (even those labeled unscented) to disguise the chemical smell of the other ingredients.

A detergent's cleaning power depends on more than its formulation. Soft water, a good dishwasher, and thoroughly rinsed dishes can make any detergent perform well.

In Consumers Union's most recent tests, the best performers were powders. In general, name-brand products cleaned better than store brands and were less likely to leave glass plates and tumblers clouded or spotty. Spots are a particular problem when you have hard water. Using a rinse agent in the dishwasher can help reduce spots and film.

The liquid detergents cleaned fairly well in the tests, but none was as good as the best powders at keeping glasses free of water spots and food debris. Powder users who try a liquid, perhaps in hopes that it will eliminate detergent left on their glasses, may find themselves trading grit for film. Grit and film, usually composed of undissolved detergent, are generally signs that the detergent is stale and has picked up moisture or that the water isn't hot enough. (For best results, detergent manufacturers recommend using water heated to 140°F; Consumers Union did in our tests.)

No matter what kind of detergent is used in the machine, it's safer to hand-wash good china. Harsh detergents can wear away overglaze, the colored, somewhat dull decoration that is applied after the main glaze on some fine china. Overglaze is fired at a lower temperature than the main glaze and thus is less durable. Gilding and other metallic decorations also tend to wear away more quickly when machine washed. A harsh detergent isn't the only danger in the dishwasher, where forceful water or a jostling pan might topple stemware or chip a saucer.

RATINGS OF DISHWASHER DETERGENTS

Listed in order of overall cleaning ability based on laboratory tests in hard water. Differences between closely ranked products were slight. Products judged about equal in quality are bracketed and listed alphabetically. Unless otherwise noted, products came in a 50-ounce container.

As published in a **February 1988** report.

Key to rating symbols: ● Excellent ◓ Very good ○ Good ◒ Fair ● Poor

Brand and model	Price	Cost per use	Plates	Glasses	Preventing spots	Gliding	Disadvantages
Electrasol	$1.99	2.9¢	◓	◓	◓	◓	—
Cascade	2.41	3.1	◓	◓	◓	◓	B
White Magic (Safeway)	2.19	2.8	◓	◓	○	◓	—
White Magic lemon (Safeway)	2.19	2.8	◓	◓	◓	○	—
Cascade lemon	2.29	3.1	◓	○	◓	◓	B
Lady Lee (Lucky)	1.99	2.2	◓	◓	○	○	—
Palmolive liquid	2.49	4.1	◓	○	○	◓	—
Sunlight lemon	1.99	2.6	◓	○	○	○	—
Cascade liquid [1]	2.34	5	◓	○	○	◓	A
Electrasol liquid	1.99	4.1	◓	○	○	◓	C
Finish	2.39	3.4	◓	○	○	◓	B
Palmolive liquid lemon	2.39	4.1	◓	○	○	◓	A
Western Family lemon	1.65	2.2	◓	◓	○	○	D
Kroger Bright	2.14	2.7	◓	◓	○	○	—
A&P	1.49	2.1	◓	○	○	◓	A,D
All	2.02	2.7	◓	○	○	○	—
Kroger Bright lemon [2]	2.39	2.2	◓	○	○	○	—
Topco	1.99	2.6	○	○	○	○	A,D
Cost Cutter (Kroger)	1.13	1.5	◓	○	○	○	A,B,D
A&P lemon	1.49	1.7	○	○	○	○	A,D
Pathmark	1.59	1.9	○	○	○	○	A,C
Pathmark lemon	1.59	1.9	○	○	○	○	A,C
No Frills (Pathmark)	1.39	1.8	○	○	○	◓	A,B,C,D

[1] Came in a 40-oz. container. [2] Came in a 65-oz. container.

Key to Disadvantages
A–Worse than most at removing lipstick from glasses.
B–Damaged colored overglaze more than most.
C–Left a heavier film than most on glasses.
D–Left more water spots than most on glasses.

Convenience

Advertising for liquids focuses on their convenience. But liquids introduce a few inconveniences of their own. They tend to separate, leaving a watery layer on top; you have to give them a good shake before you use them. Also, detergent bottles aren't like toothpaste tubes. When you run low, you can't squeeze the last bit of gel out of the container. Even balancing a bottle on its cap between uses will not increase the yield by much.

Liquids are more expensive to use than powders, a fact that is not readily apparent from the packaging. A 50-ounce jug of liquid detergent costs about the same as a 50-ounce box of a name-brand powder; both types are sold by weight. But the liquid is more dense than the powder, so you'll use more of it each time you fill the dispenser cup.

Recommendations

If you have a good dishwasher and soft water, and if you rinse your dishes before loading them into the machine, chances are any detergent will do a satisfactory job. Look for a good price; a name brand on sale can be cheaper than a supermarket's own brand. You might want to try a liquid if you live in a humid climate, where powdered products cake up, or if powdered detergents do not dissolve completely in your machine.

DISHWASHING LIQUIDS

People who do not own a dishwashing machine probably use a dishwashing liquid for all their dishwashing chores. But machine users, too, find a need for the product, even if only for their fine crystal, overglazed china, and other tableware that could be damaged by harsh chemicals in dishwasher detergents. Many people use dishwashing liquid outside the kitchen, where it excels at washing fine fabrics, children, and even the family car. Some use it as shampoo or bubble bath, since it's pleasantly scented and one of the mildest detergents available. For whatever use, consumers spend more than a billion dollars a year on dishwashing liquids—twice as much as they spend on detergents for the dishwasher.

Many supermarkets carry their own brand, and there are regional brands as well, which, along with the store brands, are usually a bit cheaper than national brands. A store's generic product is cheapest of all. But the price does not necessarily correlate with the cost of using a detergent. Used generously enough, any dishwashing liquid will get dishes clean. But depending on the concentration of the cleaning agent, one teaspoon of Brand A may clean three times as many dishes as Brand B. A $1 product is no bargain if you need three bottles to do the washing up another product can do with one $2 bottle.

Detergent effectiveness

Detergents work by loosening greasy soil and keeping it suspended so it can be rinsed away. Once saturated with soil, the suds vanish, and the detergent's cleaning power vanishes with them. When there are no more suds, the detergent has exhausted its cleaning power.

The best products are about six times more effective than the worst—a given quantity of the best will wash about six times more dishes than the same quantity of the worst. Many brands are sold in more than one color, which complicates matters. In some brands, different colors have different prices. A brand's colors usually performed identically, but not always.

Calculating cost

Consumers Union's technologists based their evaluations on an Effectiveness Index derived from the tests. They used the index to calculate the real cost of a product.

DISHWASHING LIQUID REAL-COST CALCULATOR

As published in a **March 1988** report.

As you shop, apply the Efficiency Index to a bottle of any of the tested products to find the real cost:

Price × Index = Real cost

Index: **1**
A&P Green
Kroger Lemon
Palmolive Original
Palmolive Lemon/Lime
White Magic
Joy
Sunlight
Ivory
Dawn

Index: **2.1**
A&P White
White Octagon
White Octagon Lemon
Dove
Lux

Index: **3.1**
Pathmark Lemon
Pathmark Emerald
Lady Lee Pink
Lady Lee Lemon
Sweetheart Pink
Lemon Trend
Par (Lemon)

Index: **1.4**
A&P Lemon
A&P Blue
Kroger Blue
Dermassage
Ajax

Index: **6.3**
No Frills Lemon
No Frills White
Cost Cutter Pink
Cost Cutter Lemon

Overall, the "low-priced" liquids cost quite a bit more than you might expect. Consider one product priced at 49 cents for a 32-ounce bottle. It was the cheapest detergent tested. But multiplying that price by an Effectiveness Index of 6.3 gives $3.09—the real cost of using a product with poor cleaning strength.

You can use the Effectiveness Indexes in the real-cost calculator to compute the real cost of any of the tested products, regardless of bottle size or the prices in your store. To compare bottles that are not 32 ounces, use the unit price in your calculations.

The Effectiveness Index cannot save you money if you overuse detergent, especially a highly concentrated one. Most of the bottles have a squeeze-out top, and it's easy to squeeze out more than you need. Many cleanups require no more than a full teaspoon of detergent in a sinkful of water. To be extremely efficient, measure out the detergent with a spoon. Brands with screw-on caps might encourage such economy. If a product has a screw cap with a snip-off dispensing tip, don't snip and squeeze. Unscrew the top and dispense by the spoonful, which is a less wasteful practice in the long run than giving the bottle a healthy squeeze.

Gentleness

According to claims made for some products, a dishwashing detergent is "a lotion" that "softens hands while you do dishes," "pampers your hands," or even provides "protein protection for hands that do dishes." In fact, in the same way that they remove the grease from your pots, detergents remove the skin's natural oils. Whatever their claimed content, aloe or lanolin, for example, detergents dry the skin. Some can even irritate it. You may want to wear protective gloves when washing up.

Many labels tout the presence of "real lemon juice" in the product. Lemon seems to help sell almost any cleaning product. Lemon juice can help remove some food residues, but only if the juice is present in sufficient quantity, and only if allowed enough soak time.

A typical detergent has a lemony, flowery, or herbal smell. The scent sells soap. It may also mask the odor of a detergent's ingredients, which can be disagreeable. It may even make the job more pleasant. But a scent may simply make your hands break out in a rash; switch brands if that happens.

Some products warn you not to use them with chlorine bleach. Their ingredients may react with bleach to produce noxious gases, dangerous to those with asthma and other respiratory problems. To be safe, never mix any household cleaning product with bleach.

The Rated products are biodegradable and pose no threat to the environment. If ingested, they can cause mouthburn, vomiting, or diarrhea. Keep the detergent bottle inaccessible to young children.

RATINGS OF DISHWASHING LIQUIDS

Listed by groups in order of Effectiveness Index; within groups, listed in order of increasing real cost. Except as noted, all came in a 32-oz. plastic bottle with pull-up or pop-open dispenser cap. Prices are calculated for a 32-oz. bottle, even if sold in another size.

As published in a **March 1988** report.

Product	Price	Real cost

■ *The following products had an Effectiveness Index of 1.*

Product	Price	Real cost
A&P Green Dishwashing Lotion, A Best Buy	$1.34	$1.34
Kroger Lemon Scented, A Best Buy	1.44 ①	1.44
Palmolive Original/Palmolive Lemon Lime	1.79	1.79
White Magic Liquid	1.85	1.85
Joy	1.99	1.99
Sunlight	1.99	1.99
Ivory Liquid	2.16	2.16
Dawn	2.19	2.19

■ *The following products had an Effectiveness Index of 1.4.*

Product	Price	Real cost
A&P Lemon Dish Detergent	.99	1.39
A&P Blue Dish Detergent	1.34	1.88
Kroger Crystal Blue	1.44 ①	2.02
Dermassage	1.69	2.37
Ajax	1.87	2.62

■ *The following products had an Effectiveness Index of 2.1.*

Product	Price	Real cost
A&P White Dishwashing Lotion	.99	2.08
Crystal White Octagon Regular ②	1.07 ①	2.25
Crystal White Octagon Lemon Fresh ②	1.25 ①	2.63
Dove	1.69	3.55
Lux	1.69	3.55

■ *The following products had an Effectiveness Index of 3.1.*

Product	Price	Real cost
Pathmark Lemon	.89	2.76
Pathmark Emerald	.99	3.07
Lady Lee Lotion Pink/Lady Lee Lotion Lemon	1.09	3.38
Sweetheart (Sudsy Pink)	1.16 ①	3.60
Lemon Trend	1.29	4.00
Par (Lemon Scented)	1.44 ①	4.46

■ *The following products had an Effectiveness Index of 6.3.*

Product	Price	Real cost
No Frills Lemon/No Frills White Lotion	.49	3.09
Cost Cutter Pink/Cost Cutter Lemon Freshened ②	.69	4.35

① *Calculated from price for 22- or 40-oz. bottles; 32-oz. size unavailable.* ② *Has screw-off cap.*

MACHINE DISHWASHERS

The most conspicuous difference between dishwashers of the same brand name is in the controls. The more expensive the machine, the more buttons and cycles it has. Top-of-the-line models often have a touch panel instead of push buttons or a dial; they often have an electronic timer, too. As you go down a manufacturer's line, you get progressively fewer cycles and control options. Basic models are apt to have only one cycle, a dial control, and a switch for no-heat drying.

Dish racks tend to get fancier as you go up a brand line. All dishwashers have two rolling racks of plastic-coated wire, plus a flatware basket or two. The fancier models usually have especially handy racks, such as an adjustable upper rack that can be set higher to provide extra clearance for oversized dishes below, or set lower so that tall glasses can be fitted in. With an upscale model, you may get a rack that lets you double stack cups or an extra flatware basket. Occasionally, a basic model offers one of those conveniences as an option.

Despite changing features, the wash system is often the same throughout a line. It consists of arms that rotate like lawn sprinklers to shower the dishes, a pump to circulate water through the arms and eventually down the drain, and, often, filters to trap food particles. Some brands reserve the most sophisticated and effective systems for the more expensive models.

The surest protection against internal corrosion is a stainless-steel interior. In theory, the solid plastic tub on some models should do as well. The porcelain coating on the other models will resist scratches very well, but it can be chipped by impact, exposing underlying metal to corrosion. Plastic-tub and some porcelain-tub models feature a plastic panel for the door's inner surface. Plastic is a good material for an area otherwise likely to be damaged by dropped items.

Loading and convenience

Cups and glasses typically go into the top rack and plates into the lower one, but there are exceptions. Most machines accommodate nearly twelve place settings. A few can hold thirteen to fourteen settings because their rack arrangements are more ingenious.

Some machines have fold-down shelves in their upper rack that let you make two-tier stacks of cups and squat glasses. Others have a row of pickets along the sides of the upper rack to hold additional cups. Those pickets are especially handy when you entertain. Glasses as tall as 7 to 7½ inches fit in most upper racks. In a few machines, you can angle or fold down some of the upper rack's dividers to accommodate specific items, such as a large mug or an odd-shaped bowl.

You generally slot plates into the lower rack in simple rows. But plates go into several models at right angles to each other, which may involve some rearranging if you do not anticipate the spacing required. Dinner plates typically run 9 to 10 inches in diameter; 11-inch plates, about the upper limit for common patterns, should fit any machine. There are models, however, that have a stepped upper rack that provides headroom for an oversized platter or two.

Flatware baskets generally fit into the lower rack, usually toward the front. It is wise to load knives and even forks into them prongs-down to avoid cutting yourself as you reach around the baskets to load or unload dishes. You may want to remove a flatware basket for more convenient loading on a counter; a carrying handle is a plus for that purpose. Some machines have one large basket, others have two half-size units. There's usually a covered section or two to keep baby-bottle nipples, corn-cob holders, and other small items from being swept away.

In some machines, a filter keeps troublesome bits and pieces of food from being redeposited on dishes. Many machines have a blade in the pump that cuts scraps into particles that will be washed away, in some cases with the help of a flywheel device in the pump.

Dishwasher features

There are a number of features that can enhance a dishwasher's usefulness.

Cycles. Cycle names such as Pot Scrubber, Super Scrub, and China/Crystal may lead you to think the machine can handle practically anything. It's not quite true. A dishwasher cycle is basically a combination of washes and rinses. The typical Normal cycle includes two washes and two or three rinses. Then the heating element in the bottom of the cabinet dries the dishes, unless you switch it off to save energy.

To create a Heavy or Pots-and-Pans cycle, a manufacturer might extend the wash periods, add a third wash, make the water hotter, or combine those factors. A Light cycle typically has only one wash. Water in a China/Crystal cycle may be pumped through the wash arms with reduced force.

Some models have a Sani-cycle setting meant to assure extra-hot water for the final rinse. The cycle does not make dishes any more healthful. "Sanitized" dishes are not sterilized. Even if they were, they'd quickly pick up household microbes again when you stored them in the cupboard.

To increase the number of cycles, a manufacturer may include a couple of optional phases and count each cycle more than once, or a part of an existing cycle can be renamed as a separate cycle. If a machine runs through its first wash cycle and then drains and stops, you have a Rinse-and-Hold cycle. A setting that merely turns on the heating element yields a Plate Warmer cycle.

Although Rinse and Hold might have some use for small families that accumulate dishes slowly, most other extra cycles do not add much to a washer's utility. You should think twice about subjecting good crystal or china, especially pieces with gold trim, to harsh dishwasher detergents and possible jostling, even in a special China/Crystal cycle. A Heavy cycle will not spare you effort; pots and pans are apt to emerge little cleaner than they would on the Normal cycle. Loading a dishwasher with lots of pots, pans, and baking dishes also uses the space inefficiently.

All in all, you really need only two or three cycles—Normal, Heavy, and perhaps Light—to handle all the loads you can reasonably expect a machine to wash.

Water-heating option. Some machines let you select a special cycle with extra water heating. Others allow setting the machine to boost the water temperature for the standard or other cycles. Boosting water temperature helps maintain cleaning performance if you have lowered your water heater's thermostat setting. Models without a temperature control may boost the water temperature automatically.

Drying blower. A drying blower is common on higher-priced models, and not essential. But models that have it should dry dishes a little better than would otherwise similar models.

Delayed start. If you can preset a machine for later operation, you can reduce energy costs if you have a low off-peak electricity rate. Machine noise late at night may prove annoying, however.

Rinse-conditioner dispenser. These devices inject conditioning agent into the final rinse. Conditioner helps water run off the loads, reducing spots from hard water and aiding drying.

Construction. Porcelain-coated steel resists abrasion better than solid plastic, but it can be chipped. Plastic can withstand substantial impact without damage. Stainless steel can be dented, but is the most durable interior surface of all.

Door-color options. Machines generally come with one or more reversible door panels that provide you with a choice of colors.

Convertible/portable version. These machines can be bought for immediate use as a portable, and can be converted to allow under-counter installation later.

Energy costs

Running a dishwasher takes roughly one-half to one kilowatt hour (kwh) of electricity per cycle, costing about 5 to 9 cents per load at the national average electricity rate of 8.2 cents per kwh, or less than $30 a year. Letting dishes air-dry won't save you much, only about 2½ cents a load at average electricity rates, or about $8 a year.

The largest energy cost of dishwashing is incurred at the water heater. The higher the water heater's temperature setting, the more it costs to heat a tankful of water and to keep it hot. A change from 140° to 120°F can save you about $35 a year with an electric water heater, about $12 with gas, and about $14 with oil, at national average utility rates.

Dishwashers need 140°F water to liquefy some fats and dissolve detergent fully. If the water isn't hot enough, the machine boosts the water temperature and often runs longer, at least for one wash period. On many models, you set a control to provide that boost. Others provide the boost as part of the normal cycle. The most sophisticated models are controlled with a thermostat and heat the water only when needed. It's worth trying any dishwasher with 120°F water to find out how well it performs. You can always turn the water heater back to 140°F if necessary.

You can also save money by choosing a machine with attentiveness to its water use. Some models use 12 gallons in a typical two-wash cycle, an amount that will cost about $68 a year if heated with electricity, $24 a year with gas, or $29 a year with oil. Buying a machine that uses only 9½ gallons can save you 800 gallons of water and about $5 to $14 a year in water-heating costs.

Brand reliability

The average dishwasher lasts about 11 years and is run 322 times annually. To get an indication of how reliable a given brand may be during its life span, *Consumer Reports* readers were asked how trouble free their machines have been. The findings shown here are based on the experiences of more than 135,000 responses from Consumers Union's 1986 Annual Questionnaire. All machines are built-in models that were bought new, without a service contract, between 1978 and 1986.

Repair problems increased with a dishwasher's age and frequency of use. Only 13 percent of people who wash three loads or less a week had ever needed to repair the dishwasher. But an average of four to six loads a week meant that about 18 percent of the dishwashers needed service at some time or other, and seven to nine loads a week brought the percentage to 25. In creating the repair indexes the data were adjusted to compensate for the effects of age and frequency of use.

RATINGS OF DISHWASHERS

Listed by groups in order of overall washing ability with 140°F water. Within groups, listed in order of estimated quality.
As published in a June 1987 report.

Better ← ● ◑ ○ ◐ ● → Worse

Brand and model	Price	China	Flatware	Glasses	Overall, 140° water	Overall, 120° water	140° water	120° water	Noise	Energy-efficiency	With 140° water, min.	With 120° water, min.	Water consumption, gal.	Advantages	Disadvantages	Comments
General Electric GSD2800G	$571	●	●	●	●	○	●	○	◑	○	80	95	10.5	A,C,F,G,I	—	C
KitchenAid KUDC210	499	●	●	●	●	○	●	○	○	○	80	80	9.5	—	—	E
KitchenAid KUDS21C	565	●	●	●	●	○	●	○	○	○	65	65	9.5	C,F,G	c	C,E
General Electric GSD1200G	515	●	●	●	●	○	◑	○	◑	○	80	90	11	F,G	c	—
Amana DU6000	471	●	●	●	●	○	●	○	◑	○	80	90	10	—	—	—
Wards 1066	419	●	●	●	◑	○	◑	○	○	○	75	75	12	D,G,J	—	A,B
White-Westinghouse SU550J	346	●	●	●	◑	○	◑	○	○	○	75	75	12	D,G,J	—	A,B
Frigidaire DW3300D	344	●	●	●	◑	—	◑	○	○	○	75	—	12	D,G,J	—	A,B
Gibson SU24D5KT	330	●	●	●	◑	—	—	○	○	○	75	—	12	D,G,J	—	A,B
Kelvinator DWU4005D	358	●	●	●	◑	○	◑	○	○	○	75	75	12	D,J	—	A,B
Maytag WU1000	617	◑	◑	◑	—	○	◑	◑	◑	◑	75	—	11.5	C,F,H,J	—	C,D,E,H
Jenn-Air DU471	529	◑	◑	◑	◑	○	◑	◑	◑	◑	80	120	11.5	C,F,H,J	—	D,E,H
Maytag WU502	483	◑	◑	◑	◑	○	◑	◑	◑	◑	75	85	11.5	C,F,H,J	f	D,E,F,H
Whirlpool DU6000XR	407	○	◑	○	◑	○	◑	○	◑	◑	60	110	9.5	G,J	—	E
Whirlpool DU9500XR	597	◑	◑	◑	●	◑	◑	○	◑	◑	65	110	11	G,J	c	E
Panasonic NP408U	401	○	◑	○	○	○	◑	○	○	○	70	90	10	—	h	—
Caloric DUS205	327	◑	○	○	○	○	○	○	○	◑	60	80	10.5	—	f,h	B

Brand & Model													
General Electric GSD500D	302	◑	○	◑	○	◑	85	90	11	B,G	b	I
Waste King WKD2700	559	○	○	○	○	○	65	85	11.5	F	e,g	—
Thermador THD2800	610	◑	○	◑	○	○	65	85	11.5	F	e,g	—
Sears Kenmore 16565	483	◑	○	◑	○	◑	75	95	10	E	e,h	—
Whirlpool DU3000XR	304	○	○	○	○	—	65	—	11	J	a,b,d	E,G
Magic Chef DU80	390	○	◑	○	◑	—	70	—	11.5	B,G	e	—
Hotpoint HDA897	377	◑	○	◑	○	●	70	75	9	G	e	—

Specifications and Features

All: ● Use only hot water supplied at about 15 to 125 psi. ● Require about 34½x24x24 in. (HxWxD) for installation, and 24- to 26-in. clearance to open door. ● Have switch to select no-heat drying with any wash cycle. ● Have dial or display that shows progress through cycles. ● Have heating element under lower rack that can pose a burn hazard when hot.

Except as noted all: ● Have at least Heavy, Normal, and Light wash cycles, plus a Rinse-and-Hold cycle or provision for setting same. ● Have filters that were essentially self-cleaning. ● Have a rinse-conditioner dispenser and 1 full or 2 half-size flatware baskets. ● Require 120-volt, 15-amp circuit.

Key to Advantages

A–Has systems monitor with numerous displays and printed messages about various malfunctions; also has energy-monitor display and hidden pad for locking controls to prevent tampering.

B–Accepts large dinner plates (up to 12 in.) better than most.

C–Accepts very tall glasses better than most.

D–Upper rack has pickets that allow 2-tier stacking of cups and small glasses.

E–Upper rack has removable dish cradle and additional utensil and small-item baskets.

F–Flatware basket(s) has covered section(s).

G–Flatware basket has convenient handle.

H–Dual fill valves give extra protection against accidental overfills and flooding.

I–Automatic drain action gives extra protection against accidental overfills and flooding.

J–Chassis has wheels (*Whirlpool* models) or "shoes" to make unit easier to move during installation or servicing.

Key to Disadvantages

a–Did not dry flatware as well as others.

b–Lacks Heavy cycle.

c–Has electronic or nonaccessible timer. Canceling a cycle takes about 2 min. for *Whirlpool;* takes about 1 min. for *General Electric* and *Amana* and dumps detergent from closed cup.

d–Filter likely to require routine cleaning.

e–Cannot take tall glasses as well as most.

f–Lower rack on CU's sample moved stiffly.

g–Door latch on CU's sample was very stiff.

h–Door latch on CU's sample was stiff.

Key to Comments

A–Did not dry glasses as well as most when supplied with 120° water.

B–Did not dry flatware as well as most when supplied with 120° water.

C–Has electronic timer, but canceling a cycle takes only 30 sec. or less.

D–Upper rack takes large plates; lower takes cups and glasses.

E–Some water may splash out if door is opened quickly during wash cycle.

F–Tested with optional rinse-conditioner dispenser.

G–No rinse-conditioner dispenser; tested with solid conditioner attached to dishrack.

H–Requires 20-amp circuit.

I–According to the mfr., this model was replaced by the *GSD500G,* which has 7 fills instead of 6 in normal cycle.

15

MACHINE DISHWASHER REPAIR INDEX BY BRAND

As published in a **June 1987** report.

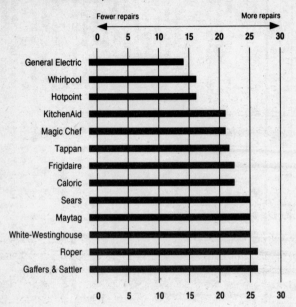

Differences between closely ranked brands in the chart are not very significant. But a difference of about five points or more is meaningful.

The analysis, of course, deals with the past, not the future. Changes in design or a company's ownership can alter a brand's long-term performance. The data apply to the brand of dishwasher; individual models within a brand could vary. Still, the data are consistent enough to improve your chances of buying a reliable dishwasher.

Floors

CARPET SHAMPOOING

The most important tool in taking care of a carpet is a good vacuum cleaner. An upright or a canister vacuum with a power nozzle is best for dislodging the grit that works its way deep into the carpet and grinds away at the fibers. A lightweight upright cleaner is all right, however, for quick pickup of surface litter.

In a room that is used routinely, it's best to do the traffic lanes a couple of times a week and the entire carpet at least once a month. Move the vacuum slowly, giving it a chance to suck up the dirt it dislodges.

Do-it-yourself cleaning

Sooner or later, vacuuming just won't do the job. That's when you have to resort to chemical cleaners. You can forestall cleaning the entire carpet by cleaning just dirty areas. Dry carpet-cleaning products are best for that. Some are powders, others are foams. You rub them in, let them dry, and vacuum.

Shampooing an entire carpet yourself is a tiring, somewhat tricky chore. Still, using a supermarket-variety cleaning shampoo can help keep carpets looking bright and stave off the need for commercial cleaning.

Most makers provide two shampoo types: a concentrated liquid that is diluted with water, and an aerosol spray foam. The liquids are applied with a sponge mop or an electric shampooer and worked into the carpet nap. Some foams also have to be worked in; others don't.

Cleaning effectiveness

A rug shampoo is primarily a surface cleaner. The main active ingredient is detergent, which is whipped into a froth by the scrubbing and left to dry. When you vacuum, you pick up dried detergent and whatever dirt it has trapped. The more thoroughly you vacuum, the more of the dirt and detergent residue you recover. Inevitably, some of the mixture will remain—and may foam up if you use a steam-cleaning machine later on.

Shampooing a relatively new rug can produce pleasing results. If the rug is in bad shape before you clean it, however, you may be disappointed with its appearance afterward. Worn areas and matted nap can become more obvious once the surface dirt has been removed.

Some shampoos claim to resist resoiling. At best, a shampoo can leave a residue that may help prevent a carpet from attracting and holding dirt. At worst, the residue can become a tacky glue that cements dirt to the fibers.

Time and effort

Carpet shampooing is a big job. The furniture should be removed or set up on foil or wax paper "booties" to protect both the furniture and the carpet from stains. Applying the shampoo to a large carpet can take hours, and the carpet will be out of service until it dries—anywhere from a couple of hours to overnight. If you can't close off the room until the carpet dries, you'll have to shampoo in sections.

Furthermore, rug shampooing takes a knack. Label instructions are simple enough, but you have to make allowances for the carpet's pile and the equipment you're using. For example, a high-pile rug should be stroked against the nap after shampooing to help the drying process and to restore the appearance of the pile. You have to learn through experience how big a patch you should tackle each time. And you have to take care not to soak the carpet, because that could induce shrinkage and might bring on stains or a mildew growth. It's easy to acquire the knack, but you ought to practice first on an area of the rug that is hidden from view. And try to keep the room well ventilated to accelerate drying.

Choose an area of the rug that is inconspicuous to check the rug dye for colorfastness before trying a new shampoo. A simple test is to moisten a white rag with shampoo (diluted if you're using a liquid) and rub it against the rug. If the cloth does not pick up color, go ahead and shampoo.

HOT WATER EXTRACTION OR "STEAM" CLEANING

◈ For house calls, professional rug cleaning companies sometimes use a "hot water extraction" method that sprays hot, wet detergent solution into the rug and then vacuums away the solution and dislodged dirt. Small hot water extraction machines can usually be rented from supermarkets and hardware stores. They are often called "steam-cleaning" machines, even though they actually use hot water.

The typical machine has two reservoirs, one for cleaning solution, the other for the dirty liquid. Depending on the machine and the amount of soil in the carpet, a tankful of cleaning solution should last from fifteen to twenty minutes.

The machine you rent will take a little practice to handle. It is smaller than the professional variety, but still cumbersome. If you follow the instructions carefully, you should do all right. The machines usually don't require more effort than an electric rotary brush shampooer.

A steam machine should work much better on very dirty or matted rugs than any ordinary rug shampoo, but will probably not do as well as a thorough professional cleaning. For lightly soiled rugs, you'll probably be just as satisfied using a shampoo with a rotary brush shampooer and a good vacuum cleaner.

Shampoo products are strong detergents that may irritate the skin or eyes. They should be used carefully. Check for spatters on furniture and woodwork. Wipe them up quickly.

Price

The price per quart has little to do with the real cost of the shampoo. That's because of the differences in the amount of shampoo it takes to do the job. The optimum amount of shampoo will produce an even application of foam, but that optimum amount can vary quite a bit from product to product. Deep-pile carpets, with their heavy dirt loads, usually require more shampoo than the label recommends, especially with a spray foam.

Recommendations

Maintain the life and good appearance of carpeting by vacuuming it thoroughly and regularly. Don't shampoo rugs more often than necessary, but do shampoo before they get very dirty or matted. Once rugs reach that state, it's unlikely that any cleaners will do a satisfactory job in one application. If your carpet is heavily soiled, you'd better call in a professional or rent a steam-cleaning machine from a local store.

If your carpeting isn't very dirty, then a shampoo may brighten it noticeably.

In order to make a difficult job more tolerable, consider renting a machine to work in the detergent foam, a wet/dry vacuum cleaner, or a machine that combines those functions.

How well the carpet is cleaned depends greatly on the skill of the operator—amateur or professional. Used carelessly, the rotating brushes of the carpet shampooer can abrade the pile. And if the carpet gets too soaked, it could shrink.

If you have an Oriental, antique, or costly varicolored wool rug, it's best to leave the cleaning to specialists in that type of rug. You have no recourse if you damage the rug when cleaning it yourself.

CARPET FIRST AID FOR STAINS FROM SPILLS

◈ Clean up spills fast. With some spilled substances—children's fruit drinks, for instance—you have only minutes before the stain sets permanently. Here are some suggestions for carpet first aid: First, before using anything, test it on a carpet scrap or in an area hidden from view—in the corner of a closet, for instance.

Have on hand a dry-cleaning solvent (from the supermarket or hardware store) for greasy, oily stains (see page 193). But be careful about using a solvent-based cleaner on a rug that has a plastic or rubber foam backing or separate padding. The solvent could soften such materials and ruin them. Use a detergent solution (one teaspoon dishwashing liquid per cup of water) for water-soluble spills. For spills that are both greasy and water-soluble, use the dry-cleaning solvent first and then the detergent solution. Do the same for unidentified spills.

Blot or scrape up as much as possible. Then cover the spill with a pad of several paper towels and stand on the towels for a minute or so. Then apply the cleaning solution—the dry-cleaning solvent to a rag or paper towel, the detergent solution directly on the carpet. Don't overwet the carpet. Blot, don't rub. Repeat those steps until the spill is cleaned up. Cover the wet spot with a half-inch pad of paper towels, weight it down, and let the rug dry.

For stains with an offensive odor such as pet urine, use a solution of one part white vinegar to two parts water, blot, then use the detergent solution. For acidic stains such as vomit or fruit drinks, use a solution of one tablespoon ammonia in a half cup of water to neutralize the acid (but don't use ammonia on wool, as it sets stains on that material).

Some people believe in the effectiveness of soda water. Perhaps the bubbles help "lift" the stain, but professional cleaners assert that soda water works no better than ordinary water.

Copious spills that penetrate through the carpet to the backing and even to the floor are a special problem. If the substance is one that smells, you may have to have the carpet lifted and cleaned professionally.

Household products that contain bleach, hydrogen peroxide, or some other oxidizing agent can cause irreversible damage. A leaking container of laundry bleach is an obvious villain. Other products are more insidious. The damage caused by acne medications containing benzoyl peroxide, for instance, often doesn't show up right away. Those medications, typically hard to wash off the hands, have ruined many a carpet. Other products to watch out for include swimming pool chemicals, mildew removers, liquid plant foods, and pesticides.

FLOOR POLISHERS

As a once- or twice-a-year proposition, floors can be polished with a rented machine, or a service company can be called in. "Self-polishing" floor wax may meet some people's standards all year round on floors that can take—and need—a water-based polish.

That's not to say ownership of an electric floor polisher is of no interest, particularly if you take pride in near-perfect floors and want to keep them buffed to a mirror sheen. If you want a machine of your own, you should have little trouble buying one that works well enough at polishing bare floors or hard-surface floor coverings. Differences are more likely to be in convenience features than in performance.

Shampooing and scrubbing

Floor polisher attachments can work quite well for wet shampooing rugs, but their use may entail some risk of damage to the rug from the brushes' abrasive action. Therefore, you should always try shampooing a small inconspicuous area of rug or carpet first to find out whether the rug can withstand the machine. Better still, rent one for a trial run. As well as checking for damage, see whether you're satisfied with the shampooing: You may find the shampooing technique difficult—and the results may not satisfy you. Also check how easily the machine can be converted from polisher to shampooer and back.

In shampooing, it's important to work a good thick foam into the pile of the rug to loosen the dirt. Moisture can promote mildew or rotting if it soaks into the carpet and underlay. Most shampooing machines have some means of agitating the shampoo into foam before it hits the rug.

If shampooing sounds like trouble, remember that rugs may not require shampooing very often. When they do, if you can take them up easily enough, they may be sent out for cleaning. Alternatively, a commercial rug-cleaning firm can shampoo them in place.

A floor-polishing machine, with or without special attachments, can be used for wet scrubbing on hard-surfaced floors. It can be a real boon on extremely dirty floors—much better than hand scrubbing or wet mopping. Damp mopping is easier and quicker for tidying up a slightly dirty floor.

A machine with vacuuming action offers a special advantage: It can suck up the dirty water, eliminating tedious mop-up. Don't be surprised if the holes in the water-pickup entrance of these machines become blocked by particles of dirt. You can minimize this problem by sweeping or vacuuming the floor before you scrub. Dirty water may also continue to drip from the machine even after you have emptied it, and even a little water on a polishing pad or brush can smear a newly waxed surface. To help prevent this, be sure the machine has dried before you use it for polishing.

Waxing

Two-brush models, the most common type, tend to leave a narrow strip of less well polished floor in the space between the brushes. To get reasonably even polishing, you have to push the machine through overlapping strokes.

Most machines have dispensers for wax and sudsy water. A dispenser is likely to be much more useful for shampooing rugs or washing floors than for waxing. First, machines tend to spread wax unevenly. Second, a solvent-based liquid wax can clog a machine's dispenser and perhaps damage it. If you do put wax in the dispenser, use a water-based emulsified liquid type. All factors considered, it's better to spread wax—liquid or paste—with an applicator and use your machine only for polishing and buffing.

Other considerations

In general, the faster the brushes rotate, the more you can expect them to spatter wax, shampoo, or water. It would seem, then, that you'd want a machine with a fairly low speed for shampooing and scrubbing and a high speed for polishing after your wax is spread. Apparently with that idea in mind, the manufacturers of many models provide two speeds. Such a machine isn't likely to perform noticeably better than a one-speed model.

If you aren't careful, a floor polisher can spin out of your hand and go careening across the floor. This is most likely to happen when the handle is vertical, so keep the handle at an angle.

It helps if there's an indication whether the motor switch is on or off before you plug in the machine. With a push-button switch there may be no way to tell.

Recommendations

Price is not a guide to effectiveness since even a cheap polisher will do the job. As you move up the price ladder you get more accessories and more features. Whether these items are needed is best left up to the individual buyer, based on his or her needs and preferences.

FLOOR POLISHES

The introduction of no-wax resilient flooring about twenty years ago promised liberation from the nuisance of periodic polishing, particularly important for people who insist on shiny floors in their homes. Judging by the popularity of no-wax flooring— much of which is relentlessly shiny—consumers were glad to avoid the polishing chore.

But as more and more no-wax floors were installed in kitchens, floor polish manufacturers saw their sales dip. The companies found out from consumers that no-wax floors weren't shiny enough to suit some people, and there were complaints about dirt building up on such floors. People were using regular polish on no-wax floors. A new product category emerged from the dissatisfaction: a combination cleaner and polish formulated for use on no-wax floor coverings.

No-wax waxes

If you have new no-wax flooring, you don't need to use a polish—even for cleaning.

On a very shiny, polyurethane-finished wood floor a polish won't make any real difference in appearance. On no-wax vinyl-surfaced floors, whose shine is a bit less glaring, a polish can add a touch of gloss. If you have a new vinyl no-wax floor and feel compelled to use a polish, you won't be doing anything but boosting the shine. The amount of protection offered by a thin film of polish is insignificant compared with the protection offered by the layer of vinyl on the flooring.

But even rugged plastics such as polyurethane and vinyl can get scratched and worn over time. It is also reasonable to assume that an accumulation of tiny scratches will eventually dull no-wax flooring a little. Polishes do have some ability to fill in tiny scratches, which would tend to improve the shine of worn areas. Until a no-wax floor is worn, however, floor polish is a waste of money. You'd be better off saving that money to make up for the extra cost of the no-wax flooring.

Although no-wax floors resist dirt well, they still get dirty. Should you buy a one-step, wash-and-wax product that "cleans as it shines," simply as a way to clean your no-wax floor? Products for no-wax floors are usually labeled as "self-cleaning"—that is, a new coat of polish wholly or partly dissolves the previous layer, and dirt is picked up on the mop along with excess polish. Products sold for no-wax floors are excellent at cleaning if the floor isn't terribly dirty to begin with, particularly if you damp mop once a week. That can make them quite clean.

Floors that need waxing

While no-wax flooring has a smooth, sealed surface, the surface of conventional vinyl asbestos tiles and other plain resilient flooring is relatively rough and porous. On such floors, polish keeps a floor cleaner and shinier partly by sealing the surface.

Polishes for resilient flooring are water-based emulsions that impart more of a satin luster than a mirror finish to a dull surface

WOOD FLOORS

❖ A lot of people have ripped up their carpets, rented floor sanders, and now have hardwood floors graced with area rugs. But there's been no resurgence in the sales of waxes for wood floors. Most people who redo wood floors make them into no-wax wood floors by giving them several coats of polyurethane varnish. The polyurethane finish requires nearly as little maintenance as a no-wax resilient flooring—vacuuming or dusting, and maybe a refinishing every few years.

Because water can damage and discolor wood, wood floor waxes are suspended in a petroleum solvent such as naphtha. Consequently, they are much more noxious substances than water-based polishes and should be used with good ventilation. (A few water-based polishes claim to be usable on wood floors, too, but it's not worth the risk: If the finish has been breached for any reason, the wood could be damaged by the water.)

Stripping old wax from wood floors requires the use of a solvent such as mineral spirits. Fortunately, waxes are excellent at cleaning, so any buildup of wax will occur slowly.

Buffing waxes must be buffed after they have dried. Doing that by hand is theoretically possible, but using a machine is easier. A one-step wood wax that requires no buffing is likely to be noticeably duller and dirtier than a buffing wax after it's been on the floor for a while.

So if you are willing to go to the trouble of moving the furniture to wax a wood floor, you might as well do it right. That would mean using a little extra effort and a buffing wax.

A wax with a coloring agent should be used only on very dark floors—those the color of end-grain walnut or rosewood. Otherwise, wax applied after some use can make scratches stand out because the wax is darker than the wood.

---

like that of resilient tiles. No product is likely to keep resilient tiles pristine. Like a polish for no-wax flooring, a product intended for regular flooring is usually resistant to water and vulnerable to alcoholic beverage spills.

Polishes that aren't good at self-cleaning require a clean floor before they're applied—otherwise, you encase the dirt and old polish in plastic.

Long ago, when floor waxes were really waxes, they required

buffing in order to develop any shine at all. In the 1930s so-called self-polishing floor waxes came along. They were the waxes that dried to a satin luster without buffing. Today, self-polishing floor polishes may still have real wax in them, but more often they are principally vinyl, acrylic, or some other plastic that dries to a shinier finish. The new formulations are better than the old waxes in one important respect: They are less slippery.

A few products say that you can use them diluted to restore shine in between full-strength applications. The diluted polishes add some shine, but not as much as a full-strength polish would. And diluted polishes remove some dirt, but not as effectively as at full strength. These products are useful as damp-mopping aids only if the floor is slightly dirty or dull.

Wax buildup

Technology has produced polishes that don't need buffing but has been less successful in eliminating the chore of stripping off old polish as the layers build up. Even polishes labeled as self-cleaning leave a small amount of old polish behind. The problem is usually most noticeable in corners, where the polish isn't worn away by traffic. And while you may be content to let the layers of wax accumulate for a long time before trying to remove it, floor polish instructions generally say that "for best results" you should strip the polish after every five or six coats, or once or twice a year.

The typical recipe for removing old floor wax is one-half cup of powdered floor cleaner and two cups of ammonia in a gallon of cool water, some fine steel wool, and a lot of elbow grease. There are also wax removers on the market, which are often recommended on the labels of their brand-mate floor polishes.

Recommendations

For taking care of new or fairly new no-wax floors, use a plain damp mop, or a little detergent and a rinse. When the floor is so worn that it looks like it really needs a polish, choose among the no-wax products by their price.

For taking care of a regular resilient floor, if shininess is important to you, buy a product that is known to give a high gloss.

HARD-SURFACE FLOOR FIRST AID FOR STAINS FROM SPILLS

◈ When using chemicals available from a supermarket or a drugstore, handle them with care and store them out of children's reach. Never mix chemicals with each other or with household cleaning products unless there are specific directions to do so. Wear rubber gloves when working with alcohol, hydrogen peroxide solution, household ammonia, acids, or chlorine bleach. To be on the safe side, it's a good idea to work in a well-ventilated room: Establish cross ventilation with open windows and doors and a window fan or air conditioner set to exhaust air.

Before using any chemical, test it on a small corner of the stain. If your procedure is wrong, the stain will not spread on the floor, nor will the floor be damaged further. If you apply steel wool to a stain, use grade 00 and rub gently. On wood, rub with the grain.

After you have tried ordinary liquid detergent (dishwashing liquid or laundry liquid) and water applied with a rag or sponge—or an all-purpose liquid cleaner sprayed from its container—here are some specific procedures that can help to remove a variety of potentially stubborn stains.

Alcoholic beverages.   Try rubbing with a clean cloth dampened with rubbing alcohol.

Blood.   Try clear, cold water first (before any detergent). If the stain remains, use caution in applying a solution of ammonia and cold water—and rinse quickly to avoid discoloration.

Candle wax or chewing gum.   Use ice cubes to chill the material to brittleness. Then carefully scrape the wax or gum from the floor, using a plastic spatula.

Cigarette burn.   For heavy stains, try scouring powder and a piece of steel wool or plastic scouring pad dipped in water. For hard-surface floors, rub with a cloth dampened with a solution of lemon juice and water.

Coffee or fruit juice.   Saturate a cloth with a solution of one part glycerine to three parts water and place it over the stain for several hours.

(Glycerine is available in drugstores.) If the spot remains, rub it gently with scouring powder and a cloth dampened in hot water.

Dyes. Rub with a cloth dampened in a solution of one part chlorine bleach and two parts water. If this doesn't work, try scouring powder and a cloth dampened with hot water.

Grease and oil. Remove as much as possible with newspaper, paper towels, or a plastic spatula. On resilient tile, rub with a cloth dampened in liquid detergent and warm water (or an all-purpose cleaner). On wood and cork, place a cloth saturated with dry-cleaning fluid (see page 193) on the stain for no more than five minutes. Then wipe the area dry and wash with detergent and water.

Ink. Try a commercial ink remover, following instructions carefully, or try rubbing alcohol.

Lipstick. Try steel wool wet with detergent and water. If the floor is hard surfaced or has a no-wax finish, or is embossed vinyl asbestos, use a plastic scouring pad instead of steel wool.

Mustard. Place a cloth soaked in hydrogen peroxide solution over the stain. Over that place an ammonia-soaked cloth. Leave in place until the stain has faded, sponge with water, and wipe dry.

Paint or varnish. On resilient tile, use liquid or all-purpose detergent with a cloth or sponge or steel wool applied very carefully. On a hard-surfaced floor, scrub with a concentrated solution of powdered detergent and water, or liquid laundry detergent applied undiluted.

Rust. Use a commercial rust remover intended for your particular type of floor.

Shoe polish or nail polish. If concentrated detergent solution doesn't work on resilient flooring, try scouring powder or steel wool. On wood and cork, steel wool should do the trick.

Tar. Use ice cubes to chill the tar to brittleness. Then scrape the tar carefully with a plastic spatula. To remove the tar stain, apply a damp cloth wrapped around a paste made of powdered detergent, chalk, and water. Leave the paste on the stain for several hours.

Tobacco. Rub with a cloth dampened in a solution of lemon juice and water. If that isn't effective, place a cloth soaked in hydrogen peroxide over the stain, and over that place an ammonia-soaked cloth. Leave in place until the stain has faded, sponge with water, and wipe dry.

Urine. Rub with a hot, damp cloth and scouring powder. For increased effectiveness, place a cloth soaked in hydrogen peroxide over the stain. Over that, place a cloth soaked in ammonia. Leave in place until the stain has faded, sponge with water, and wipe dry.

After you have successfully removed a stain, rinse the area well and allow it to dry before you apply any new finish (polish, for example). The newly finished area should blend in with the rest of the floor within a day or two.

VACUUM CLEANERS

With acres and acres of wall-to-wall carpet to tend, Americans go for the upright vacuum cleaner over the canister design by about a two-to-one margin. (The rest of the world has a distinct preference for canisters.) Other devices for collecting dirt range from the house-size to the hand-held, including central vacuum systems, compact canisters, stick vacs, battery-powered cleaners, and shop vacs (see page 74). One or another can be found in virtually every U.S. home; almost everybody who needs a vacuum already has one. Therefore, a problem arises for manufacturers: How to continue to sell the appliance.

In vacuums, as in automobiles, one answer is styling. Vacuums have been transformed from clunky, purpose-built machines to streamlined objects. Some manufacturers try to catch your eye with "European" styling. Others court upscale buyers with price-boosting features such as electronic speed control to regulate suction, self-propulsion, automatic cord rewind, or full-bag indicators. The efforts seem to work; the market for vacuum cleaners continues to grow.

Another reason for continued high sales might be that the perfect vacuum cleaner has yet to be invented. Perhaps people keep buying in hope that this or that model will finally relieve the chore of its drudgery. Meanwhile, manufacturers tinker with the design just enough to encourage that hope.

There are plenty of reasons to tinker. Compared with other major appliances, the vacuum cleaner presents many more problems of design that have yet to find clear-cut solutions. Uprights and canisters coexist because neither type is clearly, absolutely superior. Each does certain jobs better than the other. Uprights excel at carpet-cleaning and canisters at bare-floor and above-floor cleaning; canisters with power nozzles try to do both.

Similarly, smaller problems of vacuum-cleaner design can still show many solutions. For example, most full-size cleaners require a power cord. The problem: what to do with the cord when the vacuum's not being used. The storage solution on uprights is generally a pair of cleats on the handle. If the upper one flips down, the coiled cord is easier to pay out. A solution now seen on many canister models: the automatic cord rewinder. The favored design ingests the cord at the touch of a footswitch. Another solution requires you to yank the cord, as you would a window shade, to make it reel in.

Setting up

When you buy a canister vacuum, you ordinarily also get a rug and floor tool, a dusting brush, a crevice tool, and an uphol-stery nozzle, some or all of which store in or on the canister. Power-nozzle canisters typically substitute a wall/floor brush for the rug/floor tool.

To put a canister to work, you insert the hose into the hous-ing, attach one or more wands, and push a nozzle onto the wand's free end. The best wands come in metal sections that lock together with a positive click, or as permanently joined, telescop-ing tubes that lock together at any length within their range. Wands and accessories held together only by friction may prove troublesome, sometimes separating in use, sometimes being hard to uncouple for storage.

A brand-new upright may require you to join the handle sec-tions with a screw or two, or to attach the cloth outer bag. After that, you're ready to go to work—on carpets. For other chores, you usually have to buy attachments similar to the ones supplied with canisters. In most cases, you have to snap on an adapter plate underneath the upright, fit a hose into the plate, and slip a wand with attachment onto the hose. You can now drag the body of the cleaner along behind you as you work. The best upright designs have the hose for attachments plug in somewhere central on the cleaner's body.

Cleaning carpets

Vacuuming up surface trash merely tidies a carpet. If traffic has crushed the pile enough, vacuuming won't even do that. To make the carpet fibers stand straight again and to reach grit left low in the nap, a vacuum cleaner needs the mechanical assistance of a revolving brush. Deep cleaning is the measure of carpet-cleaning success.

Almost any vacuum is apt to provide satisfactory cleaning on low-pile carpets. Even the suction-only canister vacuums are at least adequate on a low-pile, hard-to-crush wool Berber. But the more luxurious the nap, the more you need a good performer to deal with it well. Striking differences in performance show up when you set to work on nylon plush with a medium pile height (about $5/16$ inch).

Overall, uprights and power-nozzle canisters clean carpet more reliably than canisters that use suction only. But the range in performance among the power-brush models is still quite large.

Revolving brushes also help dislodge surface litter—dog hair, bits of thread, spilled popcorn kernels, and the like. But most cleaners, brushes or no, pick up dog hair and threads in only a pass or two. Popcorn proves more demanding—the brushes of some uprights and power nozzles tend merely to push the popcorn around. (If the nozzle is manually adjustable, raising the height may help.)

Bare surfaces

Strong suction in a vacuum cleaner is no guarantee of deep carpet-cleaning, but suction is a good index of how well a cleaner will do on bare floors and in above-floor cleaning. As a breed, the canisters have vigorous suction. Accordingly, they are most apt to be satisfactory at such chores as dusting baseboards, window-sills, and moldings, and at tidying cobwebs from corners.

Uprights generally do not have strong suction. For their prime job—cleaning carpets—they don't need much, since their whirling brush does much of the work. The weak suction, however, makes them less than ideal for bare-surface chores. That disadvantage is coupled with another: Most uprights are rather awkward to use with attachments.

Uprights may or may not be suitable for bare-floor cleaning. One manufacturer warns against it, lest you mar floor surfaces. Other manufacturers suggest height settings for their uprights if you use them on bare floors. And other machines have a convenient provision for stopping the brush when only suction is wanted.

Some manufacturers, considerate of those who vacuum both carpets and bare floors, provide an easy way to switch between uses. Many power nozzles have a switch that stops the brush for suction-only action on bare floors. On others, you have to unplug the nozzle's power cord or replace the nozzle with a floor brush.

Lightweight items

High suction isn't always a boon. It can be a positive nuisance when you want to vacuum drapes or throw rugs, which may stick to the cleaner's nozzle or even be sucked in.

Some cleaners ignore that problem, leaving you to cope with it as best you can. Others, however, give you a suction-reducing option. The simplest design, common in canister models, is a vent, usually at the hose handle, that you can uncover to cut suction at the tool end of the wand. A more complicated solution to the problem, a variable-speed motor, is found on some canisters and uprights. In addition to reducing suction, the lower speeds also save a little electricity and spare you some noise.

Tight spots

Run a power nozzle or an upright along a wall or around the furniture and you're apt to notice that a narrow swath of carpet is left undisturbed. If there's any visible dust or litter in that swath and a pass from another direction doesn't help, you have to switch attachments or get out another cleaning appliance.

A vacuum's rotating brushes can't clean right up to obstructions—the brush supports and the shell usually take up some space at the nozzle's sides. That space typically measures one-half to three-quarters of an inch, but machines with their drive belt at one end of the brush create a "dead zone" as wide as two inches. The problem is easy to spot when you shop: Just upend the nozzle and take a look. In better designs, the belt is more central.

To offset the dead-zone effect, most cleaners have slots cut into the plate that fits over the nozzle to deliver some suction to areas the brush cannot reach.

Getting under furniture is another problem. If there are three or four inches of headroom, the canisters can reach as far as you like under beds or chairs (though you may have to lower the wand assembly toward the floor for a really deep reach). Uprights, with their bulky motor housings, typically require five or six inches of clearance.

Stairs

Space limitations make working on carpeted stairs a special, but common, challenge.

All but the most bulky canisters fit well enough on a tread. Most are designed to be stood on end for the purpose. A few models have a hose that can swivel in its canister, an advantage where space is tight.

Power nozzles can be used on stairs but are generally a bit wider and heavier than ideal—a suction-only model's rug nozzle is easier to handle. Most full-size uprights are generally far too heavy and awkward for convenience on stair treads.

Getting around

Revolving-brush nozzles should be set to suit carpets with high or low naps. If the brush is too high, the cleaner will be easy to push but won't do a good job; too low, and the cleaner will be hard to push and may abrade your rug.

Most uprights and power-nozzle models are claimed to adjust automatically to the carpet. A few accommodate various pile heights remarkably well. The brush of most automatic machines, however, may drag on any but low to medium piles. If some of your rugs have high piles, you'll probably be happier with a nozzle you can adjust yourself.

Another way to make an upright easier to push is to power its wheels. Some vacuums let you shift into power assist at the push of a switch on the handle. The effectiveness of their self-propulsion varies. A few move smoothly and easily; others, a shade jerkily, and are no easier to push than the average unpowered cleaner.

Note, by the way, that self-propulsion can mask the excessive drag that signals that a manually adjustable nozzle has been set too low. If you use a power-assisted model, you can gauge the proper nozzle setting by the degree to which the carpet's nap is stirred up. Or you can set the nozzle's height by feel in the unpowered mode before shifting into drive.

Light weight and large gliding surfaces make the power nozzles of the canister models generally easier to push than uprights on a large variety of carpets.

If electric outlets in your home are few and far between, check the cord length of the model you're considering. A number of cords are rather stingy.

Almost all uprights wheel easily across bare floors: You just lock their handles in the up position, lean them back, and trundle them along like a hand truck. On a high-pile rug, however, small wheels allow the chassis to drag. A number of uprights provide a carrying handle, which is also handy when you try to lug the cleaner upstairs. Canisters generally move along carpets and bare floors with ease but provide handles, too.

Emptying dirt

The cleaner collects dirt, but it's your job to get rid of it. A model whose bag has ample capacity keeps you from dealing

RATINGS OF VACUUM CLEANERS

Listed by type; within types, listed in order of estimated quality. Except where separated by bold rules, closely ranked models differed little in quality.

As published in a **May 1989** report.

Ratings key (Better ← → Worse): ● ◕ ○ ◔ ⬤

Brand and model	List price	Weight to the nearest ½ lb.	Deep cleaning	Suction	Noise	Dirt capacity	Dirt disposal	Switch	Cord storage
Full-size uprights									
Hoover Concept One U33199	$370/$320	20.5	●	◕	○	●	◕	●	●
Panasonic MC6230	300/290	16	◕	●	◔	◕	◕	◔	○
Eureka Ultra 7575B	230/200	15	◕	◕	○	●	◕	◕	◕
Hoover Concept Two U3323	450/360	22.5	●	◕	●	●	◕	●	○
Sears Kenmore 38710	149/133+	14	◕	◕	○	●	○	◕	◕
Eureka 1489A	130/130	12	◕	●	○	●	◕	◕	◕
Sharp EC3720	330/280	15.5	○	●	◔	○	○	◕	○
Kirby Heritage II 2HD	849/943	19.5	○	◕	○	◕	◕	◕	◕
Eureka Precision 5175A	400/349	20	○	●	●	◕	○	○	●
Eureka 5071F	350/325	17	○	◕	●	◔	○	○	○
Sanyo SCU7050	180/140	14.5	○	●	●	◔	◕	◕	●
Sharp EC3320	140/130	12.5	○	●	◔	◕	◕	○	○
Hoover Elite 200 U4455	100/70	10.5	◕	●	◕	◕	○	○	○
Panasonic MC5111	145/140	11.5	○	●	◕	◕	◕	○	○
Hoover Decade 800 U4505	260/220	17.5	○	●	◕	○	○	●	○
Oreck XL 9200S	380/320	10	○	●	◕	○	◕	◕	○
Hoover Convertible U4497900	200/180	15	○	◕	◕	●	◕	◕	○
Hoover Elite 350 U4463900	130/90	11	◕	●	◕	◕	○	○	◕
Sanyo SCU7010	140/140	12.5	○	●	○	◕	○	◕	◕
Singer SST050	100/80	10.5	○	●	○	◕	○	○	◕
Royal 886	500/320	15	◕	●	●	◔	○	●	○
Power-nozzle canisters									
Eureka Express 8295A	500/350	23	◔	◕	○	○	○	●	●
Hoover Dimension 1000 S3277040	400/350	29	◔	◔	○	○	◕	◕	●
Panasonic MC9530	410/400	27	◕	◕	◔	◕	◕	◕	●

| Type | Performance | Carpet-pile adjustment | | Carrying handle | Headlamp | Change-bag indication | Cord length, ft | Advantages | Disadvantages | Comments |
		Suction limit	Blower							
M	○	—	—	—	✔	—	24	—	m	E,F,H,N,Q
A	◕	MS	—	✔	✔	✔	33	B,E	a	—
A	○	V	—	✔	✔	—	24	—	—	—
M	○	MS	—	✔	✔	—	24	—	—	A,E,H,P,Q
A	◕	—	—	—	✔	—	18	L	—	H,J
M	◕	—	—	—	✔	—	19	C	b	M
A	○	MS	—	✔	✔	①	35	B,F	—	—
M	◕	—	✔	—	✔	—	32	E,K,N	g	F,N
M	○	MS	—	✔	✔	—	25	C	g	H
M	◕	MS	—	—	✔	—	30	C	—	A,H
A	○	—	—	—	✔	—	20	L	—	—
A	○	—	—	✔	—	—	18	—	e	—
A	◕	—	—	—	—	—	17	—	a	—
A	◕	—	—	—	—	—	18	—	—	—
M	○	—	—	—	✔	✔	30	—	—	B,E
A	○	—	—	—	✔	—	27	O	e	C,D,K
M	○	—	—	—	✔	—	20	—	c,m	E,N
M	○	—	—	—	✔	—	20	—	m	N
A	○	—	—	—	—	—	16	L	f	—
A	◕	—	—	—	—	—	15	—	a,f	J
M	●	—	—	—	✔	—	35	C,O	c	T
A	○	MS	—	✔	✔	✔	25	A,G,K,M	—	—
A	○	V	—	✔	✔	✔	22	B,E,G,M	k	—
A	○	MS	✔	✔	✔	✔	25	B,E,F,G,H,L	—	G

(Continued)

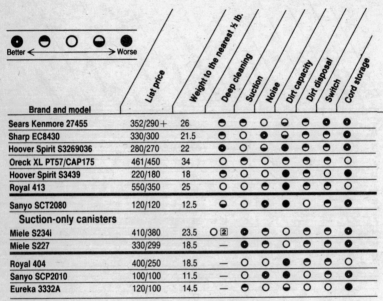

Better ← ● ◐ ○ ◑ ● → Worse

Brand and model	List price	Weight to the nearest ½ lb.	Deep cleaning	Suction	Noise	Dirt capacity	Dirt disposal	Switch	Cord storage
Sears Kenmore 27455	352/290+	26	◐	◐	○	◑	◐	●	●
Sharp EC8430	330/300	21.5	◐	○	◉	◑	◐	◐	●
Hoover Spirit S3269036	280/270	22	●	○	◐	●	◐	◐	●
Oreck XL PT57/CAP175	461/450	34	○	◐	○	◐	◐	◐	○
Hoover Spirit S3439	220/180	18	◐	○	○	●	◐	○	●
Royal 413	550/350	25	○	○	◐	●	◐	◐	○
Sanyo SCT2080	120/120	12.5	◑	○	◉	●	○	◐	●
Suction-only canisters									
Miele S234i	410/380	23.5	○ [2]	◉	◐	○	◐	◐	●
Miele S227	330/299	18.5	—	◉	◐	○	◐	◐	●
Royal 404	400/250	18.5	—	○	○	●	◐	◐	○
Sanyo SCP2010	100/100	11.5	—	○	◉	●	○	◐	◉
Eureka 3332A	120/100	14.5	—	◐	○	◑	○	○	●

1 Indicator on CU's sample did not work well. 2 When tested with accessory power nozzle S025.
(A) = automatic, (M) = manual, (MS) = multispeed motor, (V) = vent control

Specifications and Features

All: ● Remained electrically safe after 24 hours of exposure to high temperature and humidity (90°F, 85% relative humidity). None, however, should be used on wet surfaces or outdoors. ● Canisters and power-nozzle canisters come with metal wands with positive lock, floor/rug nozzle or power nozzle, wall/floor brush, upholstery nozzle, dusting brush, and crevice tool, and can reach all the way under furniture with about 3- to 4-in. clearance.

Except as noted, all: ● Use disposable dust bags. ● Clean a 10½- to 12-in. swath.

Except as noted, all uprights: ● Can reach all the way under furniture with 5- to 6-in. clearance.

Except as noted, all canisters: ● Come with hose at least 5 ft. long. ● Can store at least some tools in or on canister.

Except as noted, all power-nozzle canisters: ● Lack switch on nozzle handle to let nozzle be used on bare floor without brush's revolving; nozzle power cord must be unplugged or suction-only floor tool used instead.

Key to Advantages

A–In addition to master on/off switch on canister, has switch on power-nozzle handle that can either switch vacuum off or stop nozzle brush for bare-floor use. Handle also has

Carpet-pile adjustment

Type	Performance	Suction limit	Carpet-pile adjustment	Blower	Carrying handle	Headlamp	Change-bag indication	Cord length, ft.	Advantages	Disadvantages	Comments
M	○	MS		—	✔	✔	✔	20	A,E,G,H,I,L	—	A
A	●	MS		—	✔	—	✔	17	B,G,H,K	f	A
A	○	V		—	✔	✔	—	19	B,E,M	k	R
A	○	V	✔	✔	—	—		29	B,E,H,O,P	f,p	L,O
A	○	V		—	✔	—	[1]	15	—	k	S
M	●	—		✔	✔	—	—	25	—	e,f,l	O
A	●	—		—	✔	—	[1]	18	B	d,e,h,i,m,n	I
—	—	MS	✔	✔	—		✔	21	F,H,J,O,Q	j	—
—	—	V	✔	✔	—		✔	21	F,H,Q	h,i	—
—	—	V	✔	✔	—		—	25	D	d,h,l	—
—	—	—	—	✔	—		—	19	—	c,h,i,m	—
—	—	V	—	✔	—		—	20	H	b,c,d,i,m,o	—

canister motor-power control for reducing speed and suction.

B–Has convenient provision for stopping brush when cleaning bare floors.

C–Somewhat easier to push on carpets than most other uprights. (*Eureka 5175A* and *5071F* were tested using self-propelled option.)

D–Clip-on glides reduce drag on high-pile rugs.

E–Cleans a swath of about 13 to 14 in.

F–Interlock prevents operation without bag.

G–Power for nozzle easy to hook up. On the *Eureka* model, couplings at both ends of the suction hose also provide electrical hookup for the power nozzle. On the *Sharp,* the *Pan-asonic,* and the *Hoover,* the electrical connection is automatic only at the canister end.

H–Swiveling hose-to-canister connection improves handling and deters kinking.

I–Step-on release button detaches power nozzle conveniently from wand.

J–Telescoping wand, lockable at any length.

K–Has signal light or viewing window for monitoring rotation of brush.

L–Overload protector guards cleaner if brush jams.

M–Overload protector guards cleaner if hose clogs or bag overfills.

N–Accessory hose is reinforced.

O–Brush is adjustable for wear; on *Miele S234i,*

(Continued)

only optional power nozzle has adjustable brush.

P–Relatively long hose (about 9 ft.).

Q–Rug/floor nozzle pivots for better alignment with floor.

Key to Disadvantages

a–Relatively hard to push on high-pile shag rug.

b–Did not pick up thread from carpet as well as most.

c–Did not pick up dog hair from carpet as well as most.

d–Judged relatively likely to clog with bulky litter; the *Sanyo's* power nozzle was especially sensitive.

e–Cleans a swath of about 9 to 10 in.

f–Revolving brush is somewhat far from edge of housing; cannot clean carpet close to walls.

g–Requires about 8-in. clearance to reach all the way under furniture.

h–Cannot store tools on canister.

i–Friction-fit wands (metal on *Miele S227*, plastic on others noted) may either come apart in use or be hard to separate.

j–Accessory power nozzle relies on friction-fit between hose and wand; judged less secure than a positive lock.

k–Twist-to-lock connections at one or both ends of hose were hard to turn.

l–Relatively stiff hose (especially on the *Electrolux*) made cleaner awkward to use in close quarters and to store.

m–Hose was flimsy.

n–Relatively short hose (less than 5 ft.).

o–Poorly diffused or directed exhaust is apt to blow floor dirt about.

p–Heavy, bulky commercial model.

Key to Comments

A–Not significantly quieter at Low than at High.

B–Traps dust in transparent plastic bin.

C–Revolving brush is somewhat far from edge

of housing, but fixed side brushes assist in dislodging dirt close to walls.

D–Cleaner was hard to assemble.

E–Has spurt-of-power setting for heavy soil.

F–Can be wheeled about conveniently with the hose and above-floor attachments supplied with cleaner in place.

G–Power nozzle automatically reverses direction as nozzle is pushed or pulled; feature reduced effort to move nozzle somewhat on low-pile carpet, but didn't help on medium or high pile.

H–Self-propelled model. Feature judged a minor convenience on the *Eurekas* and somewhat helpful but a bit jerky on the *Hoovers.* On the *Sears,* effort required was no less than with most other uprights.

I–Power nozzle driven by air, not motor.

J–Cleaner goes on or off automatically when handle is lowered or raised.

K–Position of foot switch on housing favors left-handed users.

L–Power cord to nozzle not built into hose; power supplied by external cord clipped to hose.

M–Plastic handle assembly is somewhat flexible.

N–Comes with adapter, hose, and suction tools; *Kirby* also offers numerous optional attachments.

O–Comes with additional wands for above-floor accessories; some connections are friction-fit.

P–Comes with ac-powered hand vac that stores in console of cleaner.

Q–Has dual handle-release pedals; equally convenient for left- and right-handed users.

R–Replaced by *S3269070,* $300; essentially similar except tools are inside bag compartment.

S–Replaced by *S3439070,* $240; essentially similar except tools are inside bag compartment.

T–The current version of this model has been slightly modified from the *886* CU tested.

with the chore too often and saves you some money on replacement bags. Uprights generally hold a good deal more dirt than canisters.

A bag that's too full may burst or cause the cleaner's motor to overheat. Vacuuming certain fine material, such as cement dust from a cellar floor or a spilled box of talcum powder, may pose the same risks even with an unfilled bag: The bag's pores may clog and curtail the flow of air. Stay alert for hints to change the bag such as a higher-pitched whine from the cleaner's motor or a falloff in suction or performance. (But note that a clogged tool, wand, or hose can cause the same symptoms.) A specific change-bag alarm or indicator is a nicety, if it functions well.

When you shop for a cleaner, it's worth checking the convenience of its bag arrangement. Tight clearance or finicky fit make some bags less convenient than others, a point to check in the store. Some uprights have a rather crude arrangement: a bag with a sleeve that must be slipped over a wide pipe at the bottom rear of the cleaner and retained with a garterlike spring. If you get a model with a bagless dirt collector, you save some money on bags, but you have to be careful to avoid raising dust when you empty the container.

Recommendations

Uprights deal well with carpeting. Suction-only canisters, with their array of tools, are good for bare surfaces. You could buy one of each—a solution especially worth considering if you live on two levels, one largely carpeted, the other not. But a power-nozzle canister is a wiser choice.

Although discounts aren't as steep for cleaners as they are for electronic gear, real-life prices can be substantially below manufacturer's list.

Furniture

FURNITURE POLISHES

It doesn't matter much which polish you choose and use if your only aim is to keep the furniture presentable. But you should choose a polish that's easy to apply and that imparts only as much gloss as you want.

There are exceptions to that rule, however. If, for example, your dining table shows signs of blotchy wax buildup, it makes sense to switch at least for a while to a product without much wax. Or if the table's finish has worn down so much that the raw wood is exposed to moisture and dirt, then a protective layer of wax would restore its appearance a bit and defer the day when refinishing is necessary. Antiques and pieces made of very expensive wood need special consideration, since the goal is to preserve the original finish or the pattern of the wood grain.

Some products have no wax at all; others range from a little wax to nearly solid wax. Keep your own needs in mind when you select a polish. But bear in mind that the addition of a lemon scent or a switch from aerosol to pump-spray bottle does not enhance the wood.

Gloss

The shine you get from a product will depend not only on the nature of the polish, but also on the nature of the finish. For instance, no polish is likely to increase the gloss of a "piano top" high-gloss mahogany. It's already mirrorlike.

With lacquered walnut furniture that has a good-looking low luster, a "polish" should leave the wood looking just as it did when it started. That's a result that can be expected from a product that makes no bones about being a cleaner rather than a polish. It's also not so surprising from products that emphasize "no-wax" in their labeling. But many no-wax products can be buffed to a higher shine, too. No polish can turn a semigloss finish into anything like a high gloss, but some will provide a slight or moderate increase in gloss.

Since a change in gloss level, however subtle, is likely to be the most pronounced effect of using some furniture polishes, it makes sense to choose a product that will give you the gloss level you want.

Protection

A layer of polish should not only shine the wood but also resist staining, marring, and smudging.

Staining. You should be a little skeptical of claims that a polish "preserves all types of wood finishes," or "protects, beautifies fine furniture." It's really the furniture's finish and not the polish that provides the protection. Don't depend on a polish to provide any additional protection against staining.

Marring. A high-gloss surface can become marred when even something as unobtrusive as a coaster with a cup of coffee on it is pulled across the surface of the polish. Most products won't mar. Those that do will be worse on very highly polished surfaces.

A polish that claims to hide scratches and nicks in furniture does so with the help of coloring material that darkens scratches to help disguise them. That works, but you shouldn't expect the polish to be an exact match for the color of the wood. The coloring may be too dark for use on light woods.

Smudging. Of all the problems that can affect furniture finish, smudges are the least severe. In fact, smudges often heal themselves and disappear. Smudging is usually more apparent on high-gloss panels; there should be none to speak of on oiled walnut finishes.

Polishes that retain smudges can be easily restored with a couple of swipes of a cloth. But that can become a daily chore if your furniture is heavily used, especially by children.

Ease of application

Polishes in aerosol containers are by far the easiest to work with. If anything, the aerosols apply polish too easily and too liberally, leaving too much polish on the wood and wasting too much on the cloth.

Pump sprays require a little more effort than the aerosols do, but provide better control. Pumps with a trigger in front are easier to use than those with a plunger on top.

Pourable liquids and paste waxes are meant to be applied with one cloth fairly soaked with the product, then wiped and buffed with a separate dry cloth. With some brands, you have to dampen the applicator cloth with water. Damp or dry, an oily, greasy applicator cloth coats your hands quickly; you can't touch anything without fear of smearing it with polish.

The label on a few aerosols suggests a two-cloth application method: Spray some polish on one cloth, wipe on a thin coat of polish, then use a clean cloth to wipe off and buff. That's a good way to cut down on polish wasted or sprayed where you don't want it.

Any aerosol or pump-spray polish can also be used as a one-cloth dusting operation. When sprayed lightly on the cloth, any of the sprays will make the cloth tacky enough to pick up dust rather than just push it around. You're less likely to need a separate product for use between more thorough polishings.

Recommendations

If the oil or lacquer finish on a piece of furniture is worn and shabby, the cure doesn't lie with a furniture polish. What's needed is refinishing. But if the finish is in good shape, many polishes can help keep the piece looking presentable for a long time.

A good furniture polish should maintain the finish's original gloss, or lack of gloss: It shouldn't dull a high-gloss finish or put a hard, glossy shine on satin (semigloss), matte (no gloss), or natural finishes. A polish shouldn't affect the furniture's original color: A light finish should remain light and a dark finish should not be whitened. Polish should be easy to apply and buff, and it should readily remove dirt in the process. It should form a coating that protects the finish from household stains—a coating that is itself stain resistant, resists smudging, and doesn't give dirt much of a toehold. And, of course, any polish should be safe to use and store.

When using a product for the first time, try it out on an inconspicuous spot. Protect furniture finishes by making certain that lamp bases and *objets d'art* either have padded bases or are set on a cushioning material. Sponge up spills immediately to keep them from becoming stains or damaging the finish. When applying polish, it's easier and probably better to rub with the wood grain rather than against it. Use polish sparingly: You don't need to apply it each time you dust. That will help prevent unsightly polish buildup as well as make polishing easier.

Furniture polish won't protect against heat damage to the finish from hot items or from solvents such as the alcohol in a beverage, aftershave lotion, perfume, cough syrup, and the like. The best protection is a nonabsorbent barrier, such as a dish or coaster.

UPHOLSTERY CLEANERS

A commercial cleaning service may have the know-how and the hardware to rejuvenate upholstery that has lost its bloom, but commercial cleaning is expensive. It can cost close to $200 to have a pair of large upholstered chairs and a matching sofa done. A cheaper alternative is to do the cleaning on your own, with a do-it-yourself cleaner.

Cleaning codes and fabric finishes

The furniture industry has developed cleaning codes for upholstery textiles. The code is usually labeled on the furniture and on sample fabric swatches (or is part of the consumer information packet that goes with the furniture). Fabrics labeled with code W can be cleaned with water-based products. Code S means you should use a solvent-based cleaner. WS labeling indicates that you can use either type of cleaner. (No matter what the code indicates, spot-test a small, hidden area first.) Fabrics labeled code X should be professionally cleaned.

Many retailers will offer to treat the furniture you buy with a stain-repellent finish for about $25 for a chair to $60 for a sofa, and provide a warranty for the treatment. Furniture stores take a huge markup on fabric finishing. The chemicals cost just a few dollars; no great skill is used in the application. The finish is sprayed on in the warehouse, and coverage is likely to be uneven.

The typical warranty says that you should be able to remove anything short of severe stains, such as motor oil or nail polish, by following specific instructions. If you can't get rid of the stain, the retailer will send a professional to try. If that fails, the retailer will honor the warranty. But that can mean anything. It may mean only that the retailer will refund the price of the fabric finish. Read the fine print if you're considering a fabric-finish contract.

The effectiveness of fabric finishes is questionable. Fiber content, yarn texture, and construction are among the factors that determine how well the cloth takes the finish. If applied too generously, the solvents in the finishes may attack a fabric's backing and the upholstery's stitches.

In addition, a retailer-applied finish may be redundant. Fabric finishes frequently are applied at the mill, after the fabric is made.

(Check fabric swatches in the store to see which ones have been treated with a stain-repellent finish at the mill.) That assures more uniform coverage and, obviously, no damage to upholstery seams. But there's no indication that mill-applied finishes are any more effective than the ones the retailer sprays on.

Do-it-yourself cleaning

Most do-it-yourself cleaners come ready to use, but a few liquids are concentrates and must be diluted.

To work a liquid into the upholstery you need a sponge, a soft-bristle brush, a clean cloth, or a piece of terry cloth towel. With some products, the cleaner and soil are wiped off; other cleaners are vacuumed or brushed off when dry.

Some cleaners come with an applicator, usually a plastic brush or brush-and-sponge combination. Those applicators work well on vinyl, which surrenders dirt to bristles more readily than to cloth, and is none the worse for rubbing. Brushes, however, can damage flat-surfaced textiles, especially after the yarn has been tenderized by wetting with cleaner. For flat-surfaced fabrics, an old terry cloth towel makes a gentle and effective applicator. After the cleaned upholstery has dried thoroughly, brushing won't hurt it and may even improve the final result. With velvets and velours, brushing is essential to restore the fabric's nap.

A foam cleaner is simply sprayed on, but you have to squeeze a liquid out of the bottle, which can be a problem. The liquid's instructions may in fact warn against soaking the fabric. Despite the warning, it may not be possible to control the stream once you stop squeezing. The result is soaked fabric, with wet padding that may deteriorate or cause an offensive smell later on. No such problem will arise with foam cleaners.

A powdered cleaner goes on dry, but the powder is very powdery indeed. It gets on surfaces that you do not intend to clean, so you'll have to take the extra time to dust and vacuum diligently. As well as being messy to apply and remove, the powder may be an irritant: Use a dust mask, safety goggles, and gloves when working with it. If you can move the furniture outdoors for cleaning, fine. If you can't, be sure the work area is well ventilated.

Recommendations

The most effective cleaners, applied with proper care to the proper fabric, will remove dirt and leave the fabric looking brighter. Even so, a good upholstery cleaner may cause unalterable changes in the feel, shape, texture, warmth of coloring, or overall look of the fabric. After cleaning, a flat-textured fabric's finish might look blurred, uneven—almost plush—because the cleaner has raised fibers here and there. Plush pile fabrics may become matted.

Try to get by with frequent dry brushing and vacuuming for as long as you can before using a do-it-yourself upholstery cleaner. If you must use a cleaner, do the cleaning with all possible gentleness and use the least amount of cleaner that will do the job. It's far better to reapply a cleaner than to be overgenerous the first time.

House cleaning

AIR CLEANERS

Manufacturers' claims for air cleaners range from the straightforward ("offers triple filter capability for maximum air-cleaning efficiency") to the carefully worded ("in many cases, a tremendous reduction in the number of particles in the air results in substantial relief from allergic symptoms") to the excessive ("filters out virtually everything in the air but the air itself").

Air cleaners are effective at trapping dust and pollen—*if* the particles remain airborne. That's a big if. The larger particles quickly settle onto the floor or the furniture. When they're stirred up again, they may lodge in your nose or throat before they can enter the machine.

Doctors have long recommended air cleaners to allergic or asthmatic people. But, in 1987, a committee of physicians appointed by the American Academy of Allergy and Immunology concluded that no clear data exist to establish the usefulness of air cleaners in preventing or treating allergic respiratory disease.

A paper published by the committee in October 1988 described several studies of groups of allergy sufferers. A two-summer study of children at an asthma camp indicated a "strong trend" for fewer nighttime symptoms with the cleaner, but the results for each year fell just short of statistical significance. Another study showed virtually no improvement in asthma sufferers who used an air cleaner and an air conditioner compared with the use of an air conditioner alone.

For those with asthma or allergies, other measures detailed in "Dealing with allergy" (page 55) may provide far more relief than an air purifier.

Smoke and odors

Particles of smoke from tobacco or from the kitchen or fireplace are smaller than many dust particles, so they remain airborne longer. An air cleaner can do a good job of removing smoke from the air, thereby reducing eye, nose, and throat irritation. But don't expect much of an effect on smoke smell. The molecules that cause odors are gases and cannot be trapped effectively. Some of the odor molecules cling to the smoke particles, so filtration may reduce odor a bit. Eliminating the odor, however, would require far more activated carbon or other absorbent material than air cleaners contain. Just as odor molecules are beyond the practical abilities of home air purifiers, other gas molecules such as carbon monoxide, oxides of sulfur and nitrogen, and ozone are too elusive to be effectively trapped by these units.

The best way to deal with smoke, fumes, and other contaminants in household air is the old-fashioned way: Open a window. Even in winter, cracking open a window a couple of inches won't raise your heating bill by more than a few pennies an hour. In addition, a kitchen exhaust fan should effectively deal with smoke and fumes from cooking.

But if you can't open a window—because the outside air is polluted or the weather is bitter cold—or if you need to ventilate a windowless space, an air cleaner may be the only way to reduce smoke and airborne dust.

How air cleaners operate

Much of an air cleaner's effectiveness depends on how much air it can handle. That puts small models, with their small fans, at a disadvantage. But they do fit nicely on a table or desk. If such units are close to a source of smoke, they can be quite effective.

To move air, all models use a fan. Most offer two or three fan speeds; some offer continuously variable speeds. To remove particles, the machines use one or more variations on two basic technologies, mechanical filtration and electrical attraction.

High-efficiency particulate-arresting (HEPA) filters are made of densely packed fibers that are pleated to increase their surface area. The filters, developed during World War II to remove radioactive dust from the exhausts of atomic plants, are extremely effective at trapping particles. Ordinary pleated filters are smaller and more loosely packed than the HEPA type. "Electret" filters are made of polyester mesh that's electrically charged during manufacture to trap charged particles.

In electrostatic precipitators, cells with fine wires electrically charge the air and any particles it contains as the air enters the cleaner. Electrically polarized metal plates then attract the charged particles and remove them from the air, much as a magnet attracts iron filings. Ionizers charge the air in their vicinity by applying high voltage through needles or fine wires. The charged air molecules then attract airborne particles. Ionizers have a drawback: Unless the ionizer is combined with a fan and a filter of some type, the particles tend to be attracted to walls and other nearby surfaces, causing soiling.

Air cleaner effectiveness

The more air a cleaner processes, the faster it can remove pollutants. Today's models can process up to 400 cubic feet per minute (cfm). To clean the air of a large room or two, you need a model that moves a lot of air. But the rate at which the unit produces fresher air, the clean air delivery rate (CADR), is a better gauge of effectiveness. A good model (with a CADR of about 250 cfm) will clear 90 percent of the smoke from a 9-by-12-foot room in nine minutes. An average model (with a CADR of 100 cfm) might take twenty minutes. A less effective unit might be useful for a smaller room, however.

Noise

Even the most effective purifier is no bargain if its fan makes conversation difficult or keeps you awake at night. Few models are objectionably loud at their lowest fan speed, but many can be annoying at their highest speed. The lowest setting is generally preferable for continuous use.

Because an air cleaner is often used in a bedroom at night, it is a good idea to listen to the machine you are planning to buy. If you can't try it in a quiet location in the store, be sure the air cleaner is returnable if it turns out to be too noisy at home.

Ozone

Ozone, a colorless gas, is a major constituent of smog; it also forms when oxygen in the air is exposed to a strong electrical charge. At high concentrations, ozone can cause eye irritation and breathing difficulties. Long-term exposure to lower levels may affect lung function.

Air cleaners are not effective at removing ozone from the home environment.

Many manufacturers of filter-based models boast that *their* product doesn't produce ozone, clearly implying that some competing electrostatic precipitators may *produce* ozone rather than eliminate it. Consumers Union testers checked the precipitator and ionizer models—the models that use high-voltage electricity—for ozone emissions. Their instruments, which could have detected levels at or below 100 parts per billion, found none.

The U.S. Environmental Protection Administration (EPA) tested various console and tabletop air purifiers and found their ozone output negligible. The EPA has, however, recorded considerably higher ozone levels in homes that use some large electrostatic precipitators, the kind built into heating-system ducts.

DEALING WITH ALLERGY

◈ Simply setting up an air cleaner in the middle of the room is an ineffective way to reduce or prevent asthmatic attacks and other allergic and respiratory problems. So says Harold S. Nelson, M.D., a physician at the National Jewish Center in Denver who chaired a committee set up by the American Academy of Allergy and Immunology to study allergens in indoor air and air-cleaning devices.

"Most household dust is inert," he told Consumers Union. "Removing it from the air with [an air cleaner] won't help much. And as for pollen, an air conditioner is far more effective."

Dr. Nelson blames the fecal pellets of house dust mites (microscopic creatures that feed on human skin cells that are sloughed off) for many allergic reactions. The pellets are too large to remain airborne for long; they settle within minutes, so an air cleaner is rather ineffective against them.

The problem is that the mites thrive in bedding, in mattresses, pillows, and blankets. An allergy sufferer buries his or her face in the bedding, breathes in the pellets, and suffers an allergic reaction.

The best relief comes from separating the patient from the allergen. The pillows and mattress should be sealed in special allergen-proof encasing, available from surgical supply houses. Blankets and sheets should be washed often in hot water.

For the same reason, allergy sufferers should avoid lying on an upholstered couch.

Some manufacturers promote humidifiers as beneficial for allergies. Dr. Nelson believes a humidifier can do more harm than good, because house dust mites proliferate in humid conditions. He advises keeping indoor humidity relatively low, at about 20 to 30 percent.

Common advice echoed in a pamphlet put out by one air cleaner manufacturer suggests eliminating as much as possible any surfaces that can collect dust: books, stuffed toys, drapes, textured walls. "Ridiculous!" snaps Dr. Nelson. "Books, toys, and walls don't radiate allergens."

Animal dander is lighter than most dust and tends to remain airborne longer, creating a serious problem for allergy sufferers. If you must have a pet, then at least keep the bedroom off-limits. Here, an air cleaner might help, since the particles of animal dander are of a size that these machines can collect.

As for vacuuming, it's "the best way of disseminating allergens into the air," says Dr. Nelson. Allergic individuals should let someone else do the cleaning and stay out of the room for at least an hour afterward, until the dust settles.

RATINGS OF AIR CLEANERS

Listed by types. Within types, listed in order of estimated quality, based primarily on effectiveness in removing smoke and dust. Two brands were check-rated. As published in a **February 1989** report.

Better ● ◑ ○ ○ ● Worse

Brand and model	Price	Type	Smoke removal	Dust removal	Noise (high/low)	Filter access	Airflow, cfm	Fan speeds	Size (H x W x D), in.	Weight, lbs.	Comments
Room models											
✓ Smokemaster P600	$649	EP	●	●	●/○	●	400	3	20 x 14 x 17	40	—
✓ Honeywell F59A	509+	EP	●	●	◑/○	●	400	3	20 x 14 x 17	42	—
Cloud 9 300	495	HEPA	◑	◑	◑/○	◑	325	3	21 x 26 x 12	40	C,H
Hepanaire HP-50	445	HEPA	◑	◑	◑/○	●	325	Var	15 x 21 x 20	38	H
Vitaire H200	300	HEPA	◑	◑	◑/○	◑	300	Var	20 x 14 x 16	31	B,C,D
Micronaire P-500	445	EP	◑	◑	◑/○	●	325	3	15 x 12 x 15	25	—
Trion Console II	250	EP	◑	◑	◑/○	○	300	3	25 x 17 x 14	41	A
Sears Cat. No. 7330	270	EP	◑	◑	◑/○	○	300	3	25 x 17 x 14	41	A,I
Enviracaire EV1	299	HEPA	◑	◑	○/○	●	225	2	11 x 16 x 16	12	C,D,M
Cleanaire 300	425	HEPA	◑	○	○/○	◑	275	3	20 x 25 x 12	40	C,H
Cloud 9 150	325	HEPA	◑	○	○/◑	◑	250	2	13 x 24 x 12	27	C,D,H
Bionaire BT-2001	460	ION, EF	○	◑	◑/◑	●	250	3	7 x 21 x 15	25	G,I,L
Instapure AF2-W	295	PF	○	○	○/○	●	225	3	20 x 17 x 13	28	F,G,H,N
Sears Cat. No. 8398	260	EP	○	●	◑/○	●	250	Var	14 x 23 x 8	27	A,J,L
Emerson 20X12A-41001	569	EP	○	●	◑/○	●	250	Var	14 x 23 x 8	27	A,N,L
Ecologizer 99005	286	HEPA	○	○	◑/◑	○	175	3	20 x 16 x 11	20	D,L
Sears Cat. No. 8321	190	EP	◑	○	◑/◑	○	200	Var	6 x 21 x 11	16	A,B,C

Model	Price	Filter[1]						CFM	Speeds	Dimensions (in.)	Weight (lb.)	Comments
Space-Gard 2275	145	PF	●	●	O	O/●	●	300	2	14 x 12 x 12	12	B,C
Cleanaire 150	210	HEPA	●	●	O	–/O	●	125	1	9 x 15 x 15	9	B,C,M
Cleanaire 1212	305	HEPA	●	●	O	O/●	●	50	2	13 x 14 x 20	13	B,C,D,H,M

■ Two samples of the following model were inoperable as received. After adjustment, one model worked.

Model	Price	Filter[1]						CFM	Speeds	Dimensions (in.)	Weight (lb.)	Comments
Tectronic PT-410	495	EP	●	O	O	O/●	●	300	Var	23 x 21 x 12	43	A,E,H

Tabletop models

Model	Price	Filter[1]						CFM	Speeds	Dimensions (in.)	Weight (lb.)	Comments
Bionaire BT-1000	320	ION, EF	●	O	●	◐/●	●	125	3	8 x 14 x 8	13	G,I,L
Sears Cat. No. 8300	130+	EP, ION	●	◐	◐	O/●	●	150	3	4 x 16 x 10	8	C,M
Trion Table Top EAC-10	130	EP, ION	●	◐	◐	O/●	●	125	3	4 x 16 x 10	8	C,K,M
Pollenex 2201	150	EP, ION, EF	●	◐	●	◐/●	●	175	2	5 x 15 x 10	8	C,M
Tectronic PT-150	295	EP	●	●	O	O/●	●	25	Var	6 x 14 x 12	16	—

[1] EP = Electrostatic precipitator; HEPA = High-efficiency particulate-arresting filter; ION = Ionization traps particles; EF = Electret filter; PF = Ordinary pleated filter

Specifications and Features

Except as noted, all have: ● Cabinet of plastic laminate over particle board. ● Indicator light to show when fan is on. ● Easily accessible cell or filter. ● Washable prefilter.

Key to Comments

A–Design allows precipitator cell to be put in backward or in such a way that it won't make electrical contact; cell won't work, but fan runs.

B–Lacks on/off indicator light.

C–Lacks washable prefilter.

D–Has handle or handhold for easy carrying.

E–Has wheels.

F–Has digital timer that allows unit to be turned on automatically.

G–Has light to signal need for filter replacement.

H–Fan whines or hums objectionably at low speed.

I–Essentially the same as Trion Console II.

J–Essentially the same as Sears 8398.

K–Essentially the same as Sears 8300.

L–Cabinet made of metal.

M–Cabinet made of plastic.

N–According to mfr., discontinued and replaced by model AF-3 ($219), similar to tested model but with manual control.

Bionaire: Bionaire Corp., 901 North Lake Destiny Dr., Suite 215, Maitland, Fla. 32751. Cleanaire: Air Techniques Inc., 1801 Whitehead Rd., Baltimore, Md. 21207. Cloud 9: Mason Engineering & Designing Corp., 777 Edgewood Ave., Wood Dale, Ill. 60191. Ecologizer: Westclox Div., General Time Corporation, Norcross, Ga. 30092. Emerson: White-Rodgers Div., Emerson Electric Co., 9797 Reavis Rd., St. Louis, Mo. 63123. Enviracaire: Enviracaire Corp., 747 Bowman Ave., Hagerstown, Md. 21740. Hepanaire and Micronaire: Summit Hill Laboratories, P.O. Box 535, Navesink, N.J. 07752. Honeywell: Honeywell Inc., 1985 Douglas Dr. N., Golden Valley, Minn. 55422. Instapure: Teledyne-Water Pik, 1730 East Prospect St., Fort Collins, Colo. 80525. Pollenex: Pollenex Associated Mills Inc., 111 North Canal Street, Chicago, Ill. 60606. Sears: Sears Merchandise Group, Sears Tower, Chicago, Ill. 60684. Smokemaster: Air Quality Engineering, 3340 Winpart Dr., Minneapolis, Minn. 55427. Space Gard: Research Products Corp., P.O. Box 1467, Madison, Wisc. 53701. Tectronic: Tectronic Products Co., 6743 Kinne St., P.O. Box 157, East Syracuse, N.Y. 13057. Trion: Trion Inc., 101 McNeill Rd., P.O. Box 760, Sanford, N.C. 27331. Vitaire: Vitaire Corp., P.O. Box 88, Elmhurst Annex, N.Y. 11380.

Maintenance

The cost of the power to run an air purifier is negligible. Electrostatic models cost less to run because their precipitator cell can (and should) be washed each month. A HEPA filter may last one or two years, depending on use. But be prepared to pay anywhere from $49 to $106 for a replacement filter.

With most filters, the only way to see if it needs replacement is to remove and inspect it. Some models make that job easy, but a few require you to remove screws, awkward plastic rivets, or nuts and braces. (A few models have a handy indicator light that signals the need for replacing the filter.)

A filter model may give you an audible hint when its filter begins to clog: The airflow rate drops. The electrostatic models may snap and pop, but their airflow rate remains constant, no matter how much dirt accumulates on the cell.

Most manufacturers recommend washing a precipitator cell in a dishwasher. A bathtub can serve if you don't have a dishwasher. But use care; a powerful stream of water, or rough handling, could break the fine wires in the cell.

Recommendations

If you have allergies, an air purifier alone probably won't help much. "Dealing with allergy" outlines steps to take first, before you buy one of these machines.

Do not expect an air purifier to remove odors or dangerous gases. Such problems are best handled by controlling sources and improving ventilation.

A smoke problem is also best handled by removing the source or improving ventilation, if you can. But here, an air purifier can help. Even if it cannot remove all the smell and clear 100 percent of the smoke, it can help diminish the heavy concentrations that people are apt to find most irritating.

It's hard to say definitively which type of purifier, electrostatic or HEPA, is more effective. Consumers Union's tests confirmed what the engineers already knew: HEPA filters collect more of the dirt that passes through them, but an electrostatic model that treats more air per minute can clean air every bit as effectively, despite its less efficient single pass.

Except for a few brands, don't expect to find a selection of these machines in department or hardware stores or at your neighborhood drugstore. Likely sources include surgical and medical supply houses, regional distributors, and air-conditioning, heating, and plumbing contractors. If you are unable to find the model you want locally, contact the manufacturer. Addresses are listed at the end of the Ratings.

ALL-PURPOSE CLEANERS

Cleaners for use around the house have become increasingly specialized. To name a few, there are glass, bathroom, appliance, floor, toilet-bowl, vinyl, and metal cleaners. A good all-purpose liquid cleaner ought to handle many of those chores. Indeed, all-purpose cleaner labels variously claim that their products are suitable for an ambitious list of cleaning chores: appliances, cabinets, countertops, dishes, pots and pans, stove tops, laundry, screens and blinds, vinyl and aluminum siding, whitewall tires, and boats.

Yet the main target for all-purpose cleaners would appear to be small areas of concentrated dirt. Convenience in cleaning spots and smudges with full-strength cleaner seems to be the objective of flip-top squeeze bottles, pull-out dispensing caps, and trigger-spray pumps. Consumers Union's tests concentrated on the products' ability to conquer three tough, typical kinds of dirt: pencil, crayon, and grease.

The testers dirtied some 1,000 white-painted panels and let the marks set at least overnight. Then they put each panel in a scrubbing machine, where a sponge moistened with cleaner went over the stains ten times. Few cleaners performed well on all three types of dirt. Black grease was the most intractable soil, but the crayon and pencil defeated most products, too. The best products did a decent job on crayon or pencil, a couple just smeared the black grease.

RATINGS OF ALL-PURPOSE CLEANERS

Listed in order of overall quality, based on CU's tests of cleaning tough spots. Liquids (L) come in plain bottles or in squeeze bottles with some sort of special cap to make dispensing easy. The trigger-spray products (S) also make application easy. Most products come in only one size, often a 28-ounce bottle.

As published in an **August 1988** report.

Better ● ◐ ○ ◑ ● Worse

Product	Type	Price/size, fl. oz.	Overall spot cleaning	Crayon	Grease	Pencil	Marred...[1]
Pine Power	L	$3.25/28	◉	◉	◐	◉	B
Spic and Span Pine	L	2.54/28	◉	◉	○	◉	A,B
Real Pine	L	1.76/22	◐	◉	○	◉	A,B
Lysol Pine Action	L	2.66/28	◐	◐	◑	◉	A,B
Lestoil	L	1.89/28	◐	◐	○	◐	A,B
Pine-Sol	L	2.72/28	◐	◐	◑	◉	B,V
Mr. Clean Lemon Fresh	L	2.24/28	◐	○	◐	◐	A,B
Pine Glo	L	.99/28	◐	○	○	◉	A,B,L,O
Natur-Pine	L	.94/28	○	○	○	◐	B
Lysol Direct	L	1.49/26	○	○	◐	◐	A,B,L,O,V
Top Job With Ammonia	L	2.35/28	○	○	○	○	B
Pine-Sol Spray	S	1.66/22	○	○	○	○	A,B,V
Cost Cutter Pine (Kroger)	L	1.09/32	○	◑	○	◐	—
Woolworth Spray-On Wipe-Off	S	1.13/22	○	○	○	○	A,B,G,S,V
Ajax Ammonia Fresh	L	1.96/28	○	◑	◐	○	A,B
Ajax Lemon Fresh	L	1.79/28	○	◑	◐	◑	A,B
No Frills (Pathmark)	L	1.21/28	○	○	◐	◑	A,B,O,V
Scrub Free Pine Fresh	S	.99/16	○	○	◑	◐	A,B,O,V
Lysol Pine Scent	L	2.54/12	○	○	◐	◑	A,B,L,O,P
Pine Magic	S	1.60/22	○	○	○	○	A,B,V
Kroger Bright Pine Scented	L	1.79/28	○	◑	◐	○	B
Fantastik	S	1.76/22	○	○	○	◑	A,B
Formula 409	S	1.70/22	○	○	◑	○	A,B,V
Murphy Oil Soap	L	2.39/32	○	◑	○	◑	A,B
Janitor In A Drum Fresh Lemon Scent	L	1.52/32	○	◑	◐	◑	A,B,S,V

● ◐ ○ ◑ ●
Better ◀———————▶ Worse

Product	Type	Price/size, fl. oz.	Overall spot cleaning	Crayon	Grease	Pencil	Marred . . . [1]
Lysol	L	2.69/12	◑	○	○	◑	A,B,L,O,P
Pathmark Premium	S	.92/22	◑	◑	○	◑	A,B
Bo-Peep Lemon Ammonia	L	.52/32	◑	◑	◑	○	A,B,O
Clean 'n Clear	L	2.39/28	◑	◑	○	○	B,L
Walgreens Super Spray	S	1.12/22	◑	◑	○	◑	A,B
Tackle	L	1.29/26	◑	◑	○	◑	A,B,S,V
Lysol Fresh Scent	L	2.22/28	◑	◑	○	◑	A,B,V
Parson's Clear Ammonia	L	.58/28	◑	◑	◑	○	A,B,O
Grease Relief	L	1.79/22	◑	◑	●	◑	B,V
Grease Relief	S	1.64/16	◑	◑	●	◑	B

[1] *One or more cleaners variously marred aluminum (A), brass (B), glass (G), latex paint (L), oil-base paint (O), acrylic plastic glazing (P), stainless steel (S), or vinyl composition floor tile (V). Check labels for further restrictions.*

Pine oil, a solvent that is a relative of turpentine, helps penetrate and loosen greasy dirt, and it's found in substantial amounts in good all-purpose cleaners. Pine oil also confers a certain psychological benefit: A pine scent left behind confirms to anyone within smelling distance that you have cleaned.

At full strength, an all-purpose cleaner should be used gently, then promptly and carefully rinsed off. Otherwise, you risk marring the surface. Most cleaners may be diluted for cleaning walls and floors with a sponge or a mop and bucket, and all should do a respectable job. But just plain water can do a decent job on many of today's no-wax floors.

Safety

Many products are somewhat caustic; a few are alkaline enough to warrant your using rubber gloves when cleaning, or at least avoiding prolonged contact with the skin. Since the solvents and other ingredients that dissolve, emulsify, suspend, or otherwise loosen grime are powerful chemicals, any cleaner should be used carefully and kept out of children's reach. To avoid potentially hazardous chemical reactions, never mix different cleaners together.

Recommendations

Many everyday spots and stains are not very hard to remove. Most products can be diluted for washing floors or walls and should be up to the task. And spot cleaning can always be improved, within limits, with the application of elbow grease.

It wastes money to pay extra for products that claim disinfectant properties. A disinfecting cleaner cannot sterilize every surface in a home or sterilize the air. At best, such a cleaner can temporarily reduce populations of some germs in a very limited area for a limited time. Keeping a sickroom clean—with any cleaner—and washing hands after contact with a sick person are usually sufficiently hygienic. If you need stronger germicidal protection, ask your doctor for advice.

BATHROOM CLEANERS

A specialized bathroom cleaner won't clean bathroom dirt any better than an all-purpose liquid cleaner, and a bathroom cleaner doesn't fight mold and mildew as successfully as household liquid chlorine bleach.

Bathroom cleaners are relatively new products; a few are promoted, for instance, as "mildew stain removers." Others seem to contain variations on old all-purpose formulas, but like other specialized products, bathroom cleaners often cost more—ounce for ounce—than all-purpose cleaners. The high unit price is somewhat disguised by the packaging (which also contributes to the extra cost). Bathroom cleaners generally come in pump-spray bottles or aerosol containers.

Most bathroom cleaners should prove fairly potent. You can improve a cleaner's performance if you let it stand on a surface for a minute or so before wiping it off. Nevertheless, if a specialized bathroom cleaner does well, spraying on a good liquid all-purpose cleaner will do better, melting dirt away without any scrubbing.

Mildew

The inclusion of antimildew ingredients is one thing that makes a bathroom cleaner different from an all-purpose cleaner. Cleaners that are likely to be most effective on mildew contain bleach, and undiluted chlorine bleach is, not surprisingly, the most effective mold fighter of all.

Many cleaning products claim germicidal powers—a pointless boast even when true. Germs are everywhere, a condition of normal living. Killing them unselectively in an otherwise unsterile environment is futile. Any bacteria that a bathroom cleaner may wipe out will be replaced in short order.

Spots and stains

A bathroom cleaner isn't really strong enough to corrode common bathroom surfaces on mere passing contact, but it may mar certain materials if allowed to rest on them for some length of time, as might happen when spatters go unnoticed.

A cleaner won't do significant harm to tile, to acrylic plastic, or to a typical countertop material. Most cleaners will discolor aluminum and brass—particularly brass—and leave visible spots of reduced gloss on fiberglass. Note, however, that the potential exists only through oversight or misuse; products should not harm common bathroom surfaces if they're promptly rinsed and wiped off.

Much the same thing can be said about the cleaners' effect on human skin, but other tissues could be more seriously affected. Virtually all the products bear strong cautionary statements on their labels. Most advise keeping their bottles out of the reach of children. All the sprays can irritate the lungs, so some warn against use by persons with certain ailments—asthma and heart disease, for example. Ingestion is apt to lead to serious consequences; so may sprays or splashes in the eye, especially if you wear contact lenses. It's sensible to wear rubber gloves while using these products and to make sure the bathroom has good ventilation.

Recommendations

Although a specialized bathroom cleaner offers respectable cleaning performance, a good all-purpose liquid cleaner costs less and does better.

Neither a bathroom cleaner nor an all-purpose cleaner is the most effective product for eliminating mold or mildew. If dampness and the fungal growth that accompanies it are particular problems in your bathroom, you may want to seek recourse in the best and cheapest mold fighter: ordinary household bleach.

Since bleach by itself isn't a good cleaner, there's a temptation to mix it with other products. Resist the temptation; it could prove quite hazardous. Bleach reacts almost instantly with acid to produce chlorine gas; and it reacts with ammonia and related alkaline substances to produce a combination of chlorine and other noxious gases. Never mix household cleaners or, for that matter, household chemicals of any kind.

Still, that's not to say that you shouldn't also use bleach in a room regularly scrubbed down with a cleaner. Just use the two separately. Make sure that you thoroughly rinse surfaces washed with bleach—something you'll want to do anyway because unwiped bleach can mar almost any smooth surface. What little bleach remains may soak into tile grout to prevent mold from taking hold again, but not in amounts great enough to hurt you when you next use another cleaner.

DRAIN CLEANERS

Most chemical drain openers are strongly corrosive alkalies or concentrated acids. They open blocked drains by eating and boiling their way through the clog. Obviously, chemicals strong enough to dissolve grease, hair, paper, and other debris can severely damage your eyes, lungs, and skin. Accidentally swallowing even a small amount of drain opener can result in appalling injuries or death.

To say that you should use these products with extreme caution is an understatement. It's best not to use chemical drain openers at all. The mechanical devices described below are much safer than chemicals and just as effective.

Mechanical methods

Often, the best way to clear a drain is to push or pull on the clog. You can buy a plunger, a plumber's snake, or a drain auger at any hardware store. None of these tools require special expertise to use, and you can depend on any of them to eliminate most clogs. A relatively new type of product uses pressurized air or gas to push an obstruction around the bend in the drainpipe and into the clear.

Some of the products are simply pressurized cans of chlorofluorocarbon gas. To use them, you stop up the sink overflow drain with rags, then push the can's cap down on the main drain opening to release the gas. The cans are handy, but not without drawbacks. There can be problems mating the caps with drain openings; a drain that's bigger than the cap will let some of the gas escape.

Another product, the *Pango Modelo Brevettato*, works on the pop gun principle. You stop up the overflow, pump a plunger in the pistol grip, insert the "muzzle" in the drain opening, and pull the trigger. The *Pango* sends a powerful blast of air straight down the drain. It delivers quite a bit more force than the pressure cans do, and it doesn't pollute. It worked well on clogged drains.

The *Sinkmaster* resembles a small bicycle pump. By pumping

on its handle, you exert both pressure and suction, moving a clog back and forth. It worked well, but fits only drains less than 1⅝ inches in diameter.

Some devices are meant to be used with a garden hose. They are available at hardware stores and look a little like a canvas pastry bag. You attach one to the end of a garden hose that you feed down the drain. Water pressure expands the bag, sealing it in place and pushing the clog free. The bags should work well, provided you can reach the sink with the hose.

Chemical cleaners

When most chemical drain cleaners contact standing water in a blocked drain, they release heat that liquefies congealed grease. Alkalies break down grease chemically as well, gradually converting it into a water-soluble soap. Sulfuric acid chars through such debris as paper or hair.

These chemicals may also damage plumbing and surrounding surfaces. If you have plastic (PVC) pipes, the heat liberated by these products may soften them, perhaps enough to loosen a glued joint. If you have metal pipes that are old and corroded on the inside, the heat and chemical action might be enough to put a hole in them. Acid solutions can corrode or etch stainless-steel sinks and damage aluminum fixtures, countertops, or wood. They may heat porcelain enough to crack it, so they should not be used in toilets.

Safety

Despite their proven hazards, dozens of chemical drain openers dot store shelves. The biggest sellers contain lye as their principal ingredient. Other products have hydrochloric or sulfuric acid. Only one of the chemical products tested by Consumers Union is not highly hazardous. Its principal active ingredient is an enzyme designed specifically to dissolve hair, one of the major culprits in blocked bathroom drains.

The heating action and chemical attack these products pro-

RATINGS OF CHEMICAL DRAIN CLEANERS

Listed, except as noted, in groups in order of estimated quality; within groups, products equal in quality are listed in order of increasing cost per use.
As published in a **January 1988** report.

● ◗ ○ ◖ ●
Better ← → Worse

Product	Type [1]	Price	Size	Kitchen use	Bathroom use
Double Agent	Caustic liquid [2]	$2.84	16 fl. oz.	◉	◗
Crystal Drano	Dry caustic	2.81	18 oz.	◗	○
Mister Plumber	Caustic liquid	1.60	32 fl. oz.	●	◖
Liquid Drano	Caustic liquid	1.89	32 fl. oz.	●	◖
Liquid Plumr	Caustic liquid	2.06	32 fl. oz.	●	◖
Lewis Red Devil	Dry caustic	1.19	12 oz.	●	●
The Works [3]	Hydrochloric acid	1.36	32 fl. oz.	●	●
Woolworth	Caustic liquid	1.00	32 fl. oz.	●	●
K-Mart	Caustic liquid	1.38	32 fl. oz.	●	●
Rooto	Caustic liquid	2.77	32 fl. oz.	●	●
Mr. Roebic	Caustic liquid	2.99	32 fl. oz.	◉	●
Microbe Lift II	Enzyme	7.48	16 fl. oz.	—	●

■ *The following products were downrated because they were judged by far the most dangerous type tested.*

Rooto Professional [3]	Sulfuric acid	4.79	32 fl. oz.	○	○
Instant Power	Sulfuric acid	5.46	32 fl. oz.	○	○

[1] *Caustic liquid and dry caustic products rely on heat and chemical attack to clear a blocked drain; both types contain heavy concentrations of lye. The two types of acid generate heat to burn through a clog. The main active ingredient in the enzyme product was designed specifically to dissolve hair.*
[2] *Comes with packet of metal nuggets to be used with liquid.*
[3] *Some or all samples came with an easily removed label, a serious safety problem.*

duce are supposed to loosen any blockage enough to let it ease down the line. To help get a clog moving, a couple of products also depend on tiny metal pellets that generate hydrogen gas bubbles, liberating more heat and adding some force to the unblocking effort.

The labels of chemical drain openers contain multiple warnings and precautions. But some of the advice could do more harm than good.

One label tells you to use a plunger if the product doesn't clear the blockage. That advice is an invitation to disaster; it would be all too easy to splash caustic water onto your hands or into your eyes. Another says to use one tablespoon, but the container's mouth was too small to admit a tablespoon. If you're pouring it out into a spoon, be careful not to spill any—and be sure to wash the spoon afterward. Still other containers may have a shrink-wrapped label that could easily come off, leaving behind an unlabeled container of dangerous acid.

The first-aid advice on labels varies, partly because doctors themselves disagree on the proper course in cases of accidental ingestion. Some labels suggest you attempt to neutralize the chemical with baking soda (for acids) or citrus juice (for lyes) or dilute it with water. But those treatments can cause a chemical reaction that liberates more heat and gas, aggravating the injury and possibly even perforating the stomach and esophagus. Most of these chemicals are so immediately and catastrophically damaging if swallowed that home remedies are apt to be dangerous, even fatal.

The best advice in the case of accidental poisoning is: Do not try to induce vomiting; rush the person to the hospital immediately. If drain cleaner splashes in someone's eye, flush it with cool water for at least 20 minutes, then get medical help as quickly as possible. Continue rinsing the eye on the way to the hospital.

GARBAGE BAGS

Manufacturers spend a lot of money trying to convince you their bag is stronger. Some bags boast that they're multi-ply or use a high-strength plastic. One brand's secret is "linear D formula." Another uses a special "stress-flex" plastic. But even if you think you can select a strong garbage bag, you still have to sort through more choices. Manufacturers offer an awesome variety of styles, colors, even scents to attract as many customers as possible and sell more bags than the competition.

Garbage bags go by many names, such as trash, rubbish, scrap, kitchen, wastebasket, or lawn and leaf. The name, along with some fine print on the box, is supposed to help you pick the right-size bag. But you've probably grabbed at least one box of "small garbage bags" instead of the "tall kitchen bags" you wanted. Or you may have bought a bag that "holds up to 26 gallons" yet barely fits your 26-gallon can. That happens because some manufacturers measure capacities when the bags are filled to the brim; others measure them closed. Another reason may be the sizing of your can. Without industry-wide standards, some bags will not fit some garbage cans, even though the gallonage is the same for both.

Bag strength

You might think that the thickness of the plastic or the number of plies, as given on the label, would be a good guide to the quality of a bag. Not so, judging from Consumers Union's tests. The thickest bags tested were labeled 2 mils, or 0.002-inch thick. (A mil is one-thousandth of an inch.) Those brands failed the test. But bags 1.3 mils thick passed.

You might also think that the more plies, the stronger the bag. Again, not so. Double- and triple-ply bags failed the test about as often as they passed. Many packages make no mention of plies. That might mean they contain single-ply bags. Or it might mean the number of plies changes whenever a distributor changes suppliers.

Recommendations

Plastic garbage bags are unpredictable. Tests show that paying more or buying the thickest bags you can find are no guarantees you'll get a strong bag. But, in fact, you may not even need

RATINGS OF GARBAGE BAGS

All tested samples of these bags survived the tests without breaking and are listed in order of increasing price.

As published in a **May 1988** report.

These bags passed the tests

●	◐	○	◑	●
Better ←			→ Worse

Brand and model	Labeled size, gal.	Price per bag	Dispensing	Closure type	Thickness (in mils)	Plies
Tall kitchen bags (13-gallon can)						
Pathmark	13	7¢	●	K	1.01 [1]	3 [1]
Kordite	13	7	●	W	0.9	—
Glad Sheer Strength	13	7	●	K	1.01	—
Glad	13	7	●	K	1.01	3
Hefty	13	8	●	W	1.01	—
Glad Deodorant	13	8	●	K	1.01	—
Hefty Odor Guard	13	10	●	W	1.01	—
Hefty Cinch Sak	13	11	●	D	1 [1]	—
Hefty Steel Sak Drawstring	13	12	●	D	1.1	—
Small garbage bags (26-gallon can)						
Kordite Heavy Load	26	14	●	W	1.5 [1]	2
Medium garbage bags (30-gallon can)						
Glad	30	12	●	K	1.3	3
Hefty	30	13	●	W	1.3	2
Hefty Steel Sak	30	15	●	W	1.4	2
Yellobags	30	16	○	W	—	—
Hefty Cinch Sak	30	16	●	D	1.3	—
Glad Heavyweight	30	19	●	K	1.7	3
Hefty Steel Sak Drawstring [2]	30	22	●	D	1.6	—
Large garbage bags (33-gallon can)						
Hefty Cinch Sak	33	27	●	D	1.3	—
Lawn and leaf bags						
Glad	39	20	●	K	1.5	3
Hefty Cinch Sak	39	22	●	D	1.4	—
Sears Best Extra Duty	45	41	●	W	1.75	—

Some samples of each brand did not survive the tests. Some brands had more survivors than others. The bags are listed in order of decreasing break resistance.
As published in a **May 1988** report.

These bags failed the tests

● ◐ ○ ◑ ●
Better ←————————→ Worse

Brand and model	Labeled size, gal.	Price per bag	Dispensing	Closure type	Thickness (in mils)	Plies
Tall kitchen bags (13-gallon can)						
Presto Smart Shopper	13	5¢	○	W	0.85	—
No Frills (Pathmark)	13	4	●	W	—	—
Safeway	13	8	●	K	1.01 ①	3 ①
Presto Smart Shopper Heavyweight	13	5	○	W	1	—
Sears Medium Duty	13	10	●	W	1.1	—
Glad Handle Tie	13	10	●	H	1.01	3
Ruffies	13	6	○	W	1.1	—
Dora May	15	11	●	W	—	—
True Value Lemon	13	9	●	W	1	④
Small garbage bags (26-gallon can)						
Kordite	26	9	●	W	1.1	2
Ruffies	26	8	○	W	0.95 ①	—
True Value Heavy Duty	26	13	●	W	1	2
No Frills (Pathmark)	26	7	○ ⑤	W	—	—
Medium garbage bags (30-gallon can)						
Safeway Heavy Duty ⑥	30	30	● ③	K	1.7 ①	—
Glad Sheer Strength ⑥	30	11	●	K	1.1	—
Pathmark Heavy Duty	30	18	●	K	1.7	3
Pathmark	30	10	●	K	1.3	—
Glad Handle Tie	30	16	●	H	1.3	3
Presto Smart Shopper Heavyweight	30	11	○	W	1.4	—
Ruffies	30	10	○	W	1.01	—
True Value Tru Tuff ⑦	30	26	●	W	2	2
Brute	30	9	○	W	1.2 ①	—

(Continued)

Better ← ● ◒ ○ ◒ ● → Worse

Brand and model	Labeled size, gal.	Price per bag	Dispensing	Closure type	Thickness (in mils)	Plies
Large garbage bags (33-gallon can)						
Glad Sheer Strength	33	15	●	K	1.2	—
Kordite Heavy Load	33	24	●	W	1.5 [1]	2
Hefty	33	22	●	W	1.3	2
Kordite	33	12	●	W	1.2	2
Safeway	33	19	●	W	1.3 [1]	—
Sears Heavy Duty	33	18	●	W	1.3	—
Sears Best Heavy Duty	33	25	●	W	1.5	—
True Value Tru Tuff	33	34	●	W	2	2
Ruffies	33	14	○	W	1.01 [1]	—
Lawn and leaf bags						
Pathmark	39, 40	17	●	K	1.5 [1]	—
Sears Heavy Duty	36	30	●	W	1.5	—
Hefty	39	20	●	W	1.5	2
Safeway	39, 40	15	●	K	1.5 [1]	—
True Value Tru Tuff	[8]	34	●	W	1.75	2
Kordite	39	23	●	W	1.3	—
Ruffies	[8]	21	○	W	1.3 [1]	—
Dora May	[8]	20	●	W	—	—

Key to closure type: W = Wire tie; K = Plastic key-lock; D = Drawstring; H = Handle tie
[1] *Some samples varied slightly in stated thickness or number of plies, or gave no information on packaging.*
[2] *All samples fit tightly in trash can used in our tests.*
[3] *The dispensing method varied for some samples.*
[4] *Labeled as multi-ply bags.*
[5] *Some packages had to be cut open.*
[6] *Some samples fit loosely in trash can used in our tests.*
[7] *Some samples fit loosely, others tightly in trash can used in our tests.*
[8] *Labeled size in bushels (7 for True Value Tru Tuff, 6 for Ruffies, 5 for Dora May).*

a strong bag. Unless you nearly always have very heavy garbage, you may be paying for unneeded extra strength. In that case, you might consider a cheaper bag of unknown strength. If the cheaper bag turns out strong enough most of the time, but not for the occasional heavy load, consider lining the garbage can with two bags when you need to. In the long run, that can be cheaper than buying stronger bags.

GLASS CLEANERS

Modern technology has made glass-cleaning chores quite easy, what with a host of products you can pump, spray, or pour. You can even make your own home brew from one-half cup of sudsy ammonia, a pint of rubbing alcohol (70 percent isopropanol), a teaspoonful of liquid dishwashing detergent, and enough water to make one gallon.

Convenience and cost

A fragile glass bottle would provide poor packaging for a product used in a wet and slippery job. Fortunately, just about every product comes in a sensible, break-resistant container.

Your choice, for the most part, is between push-button aerosol cans and plastic bottles that spray when you pull a trigger or pump a vertical plunger. Aerosols are slightly handier; you can spray a whole window at the single push of a finger.

Some pump-spray bottles offer special niceties. The best have a nozzle with Stream, Spray, and Off positions. Stream can be a help in special cases. It has a longer reach than Spray and it's more controllable on narrow surfaces.

Costs are worth consideration. Most of the pumps offer the chance of a secondary saving. Those products, not notably expensive to start with, offer bottled refills at a saving per fluid ounce of anywhere from about 20 to 50 percent off the original pump-bottle price.

Safety

Besides water, the main ingredients in glass cleaners—ammonia, alcohol, detergent—are typically present in such small amounts that they are not hazardous. But parents of small children should take heed: One or another label lists petroleum distillates, glycols, or butyl cellosolve, for instance, as an ingredient, along with a warning to keep the product out of children's reach. Since some products do not disclose their ingredients at all, keep *all* glass-cleaning products away from children.

Adults should exercise a bit of caution on their own behalf, too; an inadvertent squirt or splash in the eye could be irritating. That small hazard is more likely with the aerosols, which shoot spray at the press of a button. But it's also possible with bottled products whose pump is left at its On position. Misdirected glass cleaner should be flushed out of the eyes promptly with fresh, cool water.

Most cleaners' labels caution you not to let them contact one or another surface: furniture, fabrics, plastics, wood, or surfaces that are painted, varnished, shellacked, or lacquered, including some automobiles' painted finishes. To be on the safe side, quickly remove drips or spray from any nonglass surface.

Recommendations

If you live in the countryside, your windows probably do not accumulate much soil. In that case, save money by using the home recipe, which performs quite well at only ½ cent per window.

In urban or semiurban areas, industrial pollution may leave heavy soil on your panes. Similarly, pollution (or heavy smoking) will cloud your car windows. While any cleaner will do an adequate job, a glass cleaner you've tried and found effective will spare you rubbing effort.

HAND-HELD VACUUM CLEANERS

A hand-held vacuum cleaner, or minivac, is useful for many cleanup chores, not just for minor messes and spills. Accordingly, manufacturers have come up with machines that are increasingly powerful and versatile. Minivacs come corded and cordless, and can be fitted with several attachments, including power brushes, crevice tools, and handle or hand extensions. Some of them can pick up liquids as well as dirt.

Some models that run off household current have revolving brushes that make them work much like an upright vacuum cleaner. Most cordless models work by suction only. There are also cordless wet-dry models. (Consumers Union did not test minivacs that plug into a car's cigarette lighter.)

Effectiveness

Plug-in models with revolving brushes can do a better job on carpeting than cordless models. They can even remove sand and gravel embedded in a rug's pile. Their performance and portability make them well suited for cleaning carpeted stairs, and they won't run down after a few minutes, as cordless models do.

A plug-in minivac—with or without revolving brushes—is the machine to use for cleaning the car, provided you can maneuver the car close to an electrical outlet. A cordless model's longer reach often exceeds its grasp; it won't do anything more than suck up loose litter from seats and floor mats.

The cordless models, however, generally perform well on bare floors, where a little suction can go a long way; the revolving brushes in some plug-in machines won't help much on wood or linoleum. One big advantage of a cordless minivac is its maneuverability. Most come with a crevice tool extension that allows them to nose into tight corners and narrow spaces, such as under a sofa.

Wet-dry minivacs generally cannot pick up dirt quite as well as many cordless cleaners, but they can suck up milk and other liquids without much effort. They will, however, leave behind a thin coating of moisture that must be wiped up by hand. The wet-dry models draw dirt and liquid into a plastic reservoir. A standpipe or labyrinth arrangement keeps the liquid from trickling out, and a baffle keeps the dirt filter from getting wet.

RATINGS OF HAND-HELD VACUUM CLEANERS

Listed by types; within types, listed in order of estimated quality. Except where separated by bold rules, closely ranked models differed little in quality. Models judged about equal are bracketed and listed alphabetically. As published in an **October 1988** report.

Better → Worse: ◉ ◐ ○ ◑ ●

Brand and model	List price	Weight, lbs.	Running time	Capacity	Dry pickup — Hard surface	Dry pickup — Carpet	Dry pickup — Emptying	Noise	Crevice tool	Advantages	Disadvantages	Comments
Cordless models												
Rowenta Super Cleanette AC-05	$75 ·	2½ [1]	◉	○	◉	◐	◉	○	✓	C,G,H,K	—	B,F
Douglas ReadiVac Powercell 5 4050	39	1½	◉	◐	◐	◐	◐	○	✓	F	g,n	—
Kirby Split Second 460984	50	1½	◉	◐	○	◐	◐	○	—	F,G	g,n	—
Douglas ReadiVac Powercell 3 4030	30	1½	○	◐	◐	◐	◐	○	—	—	g,n	—
Oreck Zip Vac XL3600	30	1½	○	◐	○	◐	◐	○	—	—	g,n	—
Bissell 2-Way 3020	50	1¾ [1]	○	○	○	○	◐	○	—	B,G	d,j,m,n	A
Black & Decker Dustbuster Plus 9334	50	1¾	◐	◐	◐	◐	◐	◐	✓	F	b,e,i	H
Black & Decker Dustbuster, Power Brush 9338	70	1¾	◐ [2]	◐	○	○ [2]	◐	◐	—	—	b,e,i	C,H
Eureka Mini Mite 84A	40	1¾	○	◐	◐	●	◐	○	—	B,G,J,L	d,n	—
Regal Regalaire K50260	80	1¾ [1]	◐	◐	○	◐	◐	○	✓	F,G,K	l,m,n	A
Black & Decker Dustbuster 9330	39	1½	◐	○	◐	○	◐	◐	—	—	b,d,e,i	—

76

Cordless wet/dry models

										A,l	b,i	H
Sears Craftsman Wet/Dry Cat. No. 17834	37	2½	●	◐	◐	◐	◐	◐	—	—	—	—
Hoover Dubl-Duty 300 S1103	45	1¾	○	○	○	○	◐	◐	—	I	e	—
Hoover Deluxe Dubl-Duty 500 S1105	55	2	◐	○	○	○	◐	●	✓	I	e	—
Sanyo Wet & Dry PC-9WD	60	2	◐	◐	●	◐	○	◐	✓	G,I	d,e,p	—

Plug-in models

										A,l	b,i	H
Panasonic Jet-Flo MC-1060	75	3¾	—	◐	◐	◐	●	◐	—	E,F	k	E,G
Hoover Help Mate S1059 [3]	43	2	—	○	●	●	◐	◐	✓	F,K	—	—
Panasonic Jet-Flo MC-1050	58	3¾	—	◐	◐	●	●	◐	—	F,K	k	—
Sears Kenmore Hand Vac Cat. No. 60131 [3]	38	2½	—	●	◐	◐	◐	◐	✓	F,K,L	f	—
Royal Prince 501	90	4¼	—	◐	●	●	●	●	✓	D,E,F,K	n,o	D,H
Hoover Brush Vac S1083	54	3	—	●	●	●	●	●	✓	F	a,k	—
Panasonic VacuuMate HV-650 [3]	33	1¾	—	◐	○	◐	●	○	✓	J	—	—
Douglas Aardvac 6745	45	3¾	—	◐	○	●	●	◐	—	E,K	h,k,n	E
Royal Dirt Devil 103	50	3	—	●	●	○	●	●	—	—	c,k,n	—

[1] When used with stick-type handle, weight is 5 lb. (Rowenta); 2; n3. lb. (Bissell), 2 lb. (Regal). [2] Without power-brush attachment. With power brush, running time is a ◐, carpet pickup a ○. [3] Suction only.

Specifications and Features

All have: ● Plastic body ● Washable filter. ● Occasional tendency for debris to fall out of nozzle after shutoff.

All wet/dry models: ● Spew liquid out of vents when filled past their liquid capacity.

Except as noted, all: ● Cordless and cordless wet/dry models are suction only ● Plug-in models have revolving brushes and can't be converted to suction-only use. ● Have single motor speed.

Key to Advantages

A—Had the largest capacity of wet/dry models; did best in liquid pick-up.

B—Nozzle opening is relatively large; capable of sucking in larger objects.

C—Nozzle relatively wide.

D—Less tendency than most of its type to scatter debris.

E—25-ft. line cord; longer than most.

F—Comes with dusting brush. For models with revolving brushes, dusting brush keeps revolving brushes away from surface you're dusting.

G—Has charging indicator light.

H—Light indicates low-battery condition.

I—Has transparent dirt container; makes it easy to see when machine needs to be emptied.

J—Particularly comfortable handle.

K—More initial suction than most in lab tests.

L—Adjustable nozzle makes it somewhat easier to maneuver this model into tight spaces.

(Continued)

Key to Disadvantages

a—On/off switch inconvenient for one-handed use.

b—Can eject grit; eye protection may be advisable.

c—Revolving brushes had a greater tendency than most to scatter debris.

d—Had more difficulty than most picking up brads and pins from carpeting.

e—Corn flakes clogged in nozzle.

f—15-ft. line cord; shorter than most.

g—Charging connector on some samples may not make contact, or may pull out of mount when vacuum is removed.

h—Dust bag very inconvenient to reattach.

i—Relatively unstable in charging-stand holder.

j—Hard to put back into charging stand.

k—Large nozzle. Can't be used in narrow spaces or for cleaning very irregular surfaces.

l—Has switch that can be pulsed or locked in the On position. Switch was overly sensitive and machine often turned on accidentally.

m—Dirt container often hard to remove, replace.

n—Messy to empty or change filter.

o—Seal holding dirt bag wasn't always effective; dirt can blow in user's face if bag is squeezed.

p—Less initial suction than most in lab tests.

Key to Comments

A—Converts to lightweight upright; floor nozzle was relatively ineffective on hard surface.

B—Converts easily to lightweight upright; was relatively effective.

C—Comes with easily removable—and moderately effective—powered brush.

D—Comes with wand, crevice tool, and dusting brush for use in suction-only mode, but was hard to convert.

E—Has headlight.

F—Can be hung on wall, with accessories, fully assembled.

G—Has 2 motor speeds (tested at highest speed).

H—Cleaner and accessories can be stored on mounting bracket.

Safety and convenience

Hand-held vacuums are safe and easy to use. The only potential hazard associated with some is blowby, a tendency to spew fine dust through the air vents around the motor and out the sides. Blowby is more of a problem with cordless models, but it's usually a minor annoyance. Wear eye protection when using a model that ejects grit or sand forcefully.

Even when fully charged, cordless models lose their effectiveness in about 10 minutes. A plug-in model won't give out until you do, so it's better suited for bigger cleaning jobs, if you don't mind extended bending and stooping. Some minivacs come with a wand or a handle that transforms them into a lightweight upright, a feature that can help reduce back strain.

Its work done, a plug-in minivac can quickly be stored in a cabinet or closet. A cordless model has to be slipped into its charging stand, which must be mounted near an electrical outlet. Several cordless models have a tiny light that glows when the machine is firmly attached to its charging connector—a good idea.

To empty the dirt from most of the cordless models, you simply remove the nose, pull the filter free, and bang it against the side of a wastebasket a couple of times. The wet-dry units can be a bit more difficult to empty, especially if they have been used to pick up a mixture of wet and dry soil. A few of the plug-in models have a cloth bag at the rear that has to be shaken out for dumping. Many minivac models drop dirt on the floor while they are being taken apart for emptying.

Recommendations

For the best all-round performance on carpets and upholstery, a plug-in minivac with revolving brushes is probably your choice. The plug-in models that work by suction only are more maneuverable than the revolving-brush units, though less effective on carpets. Because of their maneuverability and power, suction-only plug-in models work well for cleaning cars.

The cordless minivacs have the edge in convenience, if not always in performance. They can go anywhere and fit into tight spots, but they also have a limited running time. In Consumers Union's tests, the performance of many cordless models varied considerably from sample to sample. If you buy a cordless mini-vac that seems to be running slowly even when fully charged, take it back to the store and exchange it.

OVEN CLEANERS

Most oven-cleaning products contain sodium hydroxide, or lye, one of the most dangerous substances sold for household use. Baked-on oven dirt is too tough for ordinary cleaners, which can only soften or dissolve grime. Lye causes a chemical reaction, decomposing the stuck-on fats and sugars into soapy compounds you can wash away. Lye-containing oven cleaners are corrosively alkaline, with a pH of about 13 on the 14-point pH scale. Any substance that far from the neutral pH of 7 is reactive enough to cause serious burns. That's why most of the labels contain a long list of warnings.

The majority of the cleaners on the market are aerosol sprays. Sprays are quick to apply, but hard to focus. Clouds of aerosol mist deposit cleaner not only on oven walls, but on heating elements, thermostats, light fixtures—and in your lungs. Yet most product labels warn you not to inhale the "fumes," by which they mean the aerosol droplets of lye.

As explained below, some application methods and container designs protect you more than others from exposure to caustic lye. Still, any product that contains lye must be used with extreme caution. Lye can burn skin and eyes. Inhaled droplets can actually burn the throat and lungs. Before using any cleaner containing lye, you should don safety goggles, a long-sleeved shirt, and rubber gloves. If you're using an aerosol, wear a paper dust mask, to keep from inhaling the droplets, and protective goggles.

Not only should you take steps to protect yourself from the corrosive effects of lye, you should also protect nearby floors, counters, and other surfaces. Spread newspaper on the floor in front of the oven. Take care not to splash any of the cleaner on aluminum, copper, or painted surfaces outside the oven, and keep it off the heating element, gaskets, and light fixture inside. Never use oven cleaner on a continuous-cleaning or self-cleaning oven.

Another way to avoid dangerous fumes and corrosive spatters is to use an aerosol cleaner without lye. For years, the only such product on the market was *Arm & Hammer* oven cleaner. The maker of *Easy-Off* bought *Arm & Hammer*'s cleaner and renamed it *Easy-Off Non-Caustic Formula*. In contrast to the lye-containing cleaners, *Easy-Off Non-Caustic Formula* has a pH of 9.5, about what hand soap would measure. Instead of using lye to break down oven grime, *Easy-Off Non-Caustic Formula* uses a patented combination of organic salts that are activated by heat. The product doesn't have to carry a long list of warnings on its label. It won't damage kitchen surfaces. You don't have to arm yourself with rubber gloves and a face mask to use it because it isn't likely to irritate.

Packaging

An oven cleaner's packaging affects its convenience of use and safety. Oven-cleaning products come in four forms: pad, aerosol, brush-on jelly, and pump spray. All have drawbacks.

Because they don't create airborne lye particles, pads are a relatively safe way to apply oven cleaner, as long as you've covered your hands and forearms. Aerosols are easy to apply, but easy to get on gaskets, heating elements, and sometimes your face by mistake. A broad, concave button makes it harder to misdirect the spray than a small button.

Not only is it tedious to paint an entire oven with brush-on jelly using a brush that's barely an inch wide, it's almost impossible to keep from spattering the jelly. Finally, a hand-pumped spray can be a real annoyance. The adjustable nozzle produces anything from a stream to a misty, broad spray. The stream doesn't cover much and splatters, and the spray is unnecessarily diffuse and easy to inhale.

RATINGS OF OVEN CLEANERS

Listed in order of overall quality, based on cleaning tests and on judgments of safety and convenience. *SOS* is for one use only; aerosols contain enough cleaner for two full applications.
As published in a **March 1987** report.

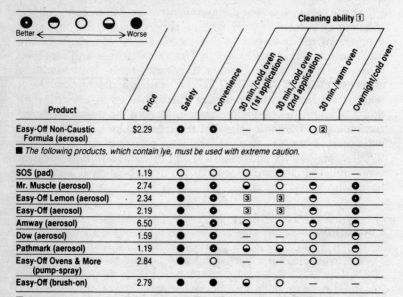

● ◑ ○ ◐ ●
Better ← → Worse

Cleaning ability [1]

Product	Price	Safety	Convenience	30 min./cold oven (1st application)	30 min./cold oven (2nd application)	30 min./warm oven	Overnight/cold oven
Easy-Off Non-Caustic Formula (aerosol)	$2.29	●	●	—	—	○ [2]	—

■ *The following products, which contain lye, must be used with extreme caution.*

Product	Price	Safety	Convenience	30 min./cold oven (1st application)	30 min./cold oven (2nd application)	30 min./warm oven	Overnight/cold oven
SOS (pad)	1.19	○	○	○	◑	—	—
Mr. Muscle (aerosol)	2.74	●	●	◑	○	◑	●
Easy-Off Lemon (aerosol)	2.34	●	●	[3]	[3]	◑	●
Easy-Off (aerosol)	2.19	●	●	[3]	[3]	◑	●
Amway (aerosol)	6.50	●	●	◑	○	◑	◑
Dow (aerosol)	1.59	●	●	—	—	○	◑
Pathmark (aerosol)	1.19	●	●	◑	◑	○	◑
Easy-Off Ovens & More (pump-spray)	2.84	●	○	—	—	○	○
Easy-Off (brush-on)	2.79	●	●	◑	○	—	—

[1] *Based on one application except where noted.* [2] *But* ● *when used twice.* [3] *Method recommended only for touch-ups.*

Recommendations

Even if you lack a self-cleaning or continuous-cleaning oven, you aren't necessarily sentenced to the hard labor of cleaning your oven. An oven in continual use can reach a steady state at which grease and grime burn off at the same rate that they accumulate. Serious spills, such as when a cake overflows its pan, can be scraped up after the oven cools. A little dirt in the oven never hurt anybody, a little oven cleaner might.

Easy-Off Non-Caustic Formula was the only product Consumers Union tested that was not hazardous. Therefore, *Easy-Off Non-Caustic Formula* is the only recommended oven cleaner. Although it is not quite as effective as some of the other cleaners, it is still a good cleaner and easy to apply. Used twice it does an excellent job.

PAPER TOWELS

Because paper towels are costly to haul long distances, most big paper companies make their towels at different mills. Some brands are the same nationwide, but there are also many regional and store brands. In a few cases, a nationally known brand name will vary from region to region.

Manufacturers try to take a bigger share of the market by selling many brands, aiming a premium brand, for example, at consumers who believe that a high price connotes high quality and a moderately priced brand at consumers who treat one roll of towels pretty much like another. One supermarket executive termed premium-priced towels "overspecified," meaning that they are thicker and heavier than they have to be. The over-specified towel gives the advertiser something to brag about and helps justify the generally higher price. That in turn pays for both the manufacturing costs and the heavy advertising and promotion expenses.

Quality

A paper towel should have good wet strength and absorbency. Combining those qualities is something of a technical achievement: Most of the papermaking processes that create strength tend to undercut absorbency, and vice versa. In addition, absorbency alone does not help much if it takes the towel a long time to get wet. You'll want a towel that absorbs liquids quickly if you're mopping up big spills or a spill on a carpet, for example.

Other properties become important for certain jobs. Some paper towels shed lint when they are used to wipe a hard surface, a shortcoming that's particularly noticeable if you use paper towels to wash windows or mirrors.

Towels printed in vivid colors can pose another problem: Some of the wet towel's color rubs off onto white cotton or white-painted panels. Since towel colors and designs change frequently, it's hard to say which brands are the most likely to run. But you can always avoid the problem by using white paper towels.

A towel that doesn't separate cleanly at the perforations can leave you with an avalanche of paper or a mere shred. That's not a common problem, provided the towel holder holds the roll securely.

Microwave towels

Ever since microwave ovens caught on, people have used paper towels to cook in them. Paper towels keep foods such as bacon or sausage from making a mess of the oven interior; the towels also help keep bread and rolls from drying out or getting soggy when they're warmed.

Some towels may have special microwave claims, and are named to make you think they are somehow special and therefore better than other brands for microwave cooking. But there's likely to be only one meaningful difference between ordinary and microwave towels: The microwave version is priced higher. Any white paper towel should work in a microwave oven.

Recommendations

The strongest, most absorbent towels are likely to be the premium-priced brands. But that doesn't make such towels the best value. For simple little spills or other small mop-ups, you might want to keep around a roll of cheap towels.

RATINGS OF PAPER TOWELS

Listed in order of estimated quality. Differences between closely ranked models were slight. Two products were check-rated.
As published in a **September 1987** report.

Better ← ● ◐ ○ ◑ ● → Worse

Product	Price per roll	Towels per roll	Sq. ft. per roll	Absorption capacity	Wet-strength	Water	Oil	Tearing ease	Linting
✓ Job Squad	$ .92	50	40	◉	◉	◉	◉	◉	○
✓ Viva (West, Midwest)	.83	90	71	◉	◉	◉	◉	◉	○
Bounty	.96	88	73	◉	◑	◉	◉	◉	◑
Bounty Microwave	1.02	88	73	◉	◑	◉	◉	◉	◑
Brawny	.77	70	73	◑	○	◑	○	◑	○
ScotTowels	.74	124	88	○	◑	○	◑	◑	○
ScotTowels Junior	.66	95	50	○	◑	○	◑	◑	○
Summit	.78	99	70	◑	◑	◉	◑	◉	○
Zee	.76	102	72	○	○	◉	◑	◉	○
Viva (East Coast, South)	.82	90	72	○	○	◉	○	◉	◑
Truly Fine (Safeway)	.88	115	78	○	○	○	○	◉	◑
Mr. Big	.52	100	69	○	○	○	●	○	○
Delta	.59	110	75	○	○	○	●	◑	○
Coronet	.71	115	79	○	◑	○	○	◉	○
Gala	.76	110	77	○	◑	◑	○	◑	○
Pathmark	.65	115	79	○	◑	◑	○	◑	○
Hi-Dri (East Coast)	1.19	200	148	○	◑	○	○	◑	◑
Hi-Dri (West Coast)	.67	100	74	○	◑	○	○	◑	◑
Pathmark	.50	130	89	○	◑	○	●	○	○
Marigold (Safeway)	.59	115	79	○	◑	◑	●	◑	◑
Cost Cutter (Kroger)	.42	108	77	◑	○	●	●	◉	○
Fleece (Kroger)	.56	108	77	◑	○	●	●	○	○
Marcal	.59	100	69	○	●	◑	○	◉	◉
A&P	.64	108	77	○	●	◑	○	◉	◑
Mardi Gras	.69	110	75	○	●	◑	○	◉	◑
No Frills (Pathmark)	.54	120	83	○	●	◑	○	◉	○
Swansoft (Kroger)	.72	108	77	○	●	○	○	◑	○

Absorption rate (Water, Oil)

For bigger jobs, such as washing windows or cleaning the stove top, you can always keep a spare roll of towels under the sink or in the broom closet. In this case, though, you should try to buy a brand that's superior in absorbency and wet strength and that's moderately priced by the square foot rather than by the towel.

A coupon or a special store sale may make an otherwise expensive brand a good buy. But don't think that towels in two-roll or three-roll packs give you a price break; most multiple-roll packs are probably no cheaper per 100 towels or per 100 square feet than single rolls of the same brand.

SCOURING CLEANSERS

Liquid and powder scouring products are abrasive, and a little bit of abrasion goes a long way. A really abrasive scourer can make the job of removing baked-on grime from ovens and barbecue grills (where appearances aren't important) easier. The same abrasive scourer will ruin the shine of expensive stainless-steel cookware or the unmarred surface of a new porcelain enamel sink or bathtub. The bigger and harder the gritty abrasive particles in a product, the more likely it is to damage the surface being cleaned.

Most scouring powders use silica, a quartz dust so hard it can scratch glass, plastic, and the glasslike enamel surface of your sink. Many of the "soft" liquid and powder cleansers use milder abrasives such as feldspar or calcium carbonate, but even the softest will do some damage.

How they work

Cleansing powders, generally, are a mixture of abrasives, soaps, detergents, bleaches, and alkaline or acidic chemicals. The abrasives help to lessen the labor needed to remove grime. The detergents or soaps help to wet the surface being cleaned, cut grease, and suspend some solids. The bleaches help to remove stains, particularly from old, abraded surfaces. The alkaline or acidic chemicals enhance the cleaning action of the detergent and have a cleaning action of their own (removing aluminum pot scrapes from porcelain enamel, for instance).

Few products claim disinfecting ability, although cleansers containing bleach are likely to have some degree of disinfectant power. Disinfecting doesn't mean much, however. Germs are everywhere. A disinfectant will kill germs, but they'll be back again as soon as you finish cleaning.

Abrasiveness

Regular use of any abrasive scouring product will gradually scratch the shiny surfaces of sinks, bathtubs, porcelain enamel, and kitchen appliances. Harsh abrasives can also damage plastic, glass, paint, and polished metals.

The least abrasive products will leave only a satiny glaze on porcelain after a good deal of rubbing. The average will leave it moderately abraded. The most abrasive products will dull porcelain quickly.

Overall, powders are more abrasive than liquids, but not always. Just about any cleanser will scratch acrylic plastic and aluminum; none can be safely used on mirror-finish metal. Generally, a scouring product that is gentle on porcelain is also gentle on plastic and aluminum.

Whatever product you use, remember that the effects of abrasion are cumulative. You might not scuff up the tub right away even if you scrub intensely, but light scrubbing over the years will eventually ruin the finish. To help minimize these effects, don't apply scourers with a heavy hand and a hard pad. Use a sponge or a soft cloth at first, and use a rougher applicator only if you can't get the cleaning results you want.

Stains

A powerful, abrasive cleanser that's good for general cleaning may not be the best for getting at stubborn stains. Stain removal depends on chemical action, usually the action of bleach. Most products are alkaline, meaning they are best at removing dirt, grease, grape juice, and other organic stains. The few acidic cleansers are useful for dissolving hard-water stains or metallic, colored spots.

Scouring products vary in their ability to remove common stains:

Aluminum scuffs.   Some sinks, especially older ones with a bit of their enamel worn off, tend to collect scuff marks from aluminum pots and pans. A good cleanser should remove those marks readily after being allowed to be in contact with the stain for approximately fifteen minutes.

Rust.   Only the special-purpose product discussed on page 90 is likely to be effective on rust or green metallic deposits.

Tea.   Chlorine bleach products should remove tea stains readily. Nonbleach products won't do it at all.

Safety

Cleaning products that contain chlorine bleach or acid should not be mixed with other cleansers. Chlorine bleach reacts with ammonia or acid and produces dangerous gases.

When you're cleaning, take off jewelry or wear rubber gloves. These scouring cleansers can dull the polish on a ring, scratch soft gems such as pearls and opals, and the chlorine bleach in some products can discolor silver.

Pads and sponges

Many scouring pads claim they can do almost any scrubbing chore. Some bill themselves as products that can handle the "tough" jobs, suggesting they are quite abrasive. In fact, some are gentle, some are tough—too tough, in fact, for many jobs.

Light-duty plastic mesh pads or reinforced sponges are probably the best choice for cleaning highly polished metals. Light-duty pads are generally safe to use on plastic-laminate countertops. Light-duty products are often labeled as well for use on nonstick-coated cookware, but repeated scourings may reduce the nonstick properties of the coated surface.

Overall, light-duty pads require a lot more rubbing than the heavy duty. They are less efficient with baked-on oven grime than powdered cleansers.

Removing gooey food residue is a different kind of chore— messy, but light duty. Plastic mesh pads and metal spirals are the most suitable type of pad for this job; they pick up the gloppy remnants and part with them easily when they are rinsed. Heavy-duty, abrasive-faced sponges and steel-wool pads are the least suitable. The former are more inclined to spread mess than pick it up; the latter won't let go of it in rinsing (and they lose any soap they contain—and therefore rust resistance—in the bargain).

It's safest to clean porcelain enamel with a cellulose sponge and powdered or liquid cleanser than with any kind of scouring pad. Light-duty scourers (plus detergent) are suitable for cleaning porcelain in good condition. Heavy-duty, abrasive-faced sponges and pads are much too abrasive for such cleaning and will prematurely age the finish. On an abraded surface, however, pads aren't able to get into the tiny hairline cracks that only a fine, powdered cleanser can reach. On that type of surface, too, metal pads are likely to leave marks.

Recommendations

You probably need more than one scourer, depending on what you have to clean. Using a highly abrasive cleanser on a new porcelain enamel sink or tub, for instance, will erode the surface and make it look old before its time. In fact, if you can clean that sink with just a wet sponge, some detergent, or a nonabrasive, all-purpose household cleaner, or a product specially formulated for the purpose—all the better. On the other hand, an old, abraded porcelain surface may require a more abrasive powdered cleanser with chlorine bleach to get into tiny cracks where the stains are.

To clean highly polished stainless-steel or aluminum cookware, try the least abrasive product—a plastic mesh pad—first. (Although here, too, if a soapy sponge or cloth will do the job, that's preferable.) Matte-finished metals can stand a little more abrasion than shiny metals. Cleansers can actually help to brighten matte-finished stainless steel, and steel wool can do some of the same for matte aluminum. Rub with the grain to minimize any abrasion.

Nonstick cookware and laminated countertops fare best with a soapy sponge or gentle abrasion—a plastic mesh pad or mesh-covered (reinforced) sponge. Save highly abrasive scrubbers for the nasty chores, such as cleaning the oven.

ZUD

◈ Scouring cleansers generally can't remove hard-water stains, rust, or the green stains that appear below the faucets in some houses with copper plumbing, but **Zud**—a special-purpose powder—claims it "works where ordinary cleansers fail."

Zud is, in fact, able to remove some rust stains that other products can't even touch. **Zud** can also remove tea stains as well as a good regular cleanser. It can also do a respectable job of dissolving aluminum scuff marks without scrubbing.

Zud doesn't work well on ordinary grime that accumulates on porcelain. Furthermore, it is quite abrasive.

Zud gets its stain-fighting power from oxalic acid, a very toxic chemical that attacks rust stains. Use **Zud** with care, and keep it safely out of the reach of small children.

TOILET BOWL CLEANERS

Stains in the toilet bowl result mainly from a buildup of minerals around the water line and under the rim. A common culprit is hard water, which has a high mineral content. As the water evaporates, mineral salts such as calcium or magnesium compounds and darker colored iron compounds are left behind, coating the upper part of the bowl and eventually hardening into a scale. Even with soft water, molds can form a brown coating in the bowl. If the ceramic surface is slick, such deposits hardly find a foothold. But if the surface has been scratched by abrasive cleaners or roughened with age, the buildup can grow rapidly.

Automatic, in-tank products are easiest to use, but generally only mask the dirt. The real cleaners are the liquid and granular in-bowl cleaners that are meant to be used with a brush.

In-bowl cleaners

Most of the in-bowl cleaners use acid to dissolve mineral scale and eradicate stains. Active agents include hydrochloric, phosphoric, and oxalic acids; some granular cleaners use sodium bisulfate, which when dissolved works like sulfuric acid. Brands with the highest total acidity have the greatest potential for cleaning. Products with lower acid content may require a bit more cleaner or a bit more muscle to do the job.

Nonacidic liquids won't be very effective at removing mineral stains. But they should work well on nonmineral stains, which are relatively easy to remove with a brush.

Ounce for ounce, the best bargain costs less than 20 cents a dose. You might try a dash of liquid all-purpose cleaner. Brushed on, it can clean a lightly soiled bowl quite satisfactorily for less.

Compared with liquids, powders are less convenient to apply around the bowl and under the rim. Most liquids come in a bottle with a flip-top spout. Unfortunately, even bottles with a recessed flip-top—supposedly child-resistant—can be opened easily by twisting off the entire cap.

The chemicals in these cleaners are powerful and should be handled carefully. Never mix an in-bowl cleaner with other household chemicals (including in-tank toilet cleaners). To do so could release toxic fumes.

In-tank cleaners

Most in-tank products subscribe to the out-of-sight, out-of-mind school of cleaning. They rely heavily on blue dye to tint the water and hide the dirt that accumulates between real scrubbings. Although blue cleaners generally contain small amounts of detergent and other ingredients to curb stains, none actually claim to clean a dirty bowl. With an in-tank cleaner, then, the question is not how well it works, but how long it lasts. Don't be too quick to change containers when the blue vanishes. Check to see if the dispensing valve has clogged or if the product is actually spent.

Some blue cleaners claim to deodorize. If you sniff packages on the store shelf, you may notice wintergreen, pine, or lemon scents. Indeed, the packages sometimes have a very strong smell. But once the cleaner dissolves in the tank, the scent is practically imperceptible.

Bleach

Some in-tank cleaners slowly dispense chlorine bleach to lighten stains and give off a scent that many people associate with cleanliness. Products containing bleach are likely to last longer than blue cleaners.

Consumers Union tested four products: *Bully Crystal Clear* and *Bully Plus Blue* are plastic dispensers of solid, organic bleach; *Sani-Flush 4 Month* and *2000 Flushes* are weighty plastic canisters filled with pebbles of calcium hypochlorite bleach.

The amount of bleach such cleaners release can vary considerably from flush to flush. Typically, it's very little—much less than a thimbleful of regular laundry bleach. They release enough chlorine to bleach stains, however, since the water may stand in the bowl for hours. Generally, such water won't harm pets, should they drink from the bowl, and neither will blue-colored water. But when a toilet isn't flushed at least once a day, the bleach can become more concentrated and may damage parts inside the tank. Some plumbing-fixture manufacturers recommend against using in-tank cleaners containing hypochlorite bleach.

RATINGS OF IN-BOWL TOILET CLEANERS

Most of these products contain acid to remove stains with some scrubbing. The weaker the acidity, the more cleaner or the more effort you may have to use. Listed in order of acidity.

As published in a **November 1988** report.

Product	Form	Price/size (oz. or fl. oz.)	Acidity	Scent
Lime-A-Way Bathroom/Kitchen ①	Liquid	$1.65/16	Very strong	Wintergreen
Sani-Flush	Granules	1.98/54	Strong	Wintergreen
Lime-A-Way Bathroom/Kitchen ②	Liquid	1.65/16	Strong	Wintergreen
Bully Foaming	Granules	2.29/34	Moderate	Fruity/chlorine
Vanish Thick Heavy Duty	Liquid	1.01/16	Moderate	Chemical/unpleasant
Lysol Toilet Bowl Cleaner	Liquid	1.59/24	Moderate	Wintergreen/peppermint
Scrub Free	Liquid	1.39/22	Weak	Floral
Lysol Cling	Liquid	1.29/22	③	Soapy/floral
Bully Swish	Liquid	1.54/24	③	Herbal/pine

① Contains phosphates.
② No-phosphate formula.
③ Nonacidic; judged appropriate for removing nonmineral stains.

Since you cannot see chlorine as you can blue dye, you might not know when to replace a bleach-based bowl cleaner. If your water is chlorinated, your nose may not tell you. You can use a drop of food coloring in the bowl to test. If the coloring lasts for more than a few minutes, it means the cleaner is spent.

Recommendations

The best way to clean the toilet bowl is to brush it frequently with a liquid all-purpose cleaner. In-bowl toilet cleaners are for more serious stains. Scrubbing with an acidic powder or liquid is the one sure way to attack the mineral matter that causes most toilet bowl stains, particularly around the rim.

RATINGS OF IN-TANK TOILET CLEANERS

These products don't do much cleaning; instead, they mask stains or lighten them.
Listed by types; within types, listed in order of cost per 100 flushes.
As published in a **November 1988** report.

Product	Form	Price/size (oz. or fl. oz.)	Flushes	Cost per 100 flushes	Scent
Blue-colored cleaners					
Bully Blu-Boy	Solid in jar	$1.09/9	1950	6¢	Ammonia/wintergreen
Royal Flush	Solid in jar	.82/9	950	9	Chemical/chlorine
Bloo Blue Spruce	Drop-in disk	1.15/1.7	900	13	Pine
Vanish Drop-Ins	Drop-in disk	1.11/1.7	700	16	Wintergreen
Topco	Liquid	.99/18	400	25	Lemon/chemical
Ty-D-Bol	Liquid	.99/12	400	25	Citrus
Pathmark	Liquid	1.07/18	250	43	Lemon/citrus
Austin's Forever Blue	Liquid	.72/12	150	48	Ammonia
Blue Vanish	Liquid	1.51/12	300	50	Spice/chemical
Chlorine-bleach cleaners					
Bully Crystal Clear	Solid in dispenser	1.25/0.7 [1]	2800	4	Chlorine
Bully Plus Blue [2]	Solid in dispenser	1.67/1.3	2150	8	Chlorine
Sani-Flush 4 Month	Solid in canister	2.27/14	2150	11	Chlorine
2000 Flushes	Solid in canister	2.42/14	2150	11	Chlorine

[1] Purchased in twin-pack for $2.49.
[2] Also dispenses blue colorant, which disappeared after approx. 600 flushes.

In-tank cleaners, blue-colored or bleaches, are easy to use, but don't expect miracles. If you start with a spotless toilet, they will only slow the buildup of new stains and keep the bowl presentable between more thorough scrubbings. In-tank bleach cleaners should not be used in a toilet that isn't flushed regularly. Enough chlorine can accumulate to damage parts inside the tank.

Finally, do not let any brand's claims to disinfect sway you. At best, a "disinfecting" cleaner can only temporarily cut the population of some germs.

Laundry

CLOTHES DRYERS

A clothes dryer is basically a simple appliance, a cabinet with a rotating drum through which a fan blows air heated by gas or electricity. The newest things in dryer design are electronic controls and moisture sensors, and they aren't all that new.

Electronic controls, with touch pads and digital displays, may give a futuristic look to a dryer. They can also add as much as $200 to its price. But when the added cost is small, as it can be, the controls may offer enough extra to justify the money.

Moisture sensors can improve the function of automatic drying cycles. A sensor samples the load's moisture directly. It should be able to shut the machine off as soon as the load is dry, avoiding wasteful overdrying. The alternative, an automatic dryness control that uses a temperature sensor, has been standard equipment on dryers for decades. A thermostat checks the load's dampness indirectly. As the clothes dry, air leaving the drum gets progressively hotter until the thermostat shuts off the heat. The timer then advances until the heat goes on again. That sort of back-and-forth continues until the heating part of the cycle has ended. A moisture sensor adds anywhere from $25 to $40 to a dryer's price. It's usually found in full-featured models. In some major brands, however, models lower in the line also feature a moisture sensor.

Note that some dryers lack an automatic drying cycle, and have only a timed cycle. An automatic drying cycle, governed either by a moisture or a temperature sensor, is a worthwhile feature. It may pay for itself by reducing overdrying and saving energy.

You probably won't notice the small differences in performance from one dryer model to the next if, like many people, you put everything from jeans and towels to undershirts and nightgowns into the washer, shift the load to the dryer, then collect it the next morning.

Performance

To cope with a variety of laundry, dryers typically offer two or three automatic cycles (named Regular, Knit/Synthetic, Permanent Press, or the like), as well as timed and unheated settings. A More Dry to Less Dry range on the automatic settings lets you adjust the setting to the laundry you're drying, using More Dry for mixed loads of heavy and light items and Less Dry for delicates, for example. (That control is also useful when you want to leave a load slightly damp, for ironing or to make corduroys look better.) In addition to the cycles, dryers generally also offer a temperature selector, with choices often given in terms of the type of fabric to be dried.

A good dryer ought to be able to dry the laundry thoroughly, without heating the fabrics too much. Conventional laundry wisdom has it that cotton can take the hottest drying temperatures, that permanent-press fabrics need a somewhat cooler cycle, and that delicates need a cycle cooler still. Too much heat not only wastes energy, but can also make a garment feel harsh, cause seams to pucker, and degrade elastic waistbands or straps.

No dryer is likely to produce temperatures too hot for cotton. On the other hand, some models cannot dry mixed loads of heavy and light fabrics completely, even at their maximum heat settings.

Most of the automatic delicate cycles run on the hot side, typically at 150° to 170°F. The electronic moisture-sensing models do best, sometimes raising temperature to only 100°F when set for minimum drying. The differences between dryers are smallest with a permanent-press load. Every model should be able to dry it thoroughly, reaching temperatures from 150° to 200°F.

All fabrics, but especially permanent-press clothes, will wrinkle if left in a warm heap. It's best to remove a load from the machine as soon as it's dry. Since that is often not feasible, dryers have a tumble-without-heat phase at the tail of any automatic cycle to reduce wrinkle problems. The cool-down is generally extended to some degree when you set the machine for permanent-press, the idea being to cool the load to room temperature. A short cool-down period causes some dryers to leave loads too warm. With most models, however, you can set an extra tumble period of 15 to 150 minutes to follow the automatic or permanent-press cycle when you put the load in to dry.

All dryers, even those with automatic dryness control, allow timed drying; the maximum times range from almost an hour to two hours. Timed drying is suggested by several manufacturers to keep from overheating small loads. Plastic and rubberized items are best dried with little or no heat; all the models provide a Fluff or Air setting. That cycle typically turns itself off in less than an hour.

Convenience

Good performance isn't the only consideration in a dryer. You also want one that's easy to live with. Some factors to note follow:

Controls. Some dryers have electronic controls, touch pads that hardly move when you press them. Those controls are not quite as informative as the rotary control on most of the other dryers.

In a rotary control, an indicator moves around a dial in clock fashion, telling you roughly where you are in the cycle. The electronic touch pads merely have little indicator lights that tell you which cycle you've chosen. The electronic controls display how much time is left only in the last few minutes of an automatic cycle. If you're using a timed cycle, the display shows exactly how many minutes have elapsed.

Whether electronic or rotary, the controls will generally let you set a timed cycle fairly flexibly for the amount of time you think a particular load needs.

Door.   Most doors swing to the right side; a few swing to the left. A number of doors are mounted high enough so that you can set a fairly tall laundry basket directly under the opening. The door of some models swings downward. That kind forms a handy shelf for loading and unloading, but slightly impedes access to the rear of the drum.

The D-shaped opening in some doors is supposed to help you remove your laundry without dropping stray items. But those models are no more convenient to unload than others with a round or rectangular opening. An oversized opening in a few models, however, can prove helpful.

Light.   You'll find a drum light useful, even in a fairly well-lit laundry room. A number of models have only a rather dim light, or none at all.

Rack.   Some dryers can be fitted with a drum rack for drying sneakers and other items without tumbling them. A few of those models also come with a detachable outside rack, a pole-and-arm device that you can use to hang shirts and other items on directly from the dryer.

Lint filter.   Your dryer will work most efficiently if you clean its lint filter after every load. That being so, the whistle or light on some dryers to indicate lint buildup has little advantage. Models with the filter in the doorsill make you stoop to get at it. A top-mounted filter is easier to remove, but it's apt to drop a bit of lint on the dryer's top as it comes out. You also must be careful not to drop anything down the opening.

Signals.   All models have a buzzer or other warning that sounds at the end of their drying cycle; the signal's loudness is adjustable in many models. The ones that let you set extra tumble time also signal periodically during the extended tumbling period.

Running cost.   Gas dryers handle clothes about as well as electric dryers, but for less than one-third the cost. At average national rates (electricity at 7.9 cents per kilowatt-hour, gas at 61.7 cents per therm, which is about 100 cubic feet), drying a 10-pound load would cost about 6 cents a load with gas, more than three times that with electricity. That estimate includes the electricity for the gas model's motor and controls.

Brand reliability

In Consumers Union's 1987 Annual Questionnaire, readers were polled about their repair experiences with clothes dryers. The "Repair index by brand" graph is based on more than 195,000 responses and shows the reliability of full-size clothes

CLOTHES DRYER REPAIR INDEX BY BRAND

As published in a **May 1988** report.

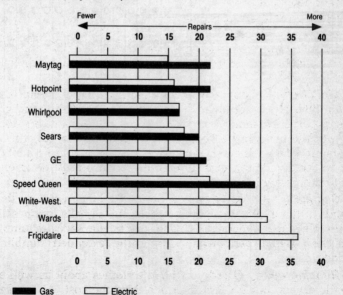

RATINGS OF CLOTHES DRYERS

Listed, except as noted, in order of estimated quality; bracketed models were judged approximately equal and are listed alphabetically.

As published in a **May 1988** report.

Better ● ◐ ○ ◖ ● → Worse

Electric models

Brand and model	Price	Dimensions (H × W × D), in.	Depth, door open, in.	Mixed-load drying (small)	Mixed-load drying (large)	Permanent-press	Delicates	Advantages	Disadvantages	Comments
Sears 66941	$648	43x29x28	42	●	○	◐	◐	A,C,D,E,F,G,I,J,L,M	—	B,C,D,F,H
Whirlpool LE9800XS	452	42½x29x28	42	◐	◐	◐	●	C,E,F,I,L,M	g	B,C,D,F,H
Sears 66921	424	43x29x28	41¾	◐	◐	●	●	A,C,F,G,I,L,M	—	B,C,D,F
Admiral DE20F8	345	44x27x27½	50	●	●	○	○	F,H,N	b,d,f,g	—
Montgomery Ward 7835	428	44x27x27½	50	◐	●	○	○	B,F,H	b,d,f,g	—
Norge DEF20-8	375	44x28¼x27½	50	●	●	○	○	F,H	b,d,f,g	—
Whirlpool LE7800XS	362	42½x29x28	41¾	●	○	◐	●	C,I,L,M	c,g	B,C,D,F
Speed Queen NE8533	422	43x27x28	47¼	○	○	○	○	A,C,E,F,O	d	B,H
KitchenAid KEYE800	465	42½x29x28	42	◐	◐	◐	○	C,D,E,I,J,L,M	g	A,B,C,D,F,I
Frigidaire DECID	379	44x28¼x27¼	53	○	○	◐	○	H,M,N	b	—
Maytag DE712	485	43¾x28½x27	47	◐	○	○	○	J,O	f	E,G
Speed Queen NE7513	397	43x27x28	47¼	◐	◐	○	○	A,F,N	b,d	—
Amana LE2500	382	42x27x28	47¼	◐	○	○	○	A,H,O,P	b,d	—
General Electric DDE9200G	418	43½x27x27½	53½	◐	◐	◐	◐	A,H,O,P	e,h,i	G
Gibson DE28A7	317	43x28¼x27¼	53	◐	○	○	○	H,M,N	a,c	—
Kelvinator DEA900C	318	43½x28¼x27¼	53	○	○	○	○	H,M,N	a,c	—

100

Model		Dimensions, HxWxD (in.)	Weight (lb.)	Ratings	Advantages	Disadvantages	Comments
Maytag DE612	454	43¾x28½x27	47	● ◐ ○ ● ○	J	e	E,G
Sears 66731	381	43x29x28	42	◐ ◐ ○ ● ●	C,I,M	e	C,D,F
White-Westinghouse DE800J	349	43¾x27x25½	48	◐ ◐ ○ ● ○	A,K,P	e	—
General Electric DDE8200G	392	43½x27x27½	53½	● ● ◐ ● ◐	A,H,P	e,i	G
Hotpoint DLB2880D	369	42½x27x27½	53½	● ◐ ○ ● ○	A,H,P	e,i	G
Gas models							
Sears 76921	468	43x29x28	41¾	● ◐ ◐ ● ●	A,C,F,G,I,M	—	B,C,D,F
Whirlpool LG7801XS	413	42½x29x28¼	42	● ◐ ◐ ● ●	C,I,M	c	B,C,D,F
General Electric DDG9280G	464	43½x27x27½	53½	◐ ◐ ◐ ◐ ◐	A,H,P	e,h,i	G
Maytag DG712	523	43¾x28½x27	47	● ◐ ● ◐ ●	J	f,g	E,G
White-Westinghouse DG800J	367	43¾x27x25½	48	◐ ◐ ◐ ● ○	A,K,P	e	—
Hotpoint DLL2880D	415	42½x27x27½	53½	● ◐ ◐ ● ◐	A,H,P	e,i	G

Specifications and Features

All have: ● Automatic dryness-control cycle. ● End-of-cycle signal. ● No-heat (air-fluff) setting. ● 4 leveling legs.

Except as noted, all have: ● Provision for at least 30 min. of added tumble time at end of permanent-press automatic-drying cycle. ● Continuously adjustable timed cycle. ● Rotary timer dial. ● Well-calibrated automatic dryness control that tells at a glance roughly where dryer is in its cycle. ● Drum light. ● Baked-enamel finish on cabinet top and drum. ● Door that opens to right. ● Venting from rear, either side, or bottom.

Key to Advantages

A—Loudness of the end-of-cycle signal can be adjusted.
B—End-of-cycle signal can be turned off.
C—Signals when lint filter is full.
D—Has fluorescent light on console.
E—Console has lighted display.
F—Comes with rack for drying items without tumbling.
G—Comes with exterior rack for hanging clothes.
H—Door is mounted high enough to clear a tall basket.
I—Oversized opening of door makes loading and unloading easier than with others.
J—Porcelain-coated cabinet top.
K—Nonglare control panel.
L—Damp-dried mixed loads well.
M—Plastic leveling legs make dryer relatively easy to move for cleaning.
N—Cooler maximum temperature than most with delicate loads.
O—Best at damp-drying delicate loads.
P—Porcelain-coated drum.

Key to Disadvantages

a—No provision for added tumbling time.
b—Cycle-selector dial turns only one way.
c—No drum light.
d—Drum light fairly dim.
e—Overdried slightly damp mixed loads when control was set at maximum-drying position.
f—Automatic-dryness control is poorly calibrated.
g—Did not completely dry 12-lb. load on automatic setting.
h—In CU's samples, fabrics snagged slightly on moisture sensor inside drum.
i—Slight gap around edge of filter assembly allows lint to bypass filter.

Key to Comments

A—Timed-dry cycle not continuously adjustable.
B—During added tumble, drum turns for some 10 to 30 sec. every 5 min.
C—Lint filter can be removed from top of cabinet.
D—Door opens downward.
E—Door opens to left.
F—Vents to rear only.
G—Vents from rear, left, or bottom.
H—Has electronic controls with touch-pad control panel.
I—Has mechanical, push-button controls.

dryers bought new over the preceding ten years. Almost three out of four were electric models, the rest gas.

The graph shows the percentage of dryers of various brands that have ever required repairs. It covers all the brands for which there were sufficient responses. The data were adjusted to compensate for age differences among dryers of different brands. Differences in score of three or more percentage points are meaningful.

While gas dryers usually proved more trouble-prone than their electric brand mates, some brands of gas dryer were more reliable than electrics of other brands.

The data, of course, apply only to brands; specific models may fare better or worse than the brand as a whole. The repair index also looks backward, necessarily ignoring the effect that changes in design, quality control, or brand ownership may have on future reliability. Nevertheless, you probably have a much better chance of avoiding repair headaches if you choose from among the brands at the top of the graph.

Recommendations

If natural gas is available to you, it's worth spending the $40 or so premium that a gas dryer commands over its electric counterpart. Energy costs are so favorable to gas models that the difference in purchase price can easily be made up in running-cost savings in the first year of use. Be sure to order a gas dryer specifically for the sort of gas (liquefied petroleum or whatever) it will burn.

FABRIC PILLING REMOVERS

There are a number of gadgets for removing "pills" from fabric. Pilling commonly occurs when fabric fibers that are worked loose by rubbing form little balls. Fibers that still hold firm in the fabric keep the pills from falling off. Loosely woven and knitted synthetics and blends are the typical candidates for pilling. Usually, the stronger synthetic fibers hold the pill to the surface. Pilling can happen to clothes, blankets, and upholstery fabrics, but sweaters seem especially vulnerable.

Some of the pill-removing gadgets work like miniature electric shavers. A battery-powered motor drives a fan-shaped cutting blade. The blade sweeps behind a screen with holes large enough for most pills to stick through and, in effect, beheads the pill. Other pill removers are lightweight stones, like pumice.

In Consumers Union's tests, the gadgets removed pills, but the effort and the results weren't always the same. It depended mostly on the type of fabric and the density of the pilling.

The shavers worked best on smaller pills, especially those on fabric that didn't have a nap. The shavers also worked better than the stone on stretchy knits, which tended to be pulled and distorted by the snaggers.

The stone worked best on large pills, especially those on firmly constructed materials such as overcoating or other heavy weaves. It also restored a nap on fabrics that had one. The tested stone emitted an unpleasant smell each time it was used, though the smell didn't linger.

Both gadgets removed pills, but the device you need depends on the fabrics that are pilling on you. If you have sweaters with light pilling and an overcoat with heavy pilling, you need both a shaver and a stone. However, one dry cleaner advised Consumers Union: "We in the dry-cleaning business have found that the fastest and most reliable way to remove pills (or slubs, as they are formally called) is to use a common twin-blade safety razor. You simply shave the pilled area as you would skin. The pills come right off."

FABRIC SOFTENERS

Detergents clean fabric fibers so effectively and rinse out so thoroughly that they can leave clothes feeling scratchy, and the tumbling action of dryers increases the buildup of static electricity on

RATINGS OF FABRIC SOFTENERS

Listed by types. Within types, listed in order of fabric-softening ability in hard water. Products rated equal in softening ability are listed in order of cling reduction. Differences between closely ranked products were slight.

As published in a **July 1987** report.

Rating key: Better ← ◉ ◓ ○ ◒ ● → Worse

Product	Type	Cost per use	Hard water Softness	Hard water Cling	Soft water Softness	Soft water Cling	Comments
In-detergent products							
Ivory Snow	Powder	24¢	◉	○	◓	●	B
Bold 3	Powder	16	◓	◓	◓	◓	A
Bold 3 (phosphate)	Powder	17	◓	◓	○	◓	—
Clean 'n' Soft (Kroger)	Liquid	21	○	◉	○	○	A
Bold 3	Liquid	26	○	◉	○	○	A
Fab	Powder	16	○	◉	◓	○	C
Sears	Liquid	28	○	◉	◓	◉	A
Sears Best	Powder	37	○	◉	○	◉	A
Solo	Liquid	25	○	◉	○	○	A
Fab	Liquid	22	◓	◓	○	●	—
Yes	Liquid	19	◓	◓	○	○	—
Purex	Liquid	21	◓	○	◓	○	—
Fab (phosphate)	Powder	17	◓	○	◓	◓	D
Liquid-in-washer products							
Snuggle	Conc.	8	◓	◉	◓	◉	—
Final Touch	Conc.	9	◓	◉	◓	◉	—
Downy	Reg.	8	◓	◉	○	◉	—
Fresh n' Soft (Kroger)	Conc.	4	◓	◉	○	◉	—
Purex StaPuf	Conc.	6	◓	◓	○	○	—
Pathmark	Reg.	2	◓	○	○	○	—
White Magic (Safeway)	Conc.	5	◓	○	○	◓	—
Lady Lee (Lucky)	Conc.	3	◓	○	◓	○	—
Par (Safeway)	Reg.	3	◓	○	◓	○	—
Downy	Conc.	8	○	◉	○	◉	—
Lady Lee (Lucky)	Reg.	3	○	◓	○	◓	—
Pathmark	Conc.	3	○	○	◓	○	—
Cost Cutter (Kroger)	Conc.	2	○	○	◓	○	—

Better ← ● ◐ ○ ◑ ● → Worse

Product	Type [1]	Cost per use	Hard water Softness	Hard water Cling	Soft water Softness	Soft water Cling	Comments
Sheet-in-dryer products							
Pathmark	Sheet	2	●	●	◐	●	—
Scotch Buy (Safeway)	Sheet	4	●	●	○	●	—
Purex Toss 'n Soft	Sheet	5	◐	●	○	●	—
Bounce	Sheet	5	◐	●	○	●	—
Arm & Hammer	Sheet	4	◐	●	○	●	—
Snuggle	Sheet	5	◐	●	○	●	—
Lady Lee (Lucky)	Sheet	4	◐	●	○	●	—
Cling Free	Sheet	6	◐	●	○	●	—
Kroger Bright	Sheet	4	◐	●	○	●	—
Purex StaPuf	Sheet	4	◐	●	○	●	—
White Magic (Safeway)	Sheet	5	◐	●	○	●	—
Cost Cutter (Kroger)	Sheet	3	◐	●	◐	●	—
Free n' Soft	Packet	5	○	○	◐	○	—

[1] *Detergents that contain fabric softeners come in either **powder** or **liquid** form. Liquid fabric softeners, used in the rinse cycle of the washer, come in two strengths—**regular** or **concentrated**. Concentrated products require less per use—two fluid ounces versus three, on average. Most softeners for use in the dryer are an impregnated **sheet** of urethane foam, polyester, or cellulose that you discard after one use. Free 'n Soft is a reusable cloth **packet** that attaches inside the dryer.*

Key to Comments
A–After three washes, laundry didn't look as white as laundry that was washed with regular detergent.
B–Soap; inherently fabric-softening.
C–New formula tested as we went to press ("Advanced Softening System" on box); softened better than formula listed.
D–New formula tested as we went to press ("Advanced Softening System" on box); performance similar to formula listed.

synthetics. By thinly coating the fibers of fabric with a waxy deposit, fabric softeners solve both problems.

First marketed in the late 1950s, fabric softeners originally came as a creamy liquid, often pink, that was added during the rinse cycle of the washing machine. Liquid fabric softeners now compete with more convenient products—sheets you throw in the dryer along with the wet laundry and detergents that include fabric softeners.

Recommendations

A rundown of what fabric softeners can do follows:

• Fabric softeners tend to work better in hard water than in soft, probably because hard water rinses clothes less thoroughly.

• Most detergent/softeners sacrifice performance for convenience. As a group, these products do no better as fabric softeners than as detergents.

• Combination products are no bargain. The typical detergent/softener costs 22 cents per wash. Subtract 16 cents for the cost of the typical detergent, and you're left with 6 cents as the cost of softening, compared with the cost of the typical dryer sheet (3 cents) and the typical liquid (4 cents).

• The best products, as a group, are dryer sheets, particularly when the wash is done in hard water. With both hard and soft water, they are unsurpassed for reducing static cling.

• Laundry washed with soap doesn't need softening. *Ivory Snow* can produce soft laundry in both hard and soft water. It won't do much for static cling, however.

Note some cautions when using fabric softeners. All the dryer sheets carry a warning to use low-heat settings for synthetics and blends, lest oily spots appear at higher heat. The same problem can occur if there are only a few items in the load. Liquids can also cause spotting if they're poured directly onto clothes. The remedy for these spots: Moisten the fabric, rub the spot with a bar of soap, and wash again.

HAND-LAUNDRY DETERGENTS

Sometimes a garment's fabric makes it more difficult to clean. Woolens can shrink or lose their shape. Silks can shrink, pucker, or fade. Some cottons can shrink or fade, too.

Sometimes the fabric's finish makes laundering difficult. Rayon, for instance, needs a finish to give it body, a finish that harsh treatment can wash away. A garment's weave, its dyes, or its construction (linings, edgings, and interface) can make cleaning an all but impossible job.

Your best guide on how to clean a fabric is the care label, which by law must be sewn into all articles of clothing. If that label says a garment must be dry-cleaned, take the advice, or you will have no recourse with the manufacturer or retailer should something go wrong. If the label permits hand-washing, you have to decide how to wash it.

On supermarket shelves, next to the regular detergents, stand many products that make special claims for cleaning wool, cotton, and silk. But make a detergent *too* specialized, and shoppers may pass it up for something that can tackle a wider variety of garments. So these cleaners also claim to work on other "fine washables," too. Increasingly, dishwashing liquids say they can double as detergent for fine washables.

The detergent edge

A detergent of any stripe is a big improvement over old-fashioned soap. In hard water—as most of the country's homes have—soaps leave behind a gray scum. Not so detergents, with their synthetic ingredients to lift soil off and keep it suspended in the wash water. Detergents generally include other ingredients to help remove grease and improve sudsing. Some have optical brighteners to make whites look whiter and enzymes to help attack stains.

You should think twice before using regular detergent on fine washables, though. Most regular detergents are quite alkaline, and that could damage natural fibers like wool and silk. The special products are supposedly gentler.

Effectiveness

In its tests, Consumers Union used a special machine to simulate very gentle hand-washing and always washed fabric test swatches in water at 70°F, a temperature warm enough to be comfortable to hands but cool enough to prevent shrinkage. Wash and rinse times were kept to four minutes each, because the less time that delicate fabrics are left soaking, the better.

Cleaning.   Although no test swatch was quite as white after laundering as it had been when brand-new, some products cleaned appreciably better than others—a difference even untrained eyes could appreciate. The product's type had little bearing on how well it cleaned. Special detergents, regular detergents, and dishwashing liquids all were represented among the best cleaners.

Brightening.   The optical brighteners found in regular detergents and most hand-laundering products adhere to fabric to give off a bluish color in sunlight or under fluorescents; that makes white cloth appear whiter than it really is. Dishwashing liquids do not have optical brighteners. Brighteners tend to work best on silk and cotton and show little effect on wool and synthetics.

Removing stains.   Generally, a detergent's stain-removal ability corresponds to its overall cleaning ability. But no product leaves every stained garment looking like new. Some stains on some fabrics are a real challenge. Silk is hardest to clean. Spaghetti sauce doesn't come out, and lightening wine stains is almost as difficult. Stains on rayon likewise prove difficult. The easiest fibers to clean are nylon and wool.

Handle with care

Heat causes shrinkage. That's why fine fabrics are typically labeled for cold or cool wash, with no drying in the dryer. Even with the water at 70°F—about the warmest you'd want to use—you can expect some shrinkage with natural fibers.

Silk crepe tends to pucker and requires ironing after washing. Rayon washes poorly; it wrinkles badly unless pressed while quite damp. Wool crepe, its weave tighter in one direction, can lose shape. If, before washing, a fabric has more "give" in one direction as you gently stretch it, you may have shrinkage problems.

RATINGS OF HAND-LAUNDRY DETERGENTS

Listed in order of estimated overall cleaning quality. Differences between closely ranked products were slight. Except as noted, all are liquids.

The "teaspoons per wash" are based on manufacturer's suggestion for two quarts of water, translated from capfuls.

As published in a **May 1989** report.

Better ← ● ◐ ○ ◑ ● → Worse

Product	Average price	Size, oz. or fl. oz.	Tsp. per wash	Cost per wash	Overall cleaning	Brightening	Comments
Softball Cot'nwash	$2.69	12	2	8¢	●	—	—
Kroger Lemon Scented Liquid	1.55	22	1	1	●	—	—
Sears Heavy-duty Laundry Detergent	4.99	128	2	1	●	○	A
Silk'n Wash	2.67	8	4	24	●	—	—
Palmolive Dishwashing Liquid	2.10	32	1	1	●	—	—
A & P Dishwashing Lotion	1.32	32	1	1	●	—	—
Pathmark Wool Wash	.99	16	1	1	●	●	—
Cheer	4.46	64	1	1	●	○	A,B
Day & Nite Mousse	3.49	12	1️⃣	3	●	●	C
A & P Wool Wash	1.15	22	1½	1	◐	—	—
Delicare	2.19	16	1	2	◐	—	—
Wisk	3.79	64	1	1	◐	○	A
Woolite Gentle Cycle	2.31	14	1	3	◐	○	A,D
Topco Wool Wash	1.34	16	2	3	◐	●	A
Woolite	2.41	16	1	3	◐	○	—

1️⃣ *"Golfball" amount of foam.*

Key to Comments
A–More alkaline than most.
B–Contains stain-fighting enzymes.
C–Foam in aerosol can.
D–Powder in box.

All the hand-wash products give directions for machine washing on the Gentle cycle. A garment's care label is your best guide about whether or not to machine-wash it. A garment is most vulnerable when being agitated, but a washer's Gentle cycle typically keeps that as brief as possible. Spinning, in which the garments are flattened and held in place by centrifugal force, won't hurt. In fact, it's less damaging than wringing the clothes by hand. When you hand-wash garments, roll them between towels and let them dry flat, away from heat and sunlight; do not wring them.

If you wash delicate fabrics in the machine, you may want to be careful about what detergent you use. Regular detergents tend to be alkaline, as are some special products. Soaking wool or silk repeatedly in any detergent that's too alkaline could eventually cause fibers to shrink or stretch.

The enzymes in regular detergents should focus on protein stains and leave the structural proteins in wool and silk alone. Still, it's prudent not to launder wool or silk in any enzyme-containing detergent unless the product's label says it's safe for hand-washables.

Recommendations

There is no reason to buy one of the specialized brands. Use a dishwashing liquid. All they lack are the optical brighteners that regular detergents and most hand-wash products contain to give whites extra dazzle. At about a penny a wash, dishwashing liquids are bargains.

If you have stains to clean, you'll have more or less luck depending on the fiber and type of stain. Generally, the top-rated detergents worked better than lower-rated products.

LAUNDRY BLEACHES

Laundry bleach can be either chlorine or nonchlorine. Liquid chlorine bleach is the old standby, having earned its place in the laundry room as well as in the bathroom and kitchen for whitening and removing stains and mildew.

Chlorine bleach also has its problems. The telltale signs of misuse or overuse of chlorine bleach are splotches of faded color or white where undiluted bleach has splashed, fabrics that have faded from vivid to dim, fraying collars, stitching that has dissolved, and sometimes the appearance of small holes in the fabric.

Excessive use of chlorine bleach can cause additional problems if your home has a septic tank for sewage disposal. Too much chlorine in a septic tank may slow down the natural decomposition of the sewage and necessitate more frequent servicing of the tank.

Nonchlorine, "all-fabric" bleaches promise the benefits of chlorine bleach without the risk, but it's easy to make a claim about a bleach. The real story unfolds in the laundry room.

Both chlorine and nonchlorine bleaches use an oxidizing agent (usually sodium hypochlorite or sodium perborate) that reacts with and, with the help of a detergent, lifts out a stain. Liquid chlorine bleaches all have about the same amount of active ingredient and there is little difference from one brand to another.

Performance

Chlorine bleaches have always been better than all-fabric bleaches at whitening clothes. They still are.

All-fabric bleaches, especially the powdered products, do whiten, but not nearly as well as chlorine bleaches. In fact, all-fabric liquid bleaches whiten hardly better than detergent alone. If you wash the laundry load successive times with an all-fabric bleach, the whitening process continues, but even four applications won't match the whitening power of a single use of chlorine bleach.

If you double the recommended amount of all-fabric powder bleach, there's some improvement. The bleach's whitening power doubles, at least for the first washing, but still falls slightly behind chlorine bleach. A second washing with a double dose of all-fabric powder won't show such dramatic results. It whitens clothes only a little bit more.

If you use hot water (140°F) rather than warm water (100°F) the bleaches will show little, if any, improvement.

Hard-to-remove stains

Some stains, such as spaghetti sauce, red wine, blood, and motor oil, seem to have an affinity for clothing and, once entrenched, leave with great reluctance, particularly with a fabric such as nylon knit.

Neither chlorine nor nonchlorine bleach can completely remove spaghetti sauce. In general, however, a good all-fabric powder surpasses chlorine bleach at removing greasy stains. That's because a powdered product contains detergents and chemical "builders" of its own and acts as a detergent "booster" as well as a bleach. Chlorine bleach removes most blood stains, but won't do well at removing wine and oil spots.

Fading

Bleach, especially chlorine bleach, can cause colors to fade.

Initially, bleach has no noticeable effect on the brightness of colors. Chlorine bleaches may not seem harsher than an all-fabric product. After a few washings, however, the chlorine begins taking its toll. Slight fading becomes evident and then, after more washings, objectionable. An all-fabric bleach, however, will continue being kind to colors.

Another concern with chlorine bleach is its tendency to gradually weaken a fabric. You would have to wash repeatedly in chlorine bleach to seriously weaken a fabric—a routine you should avoid.

Recommendations

Chlorine bleach, when used properly, is the most effective way to whiten fabrics, including many synthetics. It's ideal for the occasional whitening your wash may need, but knowing how to use chlorine bleach is essential: Improper and long-term use will take its toll on colors and fabric life. Using chlorine bleach may be tricky, but buying it is simple. The only real difference you are likely to find is price.

All-fabric powdered bleaches have the advantage of being safe with most fabrics and dyes, even over the long term. They're much more expensive to use than chlorine bleaches, and aren't as good at whitening. If you prefer them, you can get extra whitening performance out of powdered all-fabric bleaches by doubling the recommended dose. Of course, you also double the average cost per use.

A more reasonable and less costly approach might be to incorporate both chlorine and all-fabric bleach into your laundry routine. Occasional and cautious use of chlorine bleach on chlorine-safe white fabrics will deliver the whitening you need. Use all-fabric bleach to brighten colors without fading, whiten fabrics that are not safe with chlorine bleach, and remove greasy stains.

When you do use chlorine bleach, follow these guidelines:

• Bleach only when necessary, or you will get color fading and fabric deterioration.

• Before you bleach, read the garment's care label.

• Don't use chlorine bleach on wool, silk, mohair, or non-colorfast fabrics or dyes. If you're unsure about a garment's fabric content, experiment with a diluted solution of bleach on an inside seam. Any discoloration should appear in a minute or so.

• If your washer has a bleach dispenser, use it according to the manufacturer's directions. If there's no dispenser, you can fill the washing machine and add the bleach full-strength to the wash water *before* you add the laundry. Or dilute the bleach with a generous amount of water and add it to laundry that is already immersed in wash water.

• *Never* use chlorine bleach with ammonia or toilet cleaners. That combination can produce deadly fumes.

LAUNDRY BOOSTERS

Some stains do not come out in an ordinary detergent wash. Hence the occasional need for products called laundry boosters. Yet not many boosters are more effective on protein stains (for example, blood, egg, milk) than a good laundry detergent used alone in the wash cycle. No booster is likely to be superior in cleaning up sandwich stains and party stains such as red wine, dark beer, cola, purple grape juice, or pink lemonade. For soiled rags, the kind used for cleaning up around the house or for washing the car, just about any booster should be effective—but so should a regular detergent used as a presoak, or simply used in the wash cycle.

TV commercials have left the impression that "ring around the collar" is one of the toughest laundry jobs since the invention of dirt. That just isn't so. A good detergent should do the job nicely.

Convenience

Boosters are often meant for presoaking. Although that doesn't mean a lot of manual labor, it does tie up the washing machine. You could, of course, do the soaking in a bucket, but transferring the sopping laundry into the machine is messy.

Aerosols and pump sprays are easier to use. You simply spray those products on the stain, then throw the item into the machine with the rest of the wash.

Directions for other sprays call for you to rub them into the stain. That's a small chore when you're faced with one stained shirt, but think of rubbing these boosters into five shirts, grass-stained trouser knees, a cola-stained T-shirt, and other assorted stains. Rubbing can become a big chore indeed.

Hazards

If there's a chance that a booster or a boosting detergent is going to come in contact with your skin (as it would in rubbing a stain), you might want to wear rubber gloves. Gloves are almost a necessity if you have a skin rash or cuts, which can be particularly irritated by contact with one of these products. If, despite careful handling, any laundry booster product gets into an eye, rinse immediately and thoroughly with water.

Children and boosters don't mix; keep boosters and other laundry products out of their reach. In addition to the hazards of contact, there are hazards of ingestion.

All boosters can damage some household surfaces if not wiped up quickly. Aluminum and paint seem most vulnerable, with stainless steel the most resistant to staining or damage.

Recommendations

Laundry booster ads often seem to promise miracles. Some boosters do work very well on most stains, but most aren't much more effective at stain removal than detergent alone—and some are worse.

Choose a laundry booster based on its effectiveness and on your idea of convenience. Presoaking is probably the least convenient method. If you don't agree, any of the powders that are presoaks should do.

Liquid boosting detergents claim to do two jobs. They do the job of a detergent well enough, but as boosters, they are at best only average.

LAUNDRY DETERGENTS

Few products are marketed as strenuously as laundry detergents. Detergent manufacturers are constantly turning to their market-research departments and copywriters to find something that makes their detergent appear different from the detergent in all those other boxes and bottles. Detergent manufacturers also turn to their chemists to find new market niches—that's how liquid detergents got started. Because of the success of liquid detergents, many names once found only on powders are showing up on liquids, and vice versa. The manufacturers want to make sure they haven't left any sales appeal untried—or an inch of supermarket shelf space unclaimed.

Yet supermarket managers, facing an explosion of new products throughout their stores, are reluctant to expand the shelf space already allotted to detergents. The result: intense competition, not so much for your attention, but for the store managers'. To persuade supermarkets to carry a new brand, detergent companies have to promise "support" in the form of coupon and ad blitzes. To keep the brand in the public's eye, the companies have to persuade the supermarkets to feature it in a promotion, the one-week or two-week specials that supermarkets run to attract customers.

Such competition has a side effect, worrisome for detergent makers, fortunate for consumers. It undermines brand loyalty, because there's always a deal on detergents. If you're like many shoppers, you have a short list of acceptable brands and you buy whichever brand is on sale that week.

Label claims

Tide was the first heavy-duty synthetic detergent. Since its introduction more than forty years ago, detergents have been reformulated many times, sometimes with significant benefit, often to achieve a virtually invisible edge that gives the marketers something to sell. Here is the science behind the claims.

All-temperature. The dirt dissolvers in synthetic detergents are surfactants (for "surface active agents"), soaplike molecules that emulsify oil and grease and the dirt they bind, allowing them all to be washed away. There are hundreds of such chemicals, providing ample fodder for claims of "New!" and "More!" Most products contain a mixture of surfactants.

Anionic surfactants, which have a negative electrical charge, are the most widely used. They are the main ingredients in big-selling powders. Anionics are especially effective at cleaning clay and mud from cotton and other natural fibers. The hotter the water, the better they work. Like soap, synthetic anionics do not work that well in hard water. So they're often combined with water-softening compounds such as phosphates.

Nonionic surfactants, which carry no electrical charge, are much less sensitive to hardness in water, and the switch to nonphosphate formulas boosted their use. Nonionics are particularly effective at cleaning oily soils from polyester and other synthetics at cool wash temperatures. Many liquids and some powders are based on surfactants of this type.

Cationic surfactants, which carry a positive charge, are less common in detergents than in fabric softeners, where the positive charge counteracts negative charges that build up on clothes in the dryer. Their use can be expected to increase as manufacturers develop more products combining detergents and softeners.

Most detergents are formulated to clean in a wide range of temperature and water conditions.

Low suds. Anionic surfactants are high-sudsing; nonionic surfactants, low-sudsing. The amount of suds matters in a front-loading washing machine, where an excess can interfere with the agitation. In a top-loading washer, the amount of suds has no connection with a detergent's cleaning power, but an excess of suds can still cause overflow, and a mess to mop up.

No phosphates. Phosphates are used in detergents as "builders," to build up the performance of the surfactants by softening the water, dispersing dirt, and emulsifying greasy soils. But since the early 1970s, phosphate-containing detergents have been banned or restricted in several states, counties, and municipalities. They have been blamed for hastening the transformation of lakes into swamps in a process known as eutrophication. Such detergents are now unavailable to about 30 percent of the population, mostly in states around the Great Lakes and Chesapeake Bay.

The loss of phosphates dealt a blow to cleaning power. Many of the "improvements" to detergent since then have been manufacturers' attempts to duplicate its old prowess. Manufacturers often make a phosphate and a nonphosphate version of the same powder brand and sell the right one for the region. Nonphosphate powders typically use old-fashioned washing soda, with extra ingredients to make up for phosphates.

Liquid detergents probably would not exist if phosphates hadn't been restricted, since the original liquids did not clean very well at all. But they are phosphate-free (phosphates aren't very soluble or stable in liquid form). Instead of phosphates, liquid detergents contain other water-softening chemicals or extra surfactants.

Removes stains. The extra stain-removing power claimed by some products comes from enzymes, which make otherwise insoluble stains easy to wash away. Their use is increasing, to add cleaning power to detergents as phosphate use declines and wash temperatures grow colder. Two common enzymes are protease and amylase. Protease breaks down protein, as in blood or egg stains. Amylase digests carbohydrates, as in chocolate or gravy.

Brightens wash. Most detergents contain colorless, water-soluble dyes known as fluorescent whiteners or optical brighteners. The dyes convert some of the invisible ultraviolet light from the sun or fluorescent lights into visible light, which gives laundry a bit of glow. The effect does not work in incandescent light, so garments washed in a detergent with whiteners might look drab in ordinary household lighting.

Repels dirt. Soil loosened during the wash can resettle on the laundry, turning it dingy. To prevent that, laundry detergents usually contain special "antiredeposition agents," which keep dirt in suspension until it's washed away. Even the best of such agents, however, won't cope with a lot of dirt. Hence the instruction found on many detergents: "Heavily soiled items should be washed separately."

Softens. Fabric softeners wouldn't be needed if it weren't for synthetic detergents. Soap, as the *Ivory Snow* box says, "softens as it cleans"—largely because soap doesn't rinse out of textile fibers as thoroughly as detergents do. Fabric softeners coat fabric much as hair conditioners coat hair. The thin layer of waxy or soapy substance lubricates the surface of the fabric and makes it feel soft. The coating also separates a napped fabric's fibers and stands them on end, making the laundry fluff up.

It's best to apply the fabric softener in the washer's rinse cycle, after the detergent has done its work, or in the dryer. Doing it all in the wash cycle presents a problem: The positively charged surfactants used for softening tend to neutralize the negatively charged surfactants used for cleaning. Manufacturers have tried to work around this in various ways—using nonionic surfactants or excess softener in liquids, encapsulating the ingredients in powders. So far, the compromises work only at some cost in both cleaning and softening.

Static free. Just as synthetic detergents created a need for fabric softeners, clothes dryers and synthetic fabrics opened the way for a product that counteracts static electricity. The tumbling action of the dryer builds up electrical charges on the surface of synthetics. A thin coating of fabric softener disrupts the buildup by reducing friction and neutralizing the charges.

Scented. Fragrance is a common addition to detergents and fabric softeners. Scents range from what might be called "soap smell" to a biting floral reminiscent of cheap perfume. Fragrance is useful for masking the musty or otherwise unpleasant smell of the chemical ingredients. It can also give an otherwise undistinguished product something to sell. There are unscented products as well for people who are sensitive to fragrance chemicals.

Concentrated. Detergent powders contain varying amounts of filler, liquid detergents varying amounts of water and alcohol. Most liquid fabric softeners are "concentrated," too.

Concentrated products are easier to transport and store for both manufacturers and consumers. But the differing product densities make cost comparisons in the supermarket tricky, since unit costs are based on weight or volume. In Consumers Union's tests, a 72-ounce box of detergent contained anywhere between twenty and twenty-eight washes. Liquids were more constant, a 64-ounce bottle nearly always washed sixteen loads.

Hazards

Most detergents carry a warning label; its cautions should be heeded. The chemicals in any detergent can irritate the eyes, mucous membranes, or sensitive skin. Like most cleaning products, detergents should be used with commonsense care and kept out of the reach of young children. It's a good idea to avoid prolonged contact with products that are extremely alkaline or that contain enzymes.

RATINGS OF LAUNDRY DETERGENTS

Listed by types; within types, listed in order of estimated quality based on laboratory tests in hard water. Differences between closely ranked brands were slight. The best fabric-softening detergents would rank near the middle of the regular detergents in cleaning ability.

As published in a July 1987 report.

Better ● ◐ ○ ◑ ● → Worse

Effective against . . . on polyester-cotton/nylon

Product	Type (Liquid, Powder)	Dose, cup (per wash)	Cost per dose 1	Antidedeposition	Whitening	Dirt	Makeup	Spaghetti sauce	Grape juice	Grass	Tea	Ink	Motor oil	Comments
Regular products														
Liquid Cheer	L	½	28¢	●	◐/●	✓/✓	—/—	✓/✓	✓/✓	✓/✓	✓/✓	—/—	—/—	A,B
Tide	P	1	17	◐/●	◐/●	✓/✓	✓/✓	✓/✓	✓/✓	✓/✓	—/—	—/—	—/✓	A
Cheer (phos.)	P	1	16	◐/●	◐/●	✓/✓	—/✓	✓/✓	✓/✓	✓/—	✓/✓	—/—	—/—	—
Oxydol (phos.)	P	1	18	◐/●	◐/●	✓/✓	✓/✓	✓/✓	✓/✓	✓/✓	✓/✓	—/—	—/✓	D
Tide (phos.)	P	1	19	◐/●	◐/●	✓/✓	✓/✓	✓/✓	✓/✓	✓/✓	✓/✓	✓/—	—/✓	A
Liquid Tide	L	½	21	◐/●	◐/●	✓/✓	✓/✓	✓/—	✓/✓	✓/✓	✓/✓	—/—	—/—	A,B
Dash (phos.)	P	1	26	◐/●	◐/●	✓/✓	✓/✓	✓/✓	✓/✓	✓/✓	✓/✓	—/—	—/✓	D
Oxydol	P	1	15	●/●	◐/○	✓/✓	✓/✓	✓/✓	✓/✓	✓/✓	—/✓	—/—	—/✓	C
Sears	P	½	19	◐/●	◐/○	✓/✓	✓/—	—/✓	✓/✓	✓/✓	✓/—	—/—	—/—	—
Wisk	L	½	19	◐/●	◐/●	✓/✓	✓/✓	✓/✓	✓/✓	✓/✓	✓/—	✓/—	—/✓	—
Surf (phos.)	P	1	16	◐/●	◐/●	✓/✓	—/✓	—/✓	✓/—	✓/✓	✓/—	—/—	—/—	—
Era Plus	L	¼	14	◐/●	◐/◐	✓/✓	✓/—	✓/✓	✓/✓	—/—	✓/✓	✓/—	—/—	A,B
Dynamo 2	L	½	21	◐/●	◐/◐	✓/✓	✓/—	✓/—	✓/✓	—/—	✓/✓	✓/—	—/✓	A,B
Arm & Hammer (phos.)	P	1	12	◐/●	◐/◑	✓/✓	✓/—	✓/—	✓/✓	✓/✓	—/—	—/—	—/—	—
All	P	1	26	◐/●	◐/●	✓/✓	✓/✓	—/✓	✓/✓	—/—	—/✓	—/—	—/✓	—
Cheer	P	1	17	◐/●	◐/●	✓/✓	✓/✓	—/✓	✓/—	—/—	—/✓	—/—	—/—	—

Product					Comments
Fresh Start (phos.)	P	¼	17		A,B
Sears	L	½	28		B
Arm & Hammer	P	1	13		A
Fresh Start	P	¼	18		A
Dash	P	1	22		—
Arm & Hammer	L	½	14		—
Scotch Buy (Safeway)	P	1	10		C
All	L	½	16		C
Purex	P	1	12		—
Cost Cutter (Kroger)	P	1¼	9		—
Par (Safeway)	L	½	15		—
Ajax	P	1	12		B
Cost Cutter (Kroger)	L	⅝	10		B

Fabric-softening products

Product					Comments
Sears	P	¾	37		C
Yes	L	½	19		B
Purex	L	½	21		B
Fab (phos.)	P	1	17		—
Fab	L	½	22		B
Bold 3 (phos.)	P	1	17		—
Fab	P	1	16		—
Clean 'n' Soft (Kroger)	L	½	21		B
Solo	L	½	25		A,B
Bold 3	L	½	26		A,B
Bold 3	P	1	16		—
Sears	L	½	28		—
Ivory Snow	P	1¼	24		E

1 Detergent cost depends largely on whether you buy a small or large container. These figures, based on medium-size packages (64 fluid ounces for the liquids, between 65 and 80 ounces for most of the powders), give a good idea of relative cost.

Key to Comments

A—Contains enzymes; avoid prolonged contact.
B—Less alkaline than most; better for delicate fabrics.
C—More alkaline than most; avoid prolonged contact.
D—Contains bleach.
E—Soap; inherently fabric-softening.

121

Some people complain of skin rashes caused by one laundry product or another. Such symptoms are generally not serious, and they go away rapidly when the irritant is removed. Someone, somewhere, is probably sensitive to just about any product on the market. If you suspect a detergent or fabric softener of causing rashes or other such problems, stop using it and see if the symptoms subside.

Recommendations

Some detergents get clothes whiter and brighter than others, but you won't risk social disgrace if you use even the least effective product. The differences between the best and worst detergents, while enough to be noticeable, are not very significant. The scale is clean to cleanest, not dirty to clean.

The average American wash contains many different fabrics. In general, synthetics hold on to stains more tenaciously than cotton and other natural fibers. Also, detergents behave differently on polyester and nylon, whose chemistries differ radically. Polyester attracts oil, for instance, while nylon resists it. Nylon, however, tends to pick up colors from other items in the wash.

Here's a brief summary of how well detergents work:

• Modern liquid formulations have matched powders' cleaning power.

• Detergents with fabric softener do not clean as well as detergents without softener. A combination product probably won't match the performance of a regular detergent. In fact, many won't match the performance of a relatively inferior regular detergent.

• Some stains are too tough. Many products are effective on dirt, makeup, and spaghetti sauce stains. Only a few—often just the top ones—can tackle grape juice, grass stains, or tea. No product is likely to be able to get ballpoint ink out of nylon, although many are fairly effective on polyester-cotton. The situation is reversed with motor oil. None remove it from polyester-cotton, while a few work on nylon.

• You don't have to pay extra for performance. While the best detergents aren't the cheapest, neither are they necessarily the most expensive. Most of the best powders cost 16 or 17 cents per wash. The best liquids are more expensive, costing from 19 to 28 cents per wash.

LAUNDRY RECOMMENDATIONS

◈ The right way to do laundry, home-economics books tell you, is to sort it by fabric, by color, by soil level, by linting tendency, by construction, and by how the item is used. That may be the ideal way, but it's not very practical. You'll get a clean wash even with the minimalist approach: Cull out the obvious, such as oily overalls and brand-new blue jeans, and wash everything else together in warm or cold water. Your clothes may not be the whitest and brightest, but they will almost certainly be white and bright enough. If you lead a low-soil life and your laundry needs freshening more than scouring, you may not even notice any difference in cleaning.

Similarly, all detergents clean clothes. Store brands represent good value, as do national brands that are promoted on price.

Products formulated to be both detergent and fabric softener are unlikely to offer good cleaning and softening. Softener-impregnated dryer sheets offer the best combination of performance, convenience, and price. If the main reason you want a fabric softener is to reduce static cling, dryer sheets are clearly superior.

Even if you subscribe to the minimalist approach to laundry you may still want to do a special load now and then. To do a load that's all colorfast cottons, for instance, use a hot wash/cold rinse cycle, and if the dirt is really bad, first let the load soak awhile. If you use bleach, use liquid chlorine bleach. An inexpensive store brand will work as well as a nationally advertised brand. (But do not use chlorine bleach on wool, silk, mohair, or items that aren't colorfast. Check the care label or do a test on an inside seam.)

STEAM IRONS

Irons have changed. Many of today's irons beep, light up, work without a cord, or shut themselves off if you forget to. At the expensive end of the market are the so-called professional irons, with a large water chamber separate from the iron itself. At the other end are a few old-fashioned dry irons, plus the compact irons and travel irons and steamers (see page 129). The largest part of the marketplace is taken up by the full-size steam iron. List prices range from $25 or less all the way to $70 or $80 for an iron with all the new features, and more than $100 for a professional iron.

For all the improvements being made to irons, companies may not be paying enough attention to quality control. In the samples Consumers Union bought for testing, there were problems ranging from defective lights to uneven steam and leaks to total failure. The testers started out with two samples of each model of iron. At least one of those samples was defective for one-third of the models. Sometimes the second sample was, too. You should carefully inspect an iron you're buying in the store, then try out all its functions and features as soon as you get home.

Features

Irons with all the electronic innovations won't necessarily iron your clothes any better than a plain iron will. But they can make an often dreary task seem less like work.

Spray and burst of steam. These basic additions have been around for more than a decade. A built-in spray wets down a little patch in front of the iron; a burst of steam at the press of a button lets you set creases or smooth stubborn wrinkles. Both features are particularly useful for dealing with the wrinkles in clothing made of natural fibers.

Controls. The best temperature controls have complete, readable markings and are located on the top of the handle where you can set them with the hand holding the iron. Those that sit under the handle are harder to see and take two hands to work. Fabric guides give you an idea of which setting is best for different fabrics; location is not so important (it's often under the handle).

The best steam-dry controls are on the front of the iron. Many irons have the button awkwardly placed on the side.

Weight.   Some people prefer a heavy iron, others feel that a light iron is easier on the arm. Balance is probably more important than actual weight. Before you buy, pick the iron up and pretend to use it. It should feel well balanced and comfortable in your hand.

Water gauge and capacity.   Look for a see-through plastic water chamber. Very dark plastic tanks, found on some models, are nearly impossible to see through. In general, a big tank lets an iron steam longer. Most irons hold one cup of water or less.

Ease of filling.   Most irons are filled through an opening near the handle. Some have a removable water tank, which is easy to snap in and out.

Button groove.   Look for a groove that extends along the side of the soleplate.

Cord (while ironing).   Try the iron to see if the cord hits your wrist. Some cords stick straight up; designs that send the cord off to the side are better.

Automatic shutoff.   This very useful feature can remedy a memory lapse. The shutoff function is typically connected with indicator lights. Some irons even signal audibly for you to turn them off.

All the automatic shutoffs should work pretty much as claimed. But if you accidently knock an iron over onto your favorite shirt, soleplate down, it will leave at least a slight scorch mark. Chances are the shirt would be ruined, but there probably wouldn't be a fire.

Cordless irons.   Cordless irons heat up in a separate base that is plugged into the electrical outlet. Cordless irons working on the same principle were sold back in the 1920s. The product didn't catch on then and it may still be an idea that technology isn't ready for.

Cordless irons all share the same problem: An iron without a steady supply of electricity holds heat for only so long, especially when ironing moistened cotton. To keep the iron hot, cordless irons must be set back into their bases often. You can get used to that routine, but it's a nuisance, and it slows down your ironing.

The appeal of a cordless iron is understandable; many people find that the cord gets in their way. Cordless ironing suits left-handers, but they might do better to look for a cord that can be moved to the left side; there are several such models.

Temperature and steam

Fabrics wrinkle when circumstances, such as a long wait in the dryer or a long meeting in a hot conference room, overcome the fibers' inherent resilience. Ironing reshapes the fibers. Steam (or sprinkled water) makes a fabric more pliable, the pressure of the iron sets it straight, and the heat dries it out.

Because some fabrics require more heat than others to set straight, an iron needs a range of temperatures. Stiff, woody fibers derived from plants (cotton and linen) need more heat than fibers from animal sources (silk and wool) and a lot more than synthetics. A synthetic's molecules can be custom-made for resilience, but are often sensitive to high heat. Blends, including permanent-press cotton-polyester, usually take a medium temperature. (When in doubt, set the iron for the fiber that requires the lower temperature.)

Heating tests show irons to be more alike than different. The range provided by a typical iron is about 170° to 370°F. At their lowest setting, some irons are too cool even for acetate, a problem remedied by simply turning up the temperature control a bit. At their highest setting, an iron is unlikely to get hot enough to press linen totally flat, even if you use steam. Badly wrinkled linen, apparently, will respond to nothing less than dampening before ironing.

An iron usually overshoots the mark when first set for a particular temperature. The temperature stabilizes after about three minutes. Irons take much longer than that to cool down—as much as 20 minutes. Therefore, iron delicate fabrics before the linens and cottons.

Within limits, the more steam an iron produces, the better. A filled iron usually steams better than a half-filled one. Most irons steam at a slower rate as they run out of water.

Water for steam

Past experience may have taught you to use distilled water to avoid clogging your iron's steam vents with minerals. Most manufacturers say that unless you have extremely hard water—more than 180 parts per million of dissolved minerals—tap water is fine. (Note: Many manufacturers warn against using water passed through a water softener, since the minerals in such water can damage the iron.) If you use distilled water, many manufacturers suggest that you switch to tap water once in a while, as water with some minerals in it produces more steam than does pure water.

Minerals often end up as off-white, wet grit that stains clothes and dirties the bottom of the iron. To cope with that grit, some irons have a removable panel in the soleplate so you can clean the innards of the iron. Some models have a special self-cleaning feature that flushes the vents with steam and hot water. On a model with a burst-of-steam feature, you can use the burst to dislodge debris and mineral residue from the steam vents. To keep from inadvertently soiling your clothes with wet grit, shoot a spurt or two of steam into the air each time before you iron. With irons that lack either of those features, the best you can do is to fill the iron, set it on high, and iron over an old all-cotton towel for several minutes.

Many manufacturers, apparently to protect their products from outdated iron-cleaning tips, warn against using vinegar or a special iron-cleaning product. One safe way to help prevent a buildup of minerals: Store your iron empty.

Nonstick soleplates ease another cleaning problem, the accumulation of spray starch or other residues on the bottom of the iron. Take care not to scrape over metal zippers or snaps, lest you abrade the nonstick coating.

Irons draw a lot of current. To avoid blowing a fuse or tripping a circuit breaker, you shouldn't plug one into the same circuit where another electricity-hungry appliance such as a toaster oven or a blow dryer is operating. If you can't set your ironing board up next to an outlet, use a heavy-duty extension cord (*not* the 18-gauge variety commonly used for lamp cords).

RATINGS OF STEAM IRONS

Listed by types; within types, listed in order of estimated quality. Except where separated by bold rules, differences between closely ranked models were slight. Bracketed models were judged about equal and are listed alphabetically.
As published in a **March 1987** report.

Better ← ● ◐ ○ ◑ ● → Worse

Brand and model	Price	Key features [1]	Weight, lb.	Water capacity, fl. oz.	Steaming rate	Burst-of-steam rate	Setting temperature	Ease of filling	Water gauge	Nonstick soleplate
Irons with extras										
Black & Decker F440WHS	$63	A,B,S	2¾	7	○	○	○	◐	○	✔
Sanyo ACM1000	80	A,S	3	7	◐	—	●	◐	◐	✔
Norelco HD1863	48	B,S	2½	7	◐	◐	○	○	◐	—
Osrow S500	40	B,S	2¼	6	◐	●	◐	○	○	✔
Black & Decker F340BD	41	B,S	2½	6	○	◐	○	◐	○	—
Panasonic N17401	38	S	3	7	◐	—	◐	◐	◐	—
Simac 250	125	B	2¾	28	●	●	◐	◐	●	—
Sears Cat. No. 6277	45+	A,B,S	2½	4½	○	◐	○	◐	○	✔
Sunbeam 12001	69	A,B,S	2¾	5	○	◐	●	◐	○	—
Osrow S3000	60	B,C,S	2	6	◐	●	◐	○	○	✔
Sunbeam 12319	44	B,S	2½	4½	○	◐	○	◐	○	✔
Hamilton Beach 778S	80	B,C	2	5½	○	○	○	○	○	✔
Sears Cat. No. 6276	35+	B,S	2½	4½	○	◐	○	◐	○	✔
Hamilton Beach 757SW	46	B	2¼	6	○	○	○	○	○	✔
West Bend 6008	70	B,C,S	2	4	◐	◐	●	○	◐	✔
Plain irons										
Sanyo A1900	55	—	2¾	7½	◐	—	◐	○	◐	✔
Norelco HD1860	26	—	2½	6½	◐	—	○	○	◐	—
Osrow S300	30	—	2¼	6	◐	—	◐	○	○	—
Black & Decker F363BED	22	—	2¼	6	○	—	◐	◐	—	—
Sunbeam 11366	22	—	2	4½	○	—	○	●	—	—
Proctor-Silex I1300	26	—	2¼	6	○	—	○	◐	—	—
Sears Cat. No. 6203	17+	—	2¼	6	○	—	○	◐	—	—

[1] Automatic shutoff (A) turns the iron off if it isn't moved for 10 minutes or so, and shuts some irons off if they're left unmoved for about 30 seconds in the horizontal (ironing) position. Burst of steam (B) allows

Recommendations

Irons last a fairly long time. People who responded to a Consumers Union survey reported that they used their old iron for an average of eight years before buying a new one, and less than half the people gave breakdown as the reason for replacement. About an equal number, perhaps, were enticed into buying a new iron because the old one wasn't modern enough: It didn't have the features they wanted, the ads had attracted them, or it was just "time" to get a new iron.

Before you rush out to get a fancy, modern iron, consider what you iron. If you use an iron now and then to touch up permanent press, perhaps all you need is a plain steam iron. In particular, you should consider paying for an iron with extras if you iron everything from cotton to acetate, if you are as apt to press in wrinkles as press them out, or if you find the idea of a steam iron that shuts off automatically appeals to your sense of safety.

TRAVEL IRONS AND STEAMERS

Years ago, if you wanted a travel iron, the choices were limited to a few rudimentary, miniaturized models. Now, new brands and models of travel irons and steamers are cropping up all the time.

A time-honored method of smoothing rumpled clothes when you're on the road is to hang them in the bathroom with the shower turned on. The warm steam relaxes superficial wrinkles. Steamers are a logical extension of that idea, with an important improvement: You can aim the steam. A steamer is, of course,

---

you to shoot steam where you want it. A spray (S) is good for heavily wrinkled areas—at the push of a button, warm water squirts from a little nozzle in the iron's prow. All of those worked fine. Cordless (C) irons heat up in a base, which is plugged into the wall. Those irons cool off if you don't keep setting them back in their base.

RATINGS OF TRAVEL IRONS AND STEAMERS

Listed by types; within types, listed in order of estimated quality. Except where separated by bold rule, differences between closely ranked models were slight. Bracketed models were judged about equal and are listed alphabetically. As published in a **May 1987** report.

Better ◉ ◐ ○ ◑ ● → Worse

Brand and model	Price	Features	Weight, lb.	Capacity, fl. oz.	Steaming rate	Portability	Ease of filling	Temperature control	Ease of use	Ease of emptying	Advantages	Disadvantages	Comments
Travel irons													
Black & Decker Stowaway SS50	$32	S	1½	2	○	●	●	◐	◐	○	B	—	B,D,J,L
Norelco Travel Care T170	32	S,Sp	1½	1	◐	○	○	○	○	—	—	c	A,I
Panasonic NI60	27	S,V	1½	1	◐	○	◐	○	○	A	A	b,f	A,H
Franzus Air-Lite AL300	31	Sp	1½	—	—	○	○	●	○	A	A	e	A,D,F,I
Sunbeam International 10069	32	S,V	1½	1.5	◐	○	◐	◐	◐	—	—	b,h	G,H,J,M
Steamers													
Franzus Wrinkles Away WA222SE	25	V	1	3.3	◐	●	●	—	◐	A	A	b,i	A,H
Osrow Travel Iron & Steamer SB35	25	S,V	¾	5	●	○	●	—	○	—	—	b,d,g	A,C,E,N
Sunbeam Steam Valet 10079	40	V	1¼	2.9	◐	○	○	—	◐	○	C,D	a	D,G,J,K,M

(S) = steam, (Sp) = spray, (V) = works vertically.

Specifications and Features

All have: ● Approximately 8-ft. cord.
Except as noted, all have: ● Rated wattage of 300 to 500 watts. ● Recommendation to use tap water. ● Heel rest or base. ● Provision for dual voltage. ● Water indicator. ● Travel pouch with drawstring.

All travel irons: ● Have a thermostat control under handle. ● Can be used as a dry iron. ●
Except as noted, all travel irons have: ● Brushed or polished aluminum soleplate. ● Plastic upper body. ● Button grooves or notches. ● Fabric guide under handle.

All steamers: ● Have a plastic housing.

Key to Advantages

A–Dual-voltage setting easy to operate.
B–Nonstick soleplate.
C–Has detachable lint/fluff remover, detachable clothes brush, and hook for hanging.
D–Ready to steam much sooner than others.

Key to Disadvantages

a–Voltage kit costs $20 plus shipping.
b–No water indicator.
c–Water indicator is hard to see into.
d–No heel rest.
e–Metal housing gets hot enough to burn.
f–Less stable on its heel rest than other irons.
g–Housing gets hot near handle.
h–Soleplate can easily burn hand while emptying; mfr. suggests waiting until cool.
i–Takes longer to steam than others.

Key to Comments

A–Comes with adapter plug.
B–Uses separate converter with adapter plug.
C–Adaptation to dual voltage accomplished by adjusting amount of salt added to water.
D–Has zippered bag for carrying.
E–Handle doesn't fold down or come off.
F–No fabric guide.
G–Button must be pumped to get steam.
H–Handle uncomfortable.
I–Cord hits wrist.
J–Rated at 600 to 700 watts.
K–Has no base, but easy to prop up.
L–Mfr. recommends using distilled or deminer-alized water whenever possible.
M–Mfr. recommends distilled water in hard-water areas.
N–According to mfr., model discontinued and replaced by model sold under *TPI* name.

easier to use than an iron. You can remove wrinkles without taking the clothes off the hanger. You simply move the steamer over your clothes, coaxing them back to smoothness.

Although steamers are good for touch-ups—making a suit that you sat in all day look presentable again or bringing a crushed dress back to life—they cannot set a crease in trousers or put the crisp pleat back in a skirt. Creases require weight and heat. For clothes that need to be *pressed*, a miniature iron works better than a steamer.

Don't expect a small iron to work as well as a full-size iron, however. Travel irons do not get as hot or steam as much as a full-size iron. They're also lighter, have smaller soleplates, hold less water, and offer fewer features than regular irons. And any iron, regardless of size, is awkward to use on a makeshift ironing surface such as a hotel desktop padded with a towel.

Portability and convenience

Obviously, a travel iron or steamer has to pass a portability test first. If it won't fit unobtrusively in a corner of the suitcase or slide into the pocket of a garment bag, it's likely to be left behind. The travel irons and steamers in the Ratings are small and light (ranging from just under a pound to slightly more than a pound and a half) and come with either a drawstring pouch or a zippered bag. On most, the handle folds down or comes off, but even those with a fixed handle aren't ungainly.

The controls on travel irons have been miniaturized more or less successfully. Travel irons have a narrower range of temperatures than full-size irons. Without the high heat and heft of a full-size iron, they're not as good at pressing out wrinkles in linen and cotton. Heat alone may be enough to smooth delicates, but for most other fabrics you'd also need some moisture, either steam or a spray of water, to make the fabric more pliable.

Steamers have no controls. They're on when plugged in, off when unplugged.

As you'd expect, most irons and steamers make some provision for the 220-volt outlets you're likely to encounter abroad. For those that don't, you'll need a small voltage converter intended for use with a high-wattage appliance.

Travel irons and steamers are much smaller than full-size irons, so it's harder to keep your hands away from the areas that get hot. You must be careful.

Recommendations

If you select your travel wardrobe carefully, pack judiciously, and unpack promptly, you might avoid wrinkled clothes altogether. In a pinch, you can always try the shower trick.

Travel irons and steamers are make-do appliances. Travelers faced with a badly wrinkled suit and an important meeting would probably prefer a hotel's valet service or a nearby dry cleaner. But you may find a steamer just what you need to touch up a suit or knock the wrinkles out of a drip-dried shirt.

If you routinely pack cotton dresses, linen slacks, and silk blazers—the kind of clothes you know are going to wrinkle— you need a travel iron. Of those Consumers Union tested, the *Black & Decker* is the clear choice. It steamed better than any of the other irons. It's easy to carry and use, and it has a nonstick soleplate.

WASHING MACHINES

The real trend in washing machines has been toward sameness, not innovation. It's not hard to see the cause. There are no more than about half a dozen parent corporations, and brands from within a corporate family tend to be pretty much alike. In fact, unlike many other appliances, it's quite usual for today's washing machine to carry the same model number from one year to the next.

In addition to selling washers under its own nameplate, Whirlpool makes machines that sell under the *Sears Kenmore* brand. The company has another washer line under the marque of its *KitchenAid* subsidiary. Altogether, Whirlpool makes about half the washers sold in this country, thanks mostly to sales by Sears. *Amana* and *Speed Queen* are two subsidiaries of the same corporation, Raytheon. General Electric sells under its own name and under *Hotpoint.* White Consolidated parents *White-Westinghouse, Frigidaire, Kelvinator,* and *Gibson* brands. Magic Chef, an acquisition of Maytag, markets *Admiral, Norge,* and the *Ward* machines sold by Montgomery Ward.

Features

Top-of-the-line models are not the best values. Many of the less expensive brand mates of those models should perform just as well. Controls that operate with dials and levers are perfectly adequate, cheaper to service, and often more versatile than the touch-pad controls that usually come with more expensive models.

A machine's most important features are those that affect performance:

Cycle options. These are the extras that separate the high-priced from the moderately priced machines. Any machine should have these three cycles, or their equivalent: Regular, Permanent Press, and Delicate. Additional cycles are available. Soak/Prewash is for heavily soiled clothes. Extra Rinse gives you two rinses instead of one. Sequential means you can let the extra cycle proceed automatically. Otherwise, the machine stops before or afterward, as the case may be, and you set the next step yourself.

Other cycle features can be useful. An automatic bleach dispenser adds bleach to the wash cycle after water has filled the tub. A softener dispenser holds fabric softener and dispenses it during the rinse cycle so its action won't conflict with the detergent's.

Speed options. A Slow or Gentle agitation setting is good for delicate fabrics; a Slow Spin can minimize wrinkling of permanent-press garments. In some models, you choose a cycle by the type of wash and the machine automatically supplies the appropriate speed combinations.

Temperature options. You need only three wash temperatures: hot, warm, and cold, followed by a cold rinse. Although warm water is unessential for rinsing, most deluxe models offer temperature options with a warm rinse. That confers no advantage over a cold rinse, and wastes the energy needed to heat the rinse water.

Fill options. Although washing full loads is the most efficient way to do a laundry, adjusting the fill level when you do small loads helps save money, water, and detergent. A Continuous Fill setting lets you set the level anywhere on a scale from low to high.

A large tub capacity is desirable, because it's more efficient and easier to do a few large loads rather than many small ones. Although the machine may look big on the outside, tub capacity varies considerably.

Front loading

Front-loading washers have been popular in Europe, mostly because they use water and energy more efficiently. Most Americans choose top loaders, which can handle more laundry and are easier to use. Nevertheless, some people prefer front loaders. The models Consumers Union tested were from the *White-Westinghouse* line and had selling prices comparable to many top-loader models. One of the models tested has its control panel located on the front and thus can be stacked with a paired dryer if installation space is scarce.

Performance

All washers wash clothes about equally well. But some use less water. The less water you use, the cheaper it is to run the machine, since the cost of heating the water can be the greatest operating cost.

Top-loading washers typically use between 35 and 45 gallons of water for a regular cycle, sometimes a bit more for permanent-press. Front loaders use between 25 and 30 gallons. At six loads a week, an average washer would cost you about $100 a year for electrically heated water or about $35 for gas heated (using national average rates). Front loaders run about $50 for electrically heated water, $15 for gas. The most efficient models would save about 15 percent; the least efficient would cost about 15 percent extra. The washer motors themselves use a negligible amount of electricity, perhaps $4 to $8 worth a year.

Unbalanced loads

If the washload weight becomes unevenly distributed in the washtub during agitation, problems can occur during the spin cycle: The tub may bang against the machine's sides, or the machine may sense the irregular spin and shut itself off. That shutoff can be annoying if you're in a hurry, but it's better than having the tub bang against the side so hard that the washer starts to "walk" across the floor. Front loaders are best at handling severely unbalanced wash loads.

Brand reliability

The Repair Index by Brand was drawn from responses to Consumers Union's 1988 Annual Questionnaire, in which washer owners were asked about the repair history of their current machines over the past ten years.

The brand indexes cover only full-size models, and only those from brands about which enough responses were received to form a judgment. Thus, *KitchenAid* and *Amana* washers were not sufficiently represented in the survey to be counted among the brands that appear in the chart. The data were adjusted within brands to take into account differences in the ages of the machines.

WASHING MACHINE REPAIR INDEX BY BRAND

As published in a **March 1989** report.

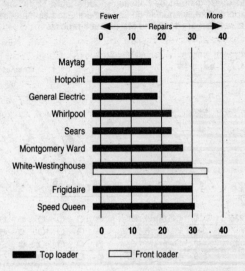

Differences of less than three points in the Repair Index are not very meaningful. Note that the data apply only to brands. Individual models may fare better or worse than their brand as a whole. Also, the data is historical and cannot take into account any design or manufacturing changes in current models. Nevertheless, the fact that the top-loading *Maytag, Hotpoint*, and *GE* washers have been most reliable should help you make a better buying decision.

Recommendations

It's easy to see why front loaders have developed a following among some consumers. The two front-loading *White-Westinghouse* models tested by Consumers Union not only excelled in our

RATINGS OF WASHING MACHINES

Listed by types; within types, listed in order of estimated quality. Except where separated by bold rules, differences between models were slight. Bracketed models were judged approximately equal in quality and are listed alphabetically.

As published in **February 1988** and **March 1989** reports.

◉ ◓ ○ ◒ ●

Better ⟵⟶ Worse

Brand and model	Price	Size (H × W × D), in.	Water use			Unbalanced-load handling	Tub capacity	Water extraction	Linting	Noise
			Total, regular cycle	Total, permanent-press cycle	Hot water, all cycles					
Top loaders										
KitchenAid KAWE800S	$500	43(51¾)x27x26¾	◓	○	○	○	◉	◓	◓	◓
Sears 28831	399	43¼(53¾)x26¾x25¾	◓	○	○	○	◉	◓	○	◓
Whirlpool LA8800XS	449	42½(51¾)x27x25¾	◓	○	○	○	◉	○	○	◓
Maytag A712	559	44(51½)x25½x27	◓	○	○	◓	◓	○	○	◉
Amana LW2500	481	42(52)x25¾x28	◓	○	○	◒	○	○	◓	○
Speed Queen NA6521	480	43(51)x25¾x28	◓	○	○	◒	○	○	◓	○
Gibson WA28M6	406	43(54½)x28¼x27¼	◒	◒	◒	◉	◒	○	◓	◓
Kelvinator AW900C	410	43½(54½)x28¼x27¼	◒	◒	◒	◉	◒	○	◓	◓
Hotpoint WLW4700B	430	42¾(50½)x27x25¼	◓	○	◓	◒	◓	○	○	○
Frigidaire WCID	442	44(54½)x28¼x27¼	◒	◒	◒	◉	◒	○	◓	◓
White-Westinghouse LA800J	483	43¾(54)x27x27	○	○	○	◉	◒	○	◓	○
General Electric WWA8500G	506	43½(50½)x27x25¼	◓	○	◓	◒	◓	○	○	○
Admiral W20F6	407	44(55½)x27x27¼	○	○	◒	◒	◓	◓	◒	◒
Norge LWF20800	426	44(55½)x27x27¼	○	○	◒	◒	◓	◓	◒	◒
Montgomery Ward LNC6635	472	44(55½)x27x27¼	○	○	◒	◒	◓	◓	◒	◒
Front loaders										
White-Westinghouse LT250J	499	36x27x27(39¼)	◉	◉	◉	◉	◒	○	◉	◓
White-Westinghouse LT800J	519	43¾x27x27(39¼)	◉	◉	◉	◉	◒	○	◉	◓

tests for operating efficiency, but they also did well at handling unbalanced loads, keeping garments free from lint, and disposing of sand. They are priced in the same league with many top-loading models. If installation space is at a premium, a stackable model merits special attention.

Despite the front loader's potential, most people will choose a top loader, and top loaders offer some overriding advantages. They're easier to load and unload. They have a bigger tub to do bigger washes, and they're easier to install and service.

Metals

METAL POLISHES

Although many metal polishes make broad claims, no one product is likely to be outstanding for use on brass, copper, stainless steel, aluminum, and chrome. In fact, very few would be worth buying for stainless steel, aluminum, or chrome.

Copper and brass

When used on copper and brass, some polishes must be washed off thoroughly because they are acidic and can stain or etch metals if left in contact with them. Others, however, may be wiped or rubbed off, for they leave at most only a slight stain if they are not completely and immediately removed. It's a good idea, therefore, to restrict your choice to a wipe-off polish for objects that can't be readily rinsed or submersed.

A good polish should make it easy to remove tarnish. It should leave an appropriate gloss and not rub off excessive finish in the process.

As a group, wipe-off brands produce a better shine. Wash-off products, however, require less elbow grease to remove tarnish than do those of the wipe-off type—a difference that you might consider important if you have to clean a heavily tarnished surface. (If you want to give a high gloss to a heavily tarnished surface, you can, of course, use both types of polish, a wash-off brand followed by a high-shining wipe-off brand.) Another advantage of a wash-off product is that, on the whole, it causes less wear than most wipe-off polishes.

Wear may not be a factor if you're cleaning a solid metal. But for things that may be only thinly coated with brass or copper, you should use the mildest cleaning method possible. This means a cloth with detergent or a wipe-off brand that's low in abrasion. You can usually find out whether the object to be cleaned and polished is solid or coated by holding a magnet against it. Objects that have a ferrous base coated with brass or copper will attract the magnet; solid brass and copper will not.

Before any brass polish can work, the metal surface must be free of any lacquer. You'll have to use a special cleaning solution to do that. You can also use nonoily nail polish remover or acetone. Any of these products is toxic and/or flammable. They must be applied cautiously and sparingly.

When the metal is clean, and after it has been polished, it's a good idea to protect the surface with a spray finish for brass or copper.

Copper-bottomed cookware

Wash-off products are particularly suited to cookware, which can be washed easily and isn't necessarily required to have a high gloss. These products should be able to remove light tarnish with little or no rubbing, and heavy tarnish with less effort than a wipe-off material. Even with the most efficient product, however, you still must use considerable elbow grease to clean a heavily coated blackened pan bottom. Steel wool will do the job more easily than polish, but leaves scratch marks on the copper. If your pans are in bad shape but you are display conscious, you might first scour the worst of the dirt off with bronze wool and then finish the job with a wipe-off polish. That will reduce the scratch marks and rub up a good gloss.

If you are looking for an excuse to avoid cleaning the tarnish off copper-bottomed cookware, you can find one in the fact that the darkened surface is more efficient for cooking than a shiny one; it absorbs heat better.

Safety

Polishes, like other household chemicals, should be kept out of the reach of children. Some brands (most often the ones labeled as containing petroleum, mineral spirits, or kerosene) carry appropriate warnings required by law.

This doesn't mean, however, that you can depend on a polish without warnings to be safe.

How to polish stainless steel, aluminum, and chrome

Stainless steel may stain with heat; aluminum becomes discolored with use, and its polished surface may dull; chrome doesn't tarnish, but it can become dirty and splotched.

Stainless steel. Ordinary cleaning in the sink will do for stainless-steel cookware except for an occasional stain from heat. To remove heat stains from the matte-finish inside of a saucepan or fry pan, a wash-off polish can do a competent job, at least as good and maybe better than soapy steel wool. If the pan's polished exterior is also stained, use a polishing product cautiously. Work as quickly as possible to avoid leaving chemicals in contact with the metal for any length of time.

Aluminum. You shouldn't expect to be able to restore a polished aluminum finish to its original glossiness. Soapy steel wool, besides being better overall in cleaning and polishing, will probably do a better job of restoring at least some of the luster than will a special aluminum cleaner. Rubbing the metal with straight, back and forth motions, rather than in circles, helps to maintain a uniform appearance.

Chrome. The chrome plating on a metal product may be so thin that it is best not to use any abrasive polish on it at all. The mildest cleaning method possible should be used for chrome-plated utensils, starting with detergent and progressing to non-abrasive plastic scouring balls.

On the chrome trim of a car, periodic applications of car wax can hold corrosion at bay. If the surface is already corroded and gentle cleaning methods don't work, you will have to resort to a moderately abrasive chrome cleaner, available in automobile supply and hardware stores.

SILVER CARE

A silver-care product can remove tarnish, polish, and treat silver with chemicals that retard further tarnishing. There are also two-way products that clean and polish but don't claim to retard tarnishing. Both types of product include a mild abrasive. You rub the polish on, wipe it off, and then buff the finish to the shine you want.

One-way products come in liquid form and clean only. They don't require tedious rubbing to remove tarnish. You just dip the silver in them or spread them onto silver surfaces. Because of the acid in the liquids, you have to handle them carefully to prevent skin irritation, rinse cleaned silver thoroughly, and tolerate a disagreeable odor as you work.

Special problems

Antique finishes. Dark-looking silver with an antique or oxidized finish is often deeply patterned. Silver polish is almost certain to remove some of the finish. Dip cleaners damage antique finishes, too, even when you wipe the liquids carefully onto the silver.

TWO OTHER WAYS TO CLEAN YOUR SILVER

◈ Cleaning and polishing heavily tarnished silver with a stick of jeweler's rouge entails coating a piece of flannel with rouge, rubbing silver surfaces with the flannel until they are tarnish-free, then buffing the silver with a piece of clean flannel. The result will be silver just about as clean and bright as you can get with the best silver polish. This method has two drawbacks: You have to rub a lot more, and the process is messy, producing quantities of red particles that can smudge clothes and furnishings. Rouge, however, is much cheaper than regular polish. Cleaning cloths are reusable until they start to come apart. You can get rouge from hobby shops or firms that supply professional jewelers. Look in the *Yellow Pages* under Jewelers' Supplies and Craft Supplies.

There is also a cheap and easy way to untarnish silver without rubbing—by a chemical process known as electrolysis. First you put the silver in a well-scoured aluminum pot (or in a nonaluminum pot with a piece of aluminum foil). Then add ¼ teaspoon baking soda and ¼ teaspoon salt dissolved in one quart of boiling water. If the tarnished objects are completely immersed and are touching the aluminum, electrolytic action will clean them in minutes. Then be sure to rinse them off well.

Electrolysis should not be used on satin or antique finishes. Electrolytic cleaning may leave a dullness on silver that only a silver polish can remove. Of course, electrolysis is just for cleaning, not for polishing. One additional caution: Do not use electrolysis on tableware that may have hollow handles. The boiling solution may soften the cement and loosen the handles.

Satin finishes. Dips are the only cleaners that remove tarnish from satin, or low-luster, finishes without making them shinier to some degree.

Staining. If you accidentally allow drops of polish to fall on silver pieces, dip cleaners are likely to leave pale stains, and some other products may leave dark stains. You have to repolish to remove the stains. Many silver table knives are made with stainless-steel blades, and—just as the label warns—drops from dip cleaners can permanently spot or even pit stainless steel if allowed to dry on the surface. To avoid damage, rinse such knives off promptly after using a dip cleaner on their silver handles.

Acidic dip cleaners, as a class, have some inherent hazards that the label may or may not mention. For example, some labels don't suggest using plastic or rubber gloves to protect your hands while cleaning, even though prolonged contact with the cleaner may irritate skin. Some labels don't warn of the danger of getting a cleaner in the eyes. Some labels fail to mention the necessity for proper ventilation when using dip cleaners—excessive inhalation of their sulfide fumes can cause headaches.

Recommendations

As a class, three-way products are higher priced than other products. Nonetheless, a good three-way product is to be preferred. Although they won't clean silver as easily as a good one-way product, they also do the polishing job—and do it well. What's more, because of their tarnish retardance, you won't have to clean the silver again quite as soon.

Dip cleaners work fast but you still may need to use a polish afterward, and polishing, after all, is like cleaning all over again.

Miscellaneous

AUDIO/VISUAL RECORDING AND PLAYBACK EQUIPMENT

Compact discs

Caring for CDs is easier than caring for LPs. Just remember that the most serious damage to a CD is a scratch in the direction the disc spins. Small scratches in the *radial* direction, across the "grooves," are completely ignored by the CD player; therefore, always wipe a CD in the radial direction. Light dust will not harm play; heavier dust can be removed by gentle strokes with a soft cloth. Smudges or deposits should be washed off under running water, with a little liquid dishwashing detergent if needed; then rinse the CD and allow the excess water to run off and *carefully* wipe it dry with a soft cloth.

If the scratches on a compact disc are wide enough, the laser beam in a CD player, which "reads" the disc, won't be able to do its job properly. The result: music punctuated with clicks and pops, or possibly a CD that cannot be played at all. There are specialty products intended to rejuvenate scratched CDs. These products probably won't work on severe scratches, but they could dramatically reduce the number of playing errors caused by light scratches. You might even be able to restore an unplayable CD to playable condition. A paste auto wax such as *Rally* is cheaper than a specialty product and can work as well.

Long-playing records

Keeping an LP dust-free is the best way to make it last longer. Records can be cleaned with a cloth-pile brush before you play them; electronics stores sell such brushes. Keep the turntable's dust cover closed except when changing records, and handle records only by the edges to prevent perspiration and skin oils from attaching dust to the record's surfaces.

When returning a record to its album, make sure that the opening in the inner sleeve doesn't coincide with the opening in the outer cover and leave the record case wide open for dust to enter. Always store records vertically to reduce the likelihood of warping and keep records away from direct sources of heat.

Stylus

Cleaning a stylus is neither difficult nor time-consuming. It's important to keep the stylus free from accumulated dust and dirt, which accelerate record wear and can cause mistracking and distortion.

Clean the stylus with a fine camel's hair or artist's sable brush lightly moistened with a little rubbing alcohol. Brush lightly from the rear to the front of the cartridge; brushing backward or sideways could bend the delicate stylus.

Audio-tape recording and playback heads

For best sound quality from an audio tape recorder, clean recording and playback heads periodically by following the manufacturer's instructions (if any are given). Use a small cotton swab, or, even better, a lint-free piece of cotton cloth wrapped around the swab. Lint-free cloth doesn't have as much of a tendency as cotton to release tiny fibers that might get into the moving parts of the machine. The swab or cloth should be lightly moistened with a cleaning agent. You can use isopropyl alcohol (rubbing alcohol), but it is probably safer and better to buy tape-head cleaner from an electronics supply store. That should ensure getting a product with a formulation developed specifically for the purpose. Tape-head cleaner is most likely to contain solvents that are safe for use on the heads as well as for the materials around the heads. Clean everything in the tape path, not just the heads: the capstan (the rotating metal shaft that moves the tape past the heads), the pinch roller (the rubberlike roller that contacts the capstan), and the tape guides.

If the deck or tape player is built so that the heads are not accessible for cleaning, you might try a special head-cleaning tape. Follow the instructions explicitly. Never use any kind of abrasive material to clean the heads.

Clean as frequently as necessary, based on how often you play tapes, the quality of the tapes, and any evidence of dirt accumulation. Once a month is probably a reasonable interval.

VCR recording and playback heads

A video head is the device that picks up the video signal from the tape. Video heads are abraded and pick up iron particles as they rub against the tape; eventually they wear out.

In tests of a VHS model and a Beta model running continuously for an extended period, with tapes changed every 200 hours, Consumers Union engineers found that the picture began to deteriorate after about 2,500 hours of play.

Replacing the heads can be expensive, running to a considerable fraction of the cost of the entire machine. There's not much you can do about normal wear of the head resulting from its spinning at high speed against the tape, and the tape moving past the head. You can try to keep the machine as free of dust as possible by covering it when the VCR is not in use and by storing tapes where they aren't likely to gather a lot of dust or other debris.

Sooner or later, however, the heads will get dirty and the picture will become "noisier" and/or fuzzier than it was when the machine was new. Cleaning the heads directly is not a do-it-yourself job. The heads are often accessible only through a maze of delicate wiring and mechanical components.

When the picture seems to need it, you might try a special VCR cleaning tape, using it cautiously and strictly in accordance with the manufacturer's instructions. Use a cleaning tape only when the picture becomes annoyingly deficient. If cleaning restores the picture, fine. If not, try the tape *once* more. If a second cleaning doesn't help, professional servicing may be necessary.

AUTO POLISHES

Wax or sealant cannot improve the glossiness of a new car's finish much. Most cars now have a clear coating that adds luster to the color underneath. But eventually sunlight, water, and air pollution age and erode the paint until the gloss fades, and the finish is no longer able to repel water and dirt. At that point, auto polish can make a dramatic improvement.

You'll find auto polish in liquid, paste, and spray versions. Many of the products are called "creams," "sealants," "glazes," and "protectors" by their makers, but they're basically just polishes. Some contain abrasives to remove stubborn stains or chalky, weathered paint from a car's finish. Most also contain waxes or silicones that can fill tiny cracks and renew the water-repellency of the finish.

The products' labels promise to make a car's finish shiny and new-looking, to whisk away ugly encrustations, and to seal against the adverse effects of sun, rain, dust, grease, and droppings from trees. That's a lot to promise for a product that, once buffed, leaves a film only thousandths of a millimeter thick.

Effectiveness

A good auto polish should improve the shine of a car's finish. Even more important, it should be durable, protecting the surface from dirt and wear for months. It should be easy to apply, of course. It should not leave behind a haze or streaks, and it should clean as well as shine.

On car surfaces that are relatively new, some polishes will shine better than others. The best ones will add noticeably. but not dramatically, to the gleam. The worst actually make the surface duller than before.

A major part of the sales appeal of auto polishes is the protection they're supposed to provide against the elements. But a polish can't protect anything once it has worn away. People who do polish their cars tend to do it twice a year, spring and fall. That may not be often enough with most polishes.

When you want to see whether a polish is holding up, look at what happens to water on the car's surface. The beads of water that form on a well-sealed surface are rounded and have a very small contact area. As the polish wears away, the beads spread and flatten. Eventually, when the polish is completely gone, water doesn't bead at all; it lies in a sheet on the surface.

Liquids are somewhat easier to apply and spread than pastes, but all the products should go on easily. Spray-on products are especially easy to apply uniformly. But be careful not to get the spray—or any polish, for that matter—on vinyl surfaces or on the windshield. The polish may damage the vinyl, and it will streak and smear the glass. (Be sure to shake a spray container before you begin; some of the ingredients may have settled to the bottom.)

Instructions on the labels of the nonspray polishes call for spreading them on with an applicator (provided with some products), then removing the excess and buffing with a dry polishing

RATINGS OF AUTO POLISHES

Listed in order of overall quality, based on how long the polish protected car finishes. When durability was equal, polishes are listed in order of ability to improve gloss on shiny finishes. A difference of one grade in gloss improvement was judged not very significant. Except as noted, all improved the gloss of dull surfaces and were easy to apply and buff out.

As published in a **June 1988** report.

Better ● ◕ ○ ◑ ● Worse

Brand and model	Form	Size, oz. or fl. oz.	Price	Protection/durability	Gloss improvement	Comments
Nu Finish	Liquid	16	$ 4.95	◉	◕	—
Blue Coral Blue Poly One-Step Sealant	Paste	16	9.64	◉	○	F
Nu Finish	Paste	14	6.65	◉	○	F
Rain Dance	Liquid	16	7.06	◉	○	F
Rain Dance	Paste	14	7.06	◉	◑	F
Meguiar's Car Cleaner	Paste	14	6.24	◕	◕	E
Simoniz II	Liquid	16	6.12	◕	◑	C,F
Blue Coral Blue Poly One-Step Sealant	Liquid	16	9.18	◕	◑	C
Meguiar's Car Cleaner	Liquid	16	6.12	○	◕	—
Turtle Minute Wax Silicone	Spray	18	4.93	○	◕	—
Mother's California Gold Original Formula	Paste	12	8.38	○	◕	—
Turtle Super Hard Shell	Paste	14	4.06	○	◕	B
Blue Coral Carnauba Premium	Paste	13	7.98	○	○	D
Wynn's Classic Car Wax	Paste	15	9.13	○	○	—
Kit	Liquid	16	3.82	○	○	D
Turtle Minute Wax Silicone	Paste	13	7.14	○	○	F
Mother's California Gold Liquid Carnauba	Liquid	15	7.81	○	○	—
Kit	Paste	12	4.54	○	◑	F
Turtle Super Hard Shell	Liquid	18	4.46	○	◑	—
TR-3 Instant Resin Glaze	Spray	20	3.99	○	◑	B
Simoniz II	Paste	14	6.37	○	◑	A,C,F
Rally	Liquid	12	3.12	○	●	A
TR-3 Resin Glaze	Liquid	16	5.65	○	●	A,B,C
Wynn's Classic High Performance Carnauba	Paste	15	10.32	◑	○	—

Brand and model	Form	Size, oz. or fl. oz.	Price	Protection/durability	Gloss improvement	Comments
Rally Cream	Paste	14	5.22	◓	○	F
Rain Dance	Spray	18	6.43	◓	○	—
Turtle Minute Wax Silicone	Liquid	16	6.38	◓	○	F
Westley's Concentrate	Liquid	16	3.39	◓	◓	—
TR-3 Resin Glaze	Paste	12	5.49	◓	◓	A,B,C
Westley's Concentrate	Paste	12	3.19	●	●	A,C

Better ◀————▶ Worse (● ◑ ○ ◐ ●)

Key to Comments
A–Tended to leave a haze on dark-colored surfaces.
B–Tended to be more difficult than most to buff.
C–Abraded finish more than most.
D–Abraded finish less than most.
E–Abraded finish least of all.
F–Applicator provided.

cloth. Buffing is likely to be fairly easy with most. But a few products, as noted in the Ratings' comments, may dry into a rather stiff coating that needs more effort than usual to buff.

A polish that has dried too long on the surface might be hard to buff. On a dry, hot day, a polish can dry very quickly, so you should tackle small sections at a time.

Judging abrasiveness

The paint, not the polish, protects a car's metal from rust. So it makes sense to polish away no more paint than is necessary to restore a smooth finish. You can see how much paint you're removing simply by looking at the buffing cloth. If it picks up much of the finish color, the polish contains an abrasive that is grinding away paint. (This test won't work on very new cars, because of the clear topcoat over the colored paint.)

A fine abrasive is useful for removing stubborn stains or a microlayer of chalky, weathered paint. For an extremely weathered finish, however, even the most abrasive polishes may not be adequate. Special, highly abrasive polishing or rubbing compounds are available for such challenging jobs. They are usually found right next to the auto polishes in the store. But do not rub too long or too hard with them, or you may rub right through the paint to the primer.

Recommendations

Whichever polish you use, be sure to wash the car thoroughly beforehand. Most road dirt is a good deal harder than a car's finish. If you polish a dirty car, you'll only grind the dirt into the paint, scratching the finish as you rub.

You may not need to polish a new car, but you should wash it often. Bird and tree droppings, salt, tar, and even plain dirt can eventually mar the finish. Frequent washing is especially important in the summer, when high temperatures increase the damaging effects of contaminants.

DRINKING WATER

Americans are becoming increasingly concerned with the quality of their water, as the booming sales of bottled water clearly show, but paying a lot for water from bottles isn't the only way to get good-tasting water. Many people have turned to activated carbon filters to upgrade their drinking water.

The carbon material is formed by exposing a carbon-containing material (usually charcoal) to high temperatures and steam in the absence of oxygen. The resulting material is honeycombed within by minuscule branching and twisting channels. The channels greatly increase the surface area to which the water is exposed and thereby account for activated carbon's impressive filtering power. As water passes through this microscopic labyrinth, contaminants stick to the walls of the channels. "Adsorption" is the technical term.

Some home-style activated carbon water filters are sink mounted and attach to the faucet outlet, others go under the sink and are connected to the cold water line there, and a few are independent of the house plumbing. Most manufacturers of home-use filters claim only that their products improve the taste and odor of water. A few claim that their products will remove toxic chemicals.

Limitations of filters

There are some important water problems that activated carbon filters will not affect. They won't help against:

Hard water. This contains large amounts of dissolved minerals, mainly magnesium and calcium. A water-softening device is needed to remove those minerals.

Other dissolved minerals. Activated carbon filters will remove dust particles, but they have only a small effect on dissolved metals such as iron, lead, manganese, or copper. They won't remove chlorides, fluorides, or nitrates at all. An "ion exchange" device, available at plumbing supply stores, can be used to remove most of those minerals, as can a "reverse osmosis" device. Reverse osmosis is a much more complex procedure.

Hydrogen sulfide. This chemical gives water the taste and odor of rotten eggs. Chlorination usually takes care of the problem; carbon filters can remove only small amounts of hydrogen sulfide.

Filtering

Despite their limitations, activated carbon filters can significantly improve water quality. First, the filters can quite effectively remove many objectionable tastes and odors. Second, they can also help clear sediments (turbidity) from tap water. Third, many home filtering units can effectively remove organic chemicals, such as chloroform, which belong to a family of chemicals known as trihalomethanes (THMs).

Three important filter characteristics follow:

Organic chemical removal. Chloroform is known to cause tumors in animals and is suspected to be a carcinogen for humans. It provides a tough test of a filter's ability to remove organic chemicals because activated carbon filters don't retain chloroform as well as they do more complex organics such as pesticides. To prevent chloroform absorbed by the filter from being returned to the water later on, avoid models that use powdered activated charcoal. Granular activated carbon is much more effective.

Chlorine removal. Chlorine contributes heavily to water's taste and odor. It is added at water treatment plants to protect public health—usually in sufficient quantity to maintain a residual amount at the tap. Even moderate amounts of chlorine can contribute to characteristic and often disagreeable tastes.

Useful flow rate. As a general rule, filtration ability depends on the flow rate of the water. Gushing water isn't filtered as well as water flowing at slower speeds. Some filters are effective only when water trickles through; others can handle much faster flow rates. A filter's "useful flow rate" is the flow rate it can tolerate while still removing contaminants adequately.

Taste

If you ask people to compare two versions of heavily chlorinated water—one version unfiltered, the other filtered—the panelists are almost certain to prefer the filtered water overwhelmingly.

Evidently, an activated carbon filter does help improve the taste of water. What's more, it doesn't have to be very effective to make the improvement noticeable.

Safety

A filter traps many contaminants, but it is not effective against bacteria. In fact, a filter can allow the bacterial levels in water to multiply many times over. Wet activated carbon, richly infused with trapped organic matter, provides bacteria with an ideal breeding ground. High bacterial levels are most likely when a filter has a saturated cartridge and when some time has passed since the filter's last use.

Tests run by the Environmental Protection Agency showed that periods of stagnation—up to five days of nonuse—will increase bacterial counts in filtered water. (A filter can go unused even in a busy household, for instance, when the family takes a weekend outing or a vacation.)

Bacteria get into the filter in the first place because disinfection at the water treatment plant doesn't kill everything. A certain number of bacteria survive and end up in tap water.

The digestive system usually adapts to the low level of "harmless" bacteria found in drinking water. Common sense suggests that drinking large doses of unidentified bacteria is best avoided.

One thing is certain: If bacteria don't get into the filter in the first place, they can't multiply inside. For this reason, filters should only be used to treat water that is microbiologically safe. (If you have questions about the safety of your water, you should ask the water company for its latest test report; if you use well water, you'll need to have it tested yourself.)

Some filters contain silver and claim to discourage growth of bacteria within the filter; but don't be impressed by any filter's "bacteriostatic" claim. The EPA has concluded that silver compounds in water filters show "no significant bacteriostatic effect" on drinking water.

Using a filter

How to use your filter is almost as important as which brand you buy. If you follow these suggestions you can maximize your filter's performance.

• Flush out the filter before the first use of the day. Open the faucet wide and let the water run for at least fifteen seconds for an under-sink model, at least five seconds for a sink-mounted filter. When you install a new cartridge, flush for several minutes to remove fine carbon particles.

• Change filters regularly. A heavily used filter is more likely to contain high bacterial levels and to discharge organic chemicals previously trapped. An exhausted filter is worse than useless.

• Don't filter hot water. A filter on the hot water faucet won't remove contaminants very well. And the hot water may liberate chemicals previously trapped on the filter.

• Use the slowest flow rate you can tolerate. The longer the water is in contact with the filter, the more impurities the carbon can attract and the cleaner your water will be.

• After installing a new cartridge, circle the date for the next replacement on your calendar. Stick to your schedule.

Recommendations

An activated carbon water filter will remove chlorine and other chemicals that impart taste and odor to water; some filters are also effective at removing organic chemicals, including chloroform and others that have little taste. Unfortunately, a wet carbon filter makes an excellent breeding ground for bacteria that can find their way into your drinking water. The potential for bacteria demands that you buy a filter only if you're willing to change the cartridge regularly.

If you simply want to clear your water of rust and dirt, then a sediment filter may suit you just fine. Such a filter contains no carbon.

If your complaint about tap water is mainly esthetic—an objectionable taste or odor—then a sink-mounted carbon filter would probably suit you.

An under-sink unit is for more serious problems such as water that tastes awful unless it's treated, or water that contains small amounts of harmful organic chemicals. These units must be permanently connected into the cold water line; this means some effort if you do it yourself and may be costly if you hire a plumber. There are also large, whole-house units with over 30 pounds of carbon that are used when a serious pollutant has been identified. Such units have a provision for regular backwashing. Check the *Yellow Pages* for Water Treatment Equipment.

PAINT-REMOVING TOOLS

Before repainting any surface you should get rid of bits of loosened paint and make sure the remaining paint isn't greasy or dirty.

When you have to deal with a paint in really poor condition, you may have to go beyond just stripping away the flaking and peeling paint. If you don't, the surface—whether that of furniture, the walls of a room, or the side of a house—may continue to deteriorate. You'll usually end up with far better-looking results if you strip off *all* the old paint.

Chemical paint removers are poisonous or highly flammable—or both. They are among the most dangerous products you can have around the house. Blowtorches and other devices that soften old paint by heating it pose a fire hazard. That leaves scrapers and sanders that you use by hand or as an accessory for an electric drill. Finishing sanders can also be used to remove paint. These methods are all slow and often strenuous to use, but for the most part they are safer.

There's a wide variety of paint-removing tools available from hardware stores, home centers, and by mail order, but no single scraper or sander will handle every paint-removal job. You may eventually need three or four different types, depending on the jobs you tackle.

Hand tools—for small jobs

There are a large number of hand tools available—scrapers, rasps, and sandpaper substitutes. Each type has its uses, however specialized. Since none is really expensive, it's a good idea to keep more than one type in your tool kit: one or two scrapers, along with a rasp or a sandpaper substitute. Within types, differences from one brand to the next are usually minimal, so you can choose according to price and availability at hardware stores and home centers.

Hook scrapers.   A hook scraper is best suited for removing loose paint from flat surfaces. It looks something like an extralarge razor with a stiff, fairly dull blade. Like a razor, it's pulled along the work surface so the edge of the blade scrapes away the paint.

The blade on a hook scraper usually has more than one usable edge. By loosening a screw, you can bring another edge into the working position. The more usable edges a scraper has, the longer you can work without having to sharpen it. A tungsten carbide blade is far harder than a conventional metal blade and will hold its edge much longer. If such a blade gets dull, you'll have to replace it or have it honed by a professional. Other blades can be resharpened simply by filing them lightly, a job you may have to do quite often.

Push scrapers.   These resemble the familiar putty knife, though they vary in details. Some have a long handle, others a short one. Some have a blunt edge; others are sharpened. You have your choice of stiff or flexible blades in several widths. The differences are of minor importance. You should try to match the shape and size of the scraper to the job at hand—a narrow-bladed scraper, for example, will be best for working in and around window frames.

Push scrapers are useful on flat surfaces and for digging paint out of corners, but they are not meant to be used on curves. In general, they are less effective than hook scrapers on all but the loosest paint. It's harder to push a scraper than to pull it.

Rasps and abrasive blocks.   These devices can scrape and sand and are generally available in a variety of sizes and abrasive grades. Rasps and blocks can also be used for sanding wood. Their shape limits their use primarily to flat surfaces, however.

Sandpaper substitutes.   Unlike rasps and sanding blocks, sandpaper substitutes are fairly flexible, so they can get into places the others can't. They may be rectangles of tough cloth coated on both sides with sheets of abrasive-coated nylon mesh, or possibly a thin sheet of metal punched with ragged holes.

The substitutes are durable and fast cutting and can be wrapped around a dowel to sand a concave surface or can be used with a sanding block. Some may leave the surface rather rough, making it necessary to do some sanding before painting.

Sponges and glass blocks. To sand moldings and other complex shapes, woodworkers often wrap sandpaper around a sponge. Sanding sponges come essentially prewrapped, with an abrasive coating covering four sides. They are springy and flexible, as you'd expect a sponge to be. They can also be rinsed out to unclog the abrasive.

Foamed glass blocks resemble chunks of hardened plastic foam. They wear away quite rapidly as they're used, leaving a residue of glass dust in the work area. What's worse, they may give off the stench of rotten eggs as you work. Sandpaper is better, and less offensive to the nose.

Drill attachments—for larger jobs

A majority of drill attachments are simply variations on the standard sanding disk, the difference being the kind of abrasive supplied. Most disks use cloth or stiff mesh coated with grit. Others are metal circles punched with holes to form a rasplike cutting surface. Yet another type is a "flap wheel" attachment, which consists of a hub fringed with flaps of abrasive paper on cloth. Some oddball attachments consist of a stiff wheel with a texture much like that of a natural sponge, stiff rubbery disks impregnated with abrasive, and a disk of material that's similar to a kitchen scouring pad.

Powered by a drill, these accessories have the ability to remove paint fairly quickly from large, reasonably flat surfaces, such as garage doors and boat hulls. These attachments can also be used to remove rust, but a hard-edged disk is suitable for use only on nearly flat surfaces. Disk attachments generally perform better than flap wheels primarily because they work faster. Wire brushes, the kind found in many drill kits, take a long time to remove paint and have a tendency to scratch wood surfaces.

A fast model should be able to strip away a square foot of paint in a little less than a minute. Even with the fastest tool, however, it would take you more than twenty hours, working strenuously, to strip a one-story house that measured 30 feet by 40 feet. That's not a weekend job.

Although speed is an important factor, there are other things to consider in choosing a drill attachment for paint removal:

Condition of surface. Some of the fastest attachments are also the harshest, leaving cleaned surfaces quite rough. If you're removing paint from a piece of furniture or a door, where appearance matters, you should look for an attachment that's reasonably gentle. One that's both fast and rough might be suitable for stripping paint from steel, concrete, or other surfaces that are hard to scratch.

Effort and comfort. All attachments produce some noise, but the disk rasps are especially loud. Other types, including most of the flap wheels, are heavy and tend to slow a drill down, making them a chore to use.

Safety

Paint removal, especially with power tools, requires certain safety precautions. To guard against the obvious hazard—flying chips of paint or grit—you should wear safety goggles or a face shield, work gloves, and a heavy jacket. Hearing protectors are also advisable.

You should also guard against health hazards that may not be immediately apparent. Older houses may have some lead-based paint on them. Removing it with a hand tool or a drill attachment will disperse small particles into the air, where they can be inhaled. Likewise, "antifouling" paints often used on boats contain toxic ingredients that might be hazardous if inhaled. In either case, you should wear a fitted respirator with a suitable filtration cartridge. If the paint is new and presents no toxicity hazard, a simple dust mask should suffice.

Recommendations

Choosing the right drill attachment for paint removal involves balancing speed against roughness, ease of use, and durability. If you're working on fine furniture, for example, you'll want an attachment that won't damage the wood; speed and durability become less important factors. On big jobs, where appearance isn't crucial, look for a tool that's fast, easy to use, and comfortable.

No drill attachment is likely to be very effective in removing paint or rust from complex surfaces. They just can't get into nooks and crannies without gouging the surface.

For large-scale jobs, you'd be better off using the services of a professional or renting the equipment you need. To scrape the old finish off a floor, you should use a large drum sander plus a smaller sander for finishing the edges.

If you have to strip old paint from a house, rent a pressure/water-spray machine, which uses a high-pressure stream of water

---

HEATERS AND ROTARY STRIPPERS

◈ Paint removal is dirty, tedious work, but it need not be dangerous. With most tools, the risk of injury is minimal. Two types of tools, however, create hazards that are hard to avoid.

A number of devices use heat to soften paint to the point where it can easily be scraped away. Some of these consist of an electric heating element, similar to that used in a number of appliances, plus a metal shield and a handle. There may also be quartz-halogen lamps, very much like a home-movie light, or propane fueled heater.

All pose a fire hazard. It is all too easy to set fire to paint with any of these heaters.

Drill attachments that are called "rotary strippers" are also unsafe. They consist of stiff wires bristling from a hub. In use, some of the wires can break off and fly away at high speed, which might injure the user or someone standing nearby.

The companies warn you not to apply pressure when using these tools, but this caution is difficult to follow.

to clear away chalking or peeling sections without harming firmly adhered paint.

Finally, for furniture and other easily transported items, you might consider a commercial paint stripper, listed in the *Yellow Pages* under Furniture Stripping.

POWER BLOWERS

Power blowers use a blast of air to whisk leaves off the lawn, sweep grass clippings from the sidewalk, or blow debris down the driveway. A power blower's roar may not endear you to your neighbors, but a blower can spare you a lot of time and sore muscles.

The current choice ranges from hand-held electric or gasoline-powered blowers to machines meant to be worn like a backpack. Many blowers can accept accessories and attachments. The most common is a kit that converts the blower into an outdoor vacuum cleaner. Another common accessory lets you use a blower to flush the leaves out of rain gutters. There's also an accessory that converts a blower to a power sprayer. One model can use its engine to power a string trimmer, a cultivator, and other lawn and garden tools.

You can spend less than $100 for a hand-held electric blower or more than $300 for a gasoline-powered backpack model. Hand-held gasoline models typically sell for $130 to $180.

Cleanup with a blower

As a type, the backpack blowers are best. The best models quickly gather leaves and combine piles. They can easily slice through large piles, moving them where you wish. The more powerful ones move more than leaves. They can denude graveled areas and push fallen branches along the ground.

A hand-held blower is less effective than a backpack model, but a gasoline-powered machine can do very well. A good electric blower can handle leaves capably. A weaker electric can pile up leaves, albeit slowly.

A gutter-cleaning attachment is available on several models. The kit consists of several tubes that stack together to reach up to a first-story gutter, up to about thirteen feet. It's best to keep the length as short as possible, because the longer extensions are harder to control. The handiest type of kit lets you swivel the nozzle from the ground. With some, you can rotate the nozzle only by lowering the entire tube to the ground. Cleaning gutters is invariably sloppy. No amount of care will control the flying mess.

Cleanup with a vacuum

Vacuum attachments, like the gutter-cleaning kits, add to a power blower's versatility. With a suction tube and vacuum bag in place, these machines can handle more than dry leaves or grass clippings on a lawn. They can clean leaves out of a ground cover, clear leaves from a flower bed, or pick up pine needles.

The vacuuming attachments are not meant for large-scale leaf removal, though. The bags hold about two cubic feet of debris, which is a little less than two bushels. The more powerful models fill their bag in less than five minutes. Emptying the bag is easy enough, but it's not something you'd want to do many times.

The vacuums are not designed to pick up anything other than pine needles, leaves, small twigs, and small pieces of paper. Stones and other hard material could damage the blade that draws material into the vacuum tube.

Comfort and convenience

Power blowers are so notoriously noisy that a number of municipalities restrict their use or ban them outright. The large backpack models produce the most racket, comparable to a chain saw. Most hand-held gasoline models generate a little more noise than a gasoline-powered lawn mower. The electric blowers are by far the least noisy. It's a good idea to protect your ears (with ear plugs or sound deadeners worn like headphones) when using a gasoline model.

The more comfortable the blower, the longer you can use it

RATINGS OF POWER BLOWERS

Listed by types; within types, listed in order of estimated quality, based mainly on leaf blowing. Bracketed models were judged about equal and are listed alphabetically.
As published in a **September 1988** report.

Better ← ● ◐ ○ ◑ ● → Worse

Brand and model	Price	Weight	Length of tube	Engine size	Claimed velocity	Leaf blowing	Comfort	Throttle convenience	Noise	Running time	Vacuum	Gutter	Extras Advantages	Disadvantages	Comments
Backpack gasoline models															
Echo PB300E	$330	18 lb.	52½	31 cc.	155 mph	●	●	○	57 min	—	1	—	A,B,C,F,H,I	—	—
John Deere 3E	309	18	52½	31	155	●	◐	○	57	—	—	—	A,B,C,H,I	—	—
Weed Eater 980	330	22	64	36	175	●	◐	●	54	—	—	—	A,B,H	h	D,E
Sears Cat. No. 79691	250	20½	68½	37.5	185	●	●	●	81	—	—	—	A,B,H,I	b,h	D,E
Green Machine 2600	340	15	59	22.5	120	○	●	◐	106	—	—	—	B,E,H,I	h,i	E,F
Homelite HB480	220	14	58	31	150	◐	○	●	34	—	—	—	B,C	a,g	E
McCulloch Super Air Stream V	230	15½	70½	21	120	◐	○	◐	34	—	—	—	A,B,C	a,i	—
Hand-held gasoline models															
Echo PB210E	230	10	38	21	135	○	○	○	30	—	1	—	B,H,I	b,e	—
John Deere 2E	179	11	38	21	135	○	○	●	30	—	—	—	B,D,H,I	b,e	—
Ryan 300	130	11	32½	31	150	○	○	●	33	—	1	—	A,B,E,H	—	B
Homelite HB180V	150	10½	38	26	150	○	●	○	64	✓	—	—	A,D	a,e,i	—
Stihl BG61AVE	190	10½	32½	20	—	○	◐	◐	30	—	—	—	B,H	c	—
Green Machine 2360	230	12	—	25.5	125	◐	●	●	34	—	—	—	E	d,i	C,G
Snapper 250BV	190	7½	33	25.5	135	◐	○	◐	26	✓	—	1	A,B,H	c,d	—
Weed Eater 960	180	11	36	28	150	◐	○	◐	26	✓	—	1	F,I	f,j	—

McCulloch Super Air Stream IV	160	10½	36	21	140	●	●	29	✓	—	A,B,D	a,c,e,j	—
Paramount GB150	130	10½	42	21	165	○	○	28	①	①	I	a,e,f,h,i,k	—
Hand-held electric models													
Weed Eater 2560	85	6½	34	—	125	●	●	—	✓	①	F	j	—
Toro 550 TBX	80	7	37½	—	135	●	○	—	✓	—	G	—	—
Green Machine 660	70	6	36	—	100	●	○	—	—	—	B	—	A
McCulloch Air Stream II	70	7	42	—	—	●	○	—	①	①	—	k	—
Paramount PB350	80	7	42	—	125	●	○	—	✓	①	—	k	—
Sears Cat. No. 79636	70+	8½	31	—	125	○	○	—	①	①	—	—	—

① Optional.

Specifications and Features

All gasoline-powered models have: ● 2-cycle engines that require a gasoline/oil fuel mix.

Except as noted, all: ● Have blower tubes whose sections stayed connected during use; those on backpack models can be rotated to change nozzle direction. ● Were easy to convert to vacuum or gutter cleaner, where such modes are available. ● Hand-held gasoline models have carrying strap, usually available as an option.

Key to Advantages

A—Has low-fuel indicator.

B—Instantaneous Off switch can be operated by hand on handle.

C—Has handle to make unit easier to carry.

D—Shoulder strap included.

E—Comes with 1 can of engine oil.

F—Gutter attachment more convenient to operate than others.

G—Has safety interlock to prevent operation while vacuum tube is being installed.

H—Comes with tools.

I—Comes with very helpful maintenance instructions (John Deere's instructions lack parts diagram, which is available only as an option).

Key to Disadvantages

a—Vibrated more than most; unit was tiring to use.

b—Sections of blower tube tended to blow apart; we had to tape them together.

c—Exhaust blows directly to the rear (or, on the Stihl, to the right); can add to discomfort in use.

d—Air intake clogged more readily than most others.

e—Air intake can snag clothing unless operator is careful.

f—Can't be refueled resting on ground; must be tilted.

g—Blower tube awkward to rotate to change nozzle direction; can hamper leaf-gathering capability.

h—Fuel-tank cap does not seal fuel tank if unit is tilted; could lead to hazardous fuel spill.

i—You must use tools to gain access to the air cleaner for servicing.

j—More difficult than others to convert to vacuum or gutter-cleaner mode.

k—Very long tube; best suited for tall people.

l—Very short tube; best suited for short people.

Key to Comments

A—Vacuum tank available for cars, workshops, and such, but it can't pick up leaves or garden debris.

B—Available with vacuum as 300BV, $150.

C—Modular unit. We purchased engine, Model 2300, and blower attachment, Model 2361. Other attachments available (not tested): string trimmer/brush cutter, weeder/cultivator, edger, snow thrower.

D—Fuel tank has line above which it should not be filled.

E—Has On/off valve that should be turned off after each use.

F—Comes with small plastic container for mixing and pouring fuel; judged too small to be useful.

G—Lacks shoulder strap; 2-handle design makes strap unnecessary.

before you tire out. A machine's low weight, good balance, and freedom from vibration contribute to comfort. As a class, the backpack blowers were the most comfortable because most of their weight rides on your back. Some machines come with a shoulder strap that usually makes them easier to handle, but the strap helps little on a blower that vibrates a lot.

The distance from where you grip the handle to the end of the nozzle is not critical with backpack models because you can swivel the tube as needed to direct the airflow. With a hand-held model, your height and the length of your arms and legs will determine the length that's most suitable for you. To get the right size, try models in the store before you buy. A tube that's too short or too long makes the blower more tiring to use and diminishes its effectiveness.

The operating controls on a blower should be easy to reach, and, on gas models, should vary the engine speed smoothly. The controls shouldn't be out of the way on the rear of the unit or be difficult to operate.

Gasoline engines

One tank of fuel should keep a blower running anywhere from about half an hour to an hour and three-quarters. Running time is especially important for a backpack-style blower that's being used for an extended period. You won't want to struggle in and out of the shoulder harness any more than necessary.

Whether an engine continues to start easily depends on how well it's maintained and tuned. The basic care is similar to that required by power lawn mowers and chain saws:

1. Keep the air filter clean and check the fuel filter regularly.
2. Do not let the engine sit for long periods with fuel in the tank.
3. Change the spark plug once a year or whenever the manufacturer recommends.

Carburetor adjustments are best left to a mechanic unless you are experienced with small engines.

Personal Care

CLEANSING CREAMS AND LOTIONS

Some products can be wiped off, others rinsed off with water. Still others can be either wiped or rinsed. But no cream or lotion can work miracles, although they may help make your skin feel more comfortable.

Most cleansing creams and lotions are oil-based formulas that act as solvents on the oils and grease that bind makeup and dirt with them. Many products contain emulsifiers that, like soap, help break down the greasy binders so they can be washed off with water.

The essential ingredients in most cleansing creams and lotions don't vary much. Most contain mineral oil. Borax is a cleansing agent common in many of the wipe-off cleaners. Detergents are often used in the rinse-off types. Ingredients such as paraffin, beeswax, and cellulose gum affect the consistency of a product so that it feels soft and is easy to spread on and remove.

Other chemicals, such as sorbitan sesquioleate and methyl-paraben, perform a variety of functions. They prevent oil and water from separating, for example, or they control mold and bacterial growth. Various oils, from avocado to lanolin to wheat germ, are also commonly added. They may supplement the mineral oil, but probably more important, from the manufacturer's point of view, they also lend the ingredients list a touch of wholesomeness.

Other ingredients in cleansing creams and lotions are also there primarily to enhance sales appeal. Often they're perfumes or dyes, for these products frequently come in flowery fragrances and sport pretty colors.

Most lotions contain water. Less water makes what's called a nonliquefying cream. When there's no water, the product is a liquefying cream. A few products are liquefying creams that turn into oily liquids when rubbed on the skin. Nonliquefying creams appear to vanish into the skin.

Important properties of cleansing creams are easy application, a comfortable feel while applying, easy removal, comfortable skin feel after use, overall convenience, and of course scent. Feel of skin after use is probably the most important characteristic. A good product shouldn't feel greasy during use, or afterward, nor should a cleansing cream leave your skin too dry or taut. Most products will clean well enough, but you may have to use a lot of some brands or even two applications to get your face clean.

You may prefer a fragrance-free cream because the quality of the scent in preferred cleaners can be less than superior, or you may object to a medicinal scent.

Packaging

Truth-in-advertising regulations perhaps have taken some of the romance out of cosmetics' sales pitches. In its place, there is some solid information in the ingredients labeling that can be particularly helpful to individuals with known allergies.

Cleansing cream marketers are cautious about making claims that their products can effect calendar-defying changes in anyone's face. Some suggest they are deep cleaning. But, in fact, the dirt and makeup these products help remove are on the surface of the skin. Cleansing creams and lotions may seem to clean more thoroughly than soap and water because they can often do their job with less scrubbing, or simply because the user thinks the creams and lotions can do a more thorough job. Some products purport to soften skin. They may, but the effect is fleeting.

A scientific pitch sells some products. There may be, for example, a little in-store calculator to determine which of a particular brand's products are appropriate for which skin types—dry, normal, or oily.

Some cleansing lotions and creams come in fairly simple, functional containers. Plastic is better than glass, because greasy hands and glass don't mix. Some containers could easily lead you to believe that they contain more of the product than is indicated on the label, particularly the ones that come in a jar within a jar. These double walls of plastic—with ample air space between the walls—create a generous appearance on the outside, but the inside has less to offer.

Recommendations

In the world of cosmetics, expensive, beautifully packaged products have a certain mystique of effectiveness and "magic" ingredients. But few, if any, live up to the billing. If you are now using an expensive, high-fashion cleansing cream, it could pay off to try an inexpensive one the next time.

FACIAL TISSUES

People expect tissues to handle all sorts of jobs—to wipe eyeglasses, remove makeup, stand in for a napkin or a towel. But you expect most from a tissue when your nose runs nonstop and your eyes water. You want one that won't turn to shreds when you sneeze into it, yet you don't want one so tough and scratchy that it chafes your nose. And you want something fairly economical

RATINGS OF FACIAL TISSUES

Listed in groups in order of estimated quality. Within groups, brands differed little in quality. Brands with identical scores are listed in order of increasing cost per 100 tissues.

As published in a **May 1989** report.

● ◑ ○ ◐ ●
Better ← → Worse

Brand and model	Tissues per box	Price	Cost per 100	Sneeze resistance	Wet strength	Softness	Comments
Puffs Plus with lotion	150	$1.54	$1.03	●	●	●	C
Helping Hand by Scott, A Best Buy	175	.87	.50	●	●	○	—
Kleenex Vogue	60	1.12	1.86	◑	◑	●	A
Kleenex Man Size	60	1.17	1.95	◑	◑	●	A
Scotties, A Best Buy	200	.89	.44	◑	●	○	—
Nice 'n Soft	175	1.02	.58	●	●	◐	—
Zee	150	.92	.61	◑	●	○	—
Truly Fine (Safeway)	175	.70	.40	◑	◑	○	—
Kachoos by Scotties	200	.88	.44	◑	◑	○	D
Puffs Family Pack	250	1.39	.56	○	○	●	B
Kleenex Dispenser Size	130	.96	.74	○	○	●	—
Lady Lee	175	.67	.38	◑	○	○	—
Kleenex Family Size	250	1.37	.55	◐	○	●	—
Coronet	150	.86	.57	●	○	◐	—
Kleenex Classic Foil	175	1.04	.59	◐	○	●	—
Kleenex Boutique	100	.92	.92	◐	○	●	—
Posh Puffs	100	1.01	1.01	◐	○	●	B
Kleenex Softique	100	1.02	1.02	◐	○	●	B
Kleenex Pocket Pack	120	1.45	1.21	◐	○	●	—
Target	175	.78	.45	○	○	○	—
Facial Tissues (K Mart)	175	.81	.46	◑	○	◐	—
Kleenex Little Travelers	65	.51	.78	◐	◐	●	D
Kleenex Casuals	90	.81	.90	◐	◐	●	—
Purse and Pocket Packs (K Mart)	120	.97	.81	◑	◐	◐	—
Janet Lee	100	.94	.94	○	◐	○	—

Better ◀— ● ◐ ○ ◑ ● —▶ Worse

Brand and model	Tissues per box	Price	Cost per 100	Sneeze resistance	Wet strength	Softness	Comments
Pathmark	280	.88	.31	○	◑	◑	—
A&P	175	.60	.34	○	◑	◑	—
Cost Cutter (Kroger)	175	.59	.34	◑	○	◑	—
Marcal Fluff Out	180	.63	.35	○	◑	◑	—
Arrow	175	.69	.39	○	◑	◑	E
A&P	100	.60	.60	○	◑	◑	—
Pathmark	200	.50	.25	○	●	◑	—
Swansoft (Kroger)	175	.69	.39	◑	◑	◑	—
Marcal Hankies	50	.37	.74	○	◑	●	—

Specifications and Features
All: ● Had adequate strength when dry. ● Had adequate ability to absorb water. ● Were suitably free from excessive linting
Except as noted, all: ● Are unscented, two-ply.

Key to Comments
A–3-ply; thicker and larger than most.
B–Scented.
C–With moisturizing lotion; not recommended for cleaning glasses, which may be smeared by the lotion.
D–Smaller than most.
E–Sneeze resistance and wet strength varied.

in the bargain. (If the tissues are the right color or packed in a box to match your decor, so much the better.)

Quality

Consumers Union tested tissues for sneeze resistance, wet strength, and softness. Since people can't be expected to sneeze on demand or to sneeze exactly the same way time after time, CU invented a mechanical sneezer to test tissues. The most sneeze-resistant tissues usually withstood the test just fine. But the worst were almost always shot through.

To measure strength when wet, CU testers clamped each tissue in an embroidery hoop, dampened it with a measured amount of water, then poured a slow, steady stream of lead shot onto the tissue. The strongest ones held more than 10 ounces of shot before they broke; they are the tissues you can count on to handle the most demanding jobs without disintegrating. The weakest tissues ruptured under about an ounce of weight. The thickest tissues tested were three-ply, and weren't the strongest. Several two-ply varieties were just as strong—some were even stronger.

Manufacturers often make facial tissues in more than one plant around the country, to cut down on shipping costs. That practice has created some differences in the same brand of paper towel purchased in different areas. But with few exceptions the tissues bought from stores in the East, South, and West were quite consistent.

Recommendations

It doesn't make much sense to spend a lot of money on a throwaway product like facial tissue. It does make sense, however, to buy tissues that are reasonably soft, suitably strong, and low in price. The softest tissues would obviously be most soothing for a prolonged cold or bout of hay fever. Those with only average softness would be fine for everyday use.

HAIR CONDITIONERS

The first hair rinse appeared on the market almost forty years ago. By the 1970s, creme rinses had been transformed into "conditioners." Today, people spend more than half a billion dollars a year on conditioners. There are "deep" conditioners, meant to be left on for fifteen or more minutes, and "instant" conditioners, meant to be rinsed out right away. There are conditioners for normal hair, oily hair, damaged hair, and hair that needs "extra body." Most of these conditioners have a companion shampoo. Some are part of a "hair-care system" consisting of a shampoo and assorted after-shampoo products.

Hair conditioners do make hair softer and easier to comb. Some are a little better than others at controlling static electricity. While all add body, fullness, and bounce to hair, some add more of those conditioning qualities than others. Most important, the price of a product bears little relationship to how well it works.

What conditioners do

Shampooing removes oil and dirt from hair. In the process, the scales that form the outer layer of the hair, the cuticle, become ruffled. When the cuticle is ruffled, hair tangles easily and may look dull. Without its natural oil coating, hair can also become static filled and frizzy. The hair's natural protective coating— sebum, an oily substance released by the scalp's sebaceous glands—eventually builds up to relieve the post-shampoo tangling and dryness. Usually, by the time it does, you're ready to wash your hair again. Conditioners have much the same effect as sebum, but without the waiting.

Conditioners reduce the roughness of the cuticle so hair combs easily, looks shinier, and feels softer. By coating each hair, they counteract static electricity, so hair is more manageable.

The conditioners that purport to be "self-adjusting" state they have more conditioning effect on hair that needs it, less on hair that does not. In fact, all conditioners work that way. Ingredients in hair conditioners form a chemical bond to the hair, especially where the cuticle has been damaged by sun, bleach, dyes, permanents, or by sheer age, which is the common cause of split ends. Hair takes what it needs and sheds the rest, no matter what brand of conditioner you are using.

Some conditioners claim to provide extra body for fine hair. Since all conditioners coat the hair, they're bound to make each strand slightly thicker. There is no consistent difference between the extra-body and regular varieties of a particular brand. Sometimes the two work virtually the same. Sometimes the regular version even out-conditions the extra-body version.

Many conditioners come in special formulations labeled for dry, normal, and oily hair. Those for dry and normal hair usually contain oils or fatty substances, such as mineral oil or lanolin. Formulations for oily hair usually contain synthetic polymers, such as silicones, acrylics, and epoxy derivatives. But again, those special formulations appear to have little relationship to how well a conditioner conditions.

The products that purport to "nourish" hair may contain substances such as protein, wheat germ, milk, egg, or honey. But hair, once it's outside the scalp, is not a living thing. It can't be nourished. (A poor diet or poor health, however, can result in poor-looking hair.)

No conditioner can permanently repair damaged hair. It may hide split ends temporarily by gluing them together. Protein in the conditioner may even fill in gaps in damaged hair, until you shampoo again. The only way to eliminate damaged hair is to cut it off.

Effectiveness

Not everyone needs to condition hair after shampooing. People with short, healthy hair that has not been color treated or permed may never need a conditioner. Some people may need to condition hair only in winter, when there's less moisture in the air, or in summer, when exposure to salt water or chlorinated pools makes the hair feel dry.

In CU tests that involved shampooing and conditioning, all the conditioners worked well. Although some of them conditioned hair more than others—gave it more shine, bounce, body, fullness, and tangle-free combing—the best hair conditioner is not necessarily better than a poor one. It simply provides the greatest degree of conditioning, perhaps more conditioning than your hair actually needs. It would work best for hair that's dry, frizzy, or damaged. Soft hair or oily hair, however, may look limp or greasy if overconditioned. People with that type of hair may not need a conditioner at all.

Recommendations

If your hair is more tangled than you think it should be after shampooing, if it tends to be unmanageable or ridden with static electricity, or if you'd like it to feel a bit softer or look shinier, your hair may need more conditioning. If, on the other hand, your hair looks limp and somewhat greasy right after shampooing, you're probably conditioning too much.

You do not need to buy a more expensive product; all conditioners work well. If you like the product you're currently using and it's doing the job it's intended to do, you still might want to change because you're paying more than you have to.

HAND AND BATH SOAPS

Differences in cleaning effectiveness among soaps are slight, regardless of their perfume or fancy packaging. Soap is merely a cleanser that removes dirt, oil film, and bacteria from your skin.

One real difference between soaps is price. An expensive bar may sell for nearly forty-five times the price of the cheapest. A related difference might be called "durability"—how quickly or slowly the soap disappears from the soap dish or container. That translates into how much the product costs in actual use. Lathering is another consideration, as is free fatty matter (one measure of "moisturizing" ability) and pH content (alkalinity). Fragrance is a quality that induces many people to pay a premium for certain soaps.

Buying soap

Comparison shopping for soap is difficult. You'll find a multitude of prices, sizes, packages, even shapes. Unit pricing, which lets you compare price per ounce, is one helpful guide out of this maze. Even so, per-ounce prices may be misleading. A better measure of value is the number of hand washings a soap delivers.

How many hand washings you get from a soap depends on its dissolution rate, how fast it disappears. Some bars of soap, like some rolls of toilet paper, seem to vanish overnight.

How many hand washings you get also depends on how you use the soap. Although it may sound peculiar, with bar soap you tend to use more of a brand that dissolves either very slowly or very quickly and less of a brand that has an average dissolution rate. The bars that have a very slow dissolution rate take more rubbings to get your hands clean, and hence deliver fewer washings; the fast dissolving soaps give fewer washings because they tend to dissolve under the faucet.

In general, liquid soaps are more expensive than bars. How fast liquid soap disappears depends largely on its container. Most have pump dispensers, which serve up varying amounts of soap. A few liquid soaps come in a squeeze container, letting you squeeze out as much as you like.

Lather

Some soaps lather more profusely than others, but lathering has little to do with a soap's cleaning ability. Lathering is actually a result of the water interacting with soap and depends upon the chemical makeup of the soap. Soft water, which contains few minerals, makes soap lather easily. In hard water, soaps that contain detergent lather better than plain soap. Some people like a lot of bubbles, some just a few. In fact, most soaps lather copiously, except possibly plain soap in hard water.

Soap chemistry

Soap is irritating to the skin, not soothing to it. Soap removes dirt and natural oil, which is very drying. In an attempt to make soap less drying and therefore less irritating, some makers have added extra fats—such as lanolin, moisturizing cream, or cocoa butter—and have made much of their moisturizing formulas in their advertising. Most soaps have about the same amount of "free fatty matter"—less than 2 percent—and even a super-fatted soap does not moisturize well since its cleaning ingredients have a drying effect. A moisturizing lotion applied immediately after bathing works better.

Soap can irritate because it is alkaline. Most soaps are moderately alkaline, with a pH of about 10. Despite what ad copy may say about pH, it doesn't matter for most people. Normal skin quickly returns to its natural acidic level after being soaped. Granted, some people may be sensitive to an alkaline soap. If you are one of those individuals you may want to consider an essentially neutral soap.

When TV and magazine ads aren't promoting "moisturizing" soap or neutral pH soap, they're often selling "deodorant" soap. These soaps contain antiseptics such as triclocarban or triclosan. The antiseptics reduce skin bacteria and thereby slow the development of odor. Unfortunately, deodorant soaps may do far more than mask B.O. They may cause a rash or other allergic reaction if you have sensitive skin. Furthermore, the antiseptics in a deodorant soap can be absorbed through the skin into the bloodstream. The amount absorbed is minimal, but no one knows whether these amounts present any danger in the long run. You may want to avoid regular use of deodorant soap. Bathing with plain old soap can be just as effective for most people.

Scent

Perfume isn't new to soap. Since the beginning of soap making, it has been used to mask the unpleasant odors of other ingredients. Perfume is, of course, another way to get you to buy one brand over another. According to a paper delivered at a symposium of the American Society of Perfumers, scent influences consumers to perceive performance differences where none exist. The paper referred to a test in which "consumers perceived the product with the preferred perfume to be superior even when all attributes are equivalent."

Despite perceived differences or individual preferences, even the strongest soap fragrance won't last long on your skin after bathing. The nature of soap is such that it removes most of its own traces from your skin when you rinse.

Recommendations

When it comes to ordinary cleaning, all soaps are equal. Your choice of brands, then, should be determined by economy and by personal needs and preferences and not by the ads.

Healthy skin can handle just about any soap. Sensitive or dry skin may fare better with soaps that do not have added perfume or antiseptics. Many soaps have an ingredients list, so you may be able to avoid a brand that contains an ingredient to which you're sensitive. If you have oily skin it's more important to keep your skin clean—no matter how often that means washing—than to use any particular brand of soap.

Soap can cost you anywhere from about $.25 to over $10 per 100 hand washings. On average, bar soap is cheaper than liquid soap. A more expensive bar soap, however, costs about as much to use as most liquid soap.

You needn't feel guilty about choosing an expensive soap over a cheap soap because you prefer its aroma, but you should be aware of how much you're paying. Consider two bars that weigh the same and dissolve at the same rate. One sells for $2.58 a bar, ten times as much as a cheap personal-size bar. At fifteen bars a year, a preference for the scent of the more expensive soaps would cost you an additional $35 annually.

Whether you bargain shop for soap or treat yourself to the most expensive, you can make a bar of soap last by minimizing the time it spends in water. Use a raised soap dish and remove a bar from the bath water promptly. According to folklore, unwrapping a bar of soap and allowing it to "harden" will lengthen its life. That's just wishful thinking. The only benefit you'll reap from stockpiling unwrapped soap is that it may make your closet or bathroom smell nice.

SHAMPOOS

Shampoo advertising would have you believe that shampoo can add glamour and romance to your life. The ads would also like you to believe that different types of hair have different needs. There's shampoo for oily hair, normal hair, and dry hair. There are brands for permanent-waved hair and for chemically treated hair. Limp hair must be a common problem: The market is rife with shampoos that offer extra body.

Lest you think that all shampoos share common ingredients, advertisers try to impress you with scientific names such as allantoin calcium pantothenate, ammonium lauryl sulfate, and sodium lauryl sulfate.

Marketing experts invite you to participate in the science of hair care by offering "systems," two-step programs that consist of shampoo (step one) and conditioner (step two). The systems accomplish pretty much the same thing as bottles of shampoo and conditioner that you buy independently, but they may make you feel more in control. To appeal to busy people, other manufacturers promote one-step shampoos, products that incorporate conditioners.

If you don't trust your own judgment, you can turn to the professionals. Some brands are sold only in hairstyling shops. Or you can rely on shampoos that have a mind of their own, the ones that purport to be self-adjusting shampoos, providing heavy-duty cleaning or gentle cleaning depending on what your hair needs at the time. Of course, advertisers have long found fear of dandruff a valuable marketing tool. It must work: *Head & Shoulders* is the best-selling brand of all.

Shampoo ingredients

Despite the fancy ingredients and heavy-handed selling, shampoos can be relied on to do only one thing: They clean hair. All shampoos work in roughly the same way:

Cleaning agents. Surfactants are the working ingredients in all shampoos. They attract excess oil and dirt so that the offending compounds can be rinsed away along with the suds.

Soap is a surfactant, but in hard water it's not a good one for shampoo. Soap reacts with the minerals that make water hard, leaving a dulling film on the hair. (If you must use soap in a pinch, an acidic rinse such as lemon juice or vinegar will remove the film.) Alternatives to soap, generally lumped together under the heading "detergent," do not leave a film. There are dozens of detergents, each with its own properties.

Baby shampoos generally contain mild surfactants. Using mild surfactants and other relatively gentle ingredients helps prevent the shampoo from stinging if it gets in the eyes. Other surfactants are stronger. Ammonium lauryl sulfate and sodium lauryl sulfate are among the most common. They're especially effective at penetrating and removing oil and attacking mousse, gel, and hair spray residues. In addition, there are surfactants that clean with little foam, and others that produce volumes of lather. Both varieties clean equally well.

Manufacturers generally use several surfactants in a single brand of shampoo. The number of possible combinations provides ample room for manufacturers to claim special formulas. It also provides the opportunity to formulate shampoos supposedly tailored for dry, normal, and oily hair.

More than half (62 percent) of the people who responded to a 1988 Consumers Union survey said they choose shampoo formulated for their hair "type." But whether you can tell the difference between one formula and another is doubtful. In blind tests, Consumers Union testers found that panelists who described their hair as dry were just as likely to prefer oily-formula shampoos as dry-formula ones. Panelists with oily hair liked some dry-hair products as well as some oily-hair products.

Conditioners. Without conditioners, the detergents in a shampoo would strip away much of the natural oil from your hair, leaving it tangled, full of static, and perhaps dull. To avoid such problems, shampoos often contain conditioners such as lanolin derivatives or balsam. Many shampoos also contain quaternaries, another type of conditioner. These neutralize the negative charge of static electricity that washing and combing imparts to hair.

pH balance. Healthy skin has a slightly acidic pH. Since some detergents are alkaline, manufacturers add acidic ingredients such as citric acid to neutralize the shampoos. The fact is, most shampoos have a fairly neutral pH, whether or not their labels say so.

Protein. Hair that's shiny, silky, and bouncy is healthy hair. Unhealthy or damaged hair can result from the use of chemicals such as permanent-waving solutions, bleaches, and hair dyes, which must penetrate the cuticle of the hair to do their work. Heat from hair dryers and electric curling devices and overexposure to sunlight or swimming pool chlorine can damage hair, too. A common result is split ends.

A pair of scissors is the only cure for damaged hair. But many shampoos contain substances that purport to help damaged hair look better. Protein is one such ingredient. It actually cements split ends together temporarily. It also helps entire strands of hair to cling to one another so your hair feels fuller and less limp.

Special effects. The only way shampoos can improve the color or brightness of hair is by cleaning it. Color enhancers such as henna, chamomile, or other botanicals used in shampoos do not have much effect. What little there is in the shampoo will go down the drain with the rinse water.

Shampoos that state they are self-adjusting don't do anything other shampoos don't do. Detergents work where there is oil and dirt; they do not work where there is no oil or dirt. Hence, all shampoos could claim, accurately, that they are self-adjusting.

Antidandruff ingredients. Dandruff is a scalp condition, not a hair problem. It's the normal shedding of skin cells that occurs all over the body every day. The flakes are just more noticeable when they lodge in the hair or settle on the shoulders.

Dandruff is more of a problem for people who wash their hair only once a week. Washing your hair three or four times a week—no matter what shampoo you use—generally keeps the flakes under control. If it doesn't, a shampoo with antidandruff ingredients might help.

If one brand doesn't work, try another with a different antidandruff ingredient. But keep in mind that severe flaking could be a symptom of seborrheic dermatitis or psoriasis. A doctor can make the diagnosis and perhaps prescribe special treatment beyond conventional dandruff shampoos.

RATINGS OF SHAMPOOS

Listed in order of estimated quality based on CU tests. All cleaned hair well, and two products were check-rated.

As published in a **February 1989** report.

Product	Overall score (out of 100)	Price	Size	Cost per use ②	Fragrance	Comments
✓ Pert Plus Extra Body For Fine Hair	96	$3.31	15 fl. oz.	6¢	Spicy/woody	A,B,C,D,E
✓ Pert Plus Normal Hair	95	3.31	15	6	Spicy/woody	A,B,C,D,E
Nexxus Therappe	74	7.73	16	13	Coconut	K
Agree Extra Body Formula	72	3.23	15	6	Herbal	A,K
Ivory Fresh Scent Normal Hair	71	2.08	15	4	Sweet	—
Ivory Fresh Scent Oily Hair	71	2.08	15	4	Sweet	—
Ivory Fresh Scent Extra Body For Fine Hair	70	2.08	15	4	Sweet	—
Jhirmack E.F.A. Dry, Permed, Color Treated Hair	70	4.24	12	10	Citrus/tangerine	K
Pantene Extra Body For Fine Hair Thickening Formula	69	3.73	7	14	Herbal	—
Agree Regular Formula	69	3.23	15	6	Herbal	K
Perma Soft For Permed Hair Regular Formula	69	3.46	15	6	Floral/herbal	K
Halsa Swedish Botanical Formula Walnut Leaves	68	2.02	15	4	Herbal	—
Wella Balsam Conditioning For Extra Body	68	2.10	16	4	Citrus/floral	L
Revlon Flex Oily	68	2.15	15	4	Sweet/spicy	—
Johnson's Baby Gentle Conditioning Formula	68	3.92	15	7	Sweet/floral	—
Alberto VO5 Normal	68	1.35	15	2	Herbal/green leafy	—
Finesse Extra Body	68	3.45	15	6	Herbal	—
Silkience Self-Adjusting Extra Body	68	3.12	15	6	Medicinal/soapy	—
Redken Glypro-L For Fine/Normal Hair	67	10.58	16.9	17	Faint medicinal	K
CVS Balsam & Protein Treatment For Extra Body	67	1.49	16	3	Sweet/spicy	—
Wella Balsam Conditioning For Normal Hair	67	2.10	16	4	Citrus/floral	L

Product	Overall score (out of 100)	Price	Size	Cost per use ②	Fragrance	Comments
Helene Curtis Salon Selectives Level 7 Deep For Normal To Oily Hair	67	2.38	15	4	Fruity	K
Suave Full Body Normal/Dry Hair	67	1.56	16	3	Woody/spicy	—
Silkience Self-Adjusting Regular	67	3.12	15	6	Medicinal/soapy	—
CVS Balsam & Protein Treatment For Normal To Dry Hair	67	1.49	16	3	Sweet/spicy	L
Revlon Flex Normal To Dry	67	2.15	15	4	Sweet/spicy	—
Avon Natural Brilliance	67	2.49	16	4	Faint floral	—
Suave Moisturizing Regular	67	1.56	16	3	Woody/spicy	—
Alberto VO5 Extra Body	67	1.35	15	2	Herbal/green leafy	—
White Rain Regular	66	1.65	18	2	Floral/faint herbal	—
Clairol Condition Revitalizing Formula For Normal Hair	66	1.99	15	4	Sweet/spicy	—
K Mart Balsam Treatment Normal To Dry Hair	66	1.28	16	2	Sweet/spicy/herbal	—
Breck Balanced Cleaning & Conditioning For Normal Hair	66	1.63	15	3	Herbal/spicy	—
Head & Shoulders Normal To Dry [bottle]	66	4.20	15	8	Sweet/slightly spicy	—
Revlon Flex Extra Body	66	2.15	15	4	Sweet/spicy	—
Breck Extra Conditioning For Dry, Damaged Or Color Treated Hair	66	1.63	15	3	Herbal/spicy	—
Suave Extra Gentle Extra Body	66	1.56	16	3	Woody/spicy	—
Perma Soft For Permed Hair Extra Body Formula For Fine/Limp Hair	66	3.46	15	6	Floral/herbal	K
Clairol Condition Extra Body Formula For Fine Limp Hair	66	1.99	15	4	Sweet/spicy	—
Halsa Swedish Botanical Formula Chamomile	66	2.02	15	4	Herbal	—
Affinity	66	3.24	15	6	Floral	K
Pantene For Normal Hair Daily Use Formula	65	3.73	7	14	Floral/hyacinth	—
Truly Fine Balsam and Protein Treatment For Normal To Dry Hair (Safeway)	65	1.47	15	3	Spicy	—

(Continued)

Listed in order of estimated quality based on CU tests. All cleaned hair well. As published in a **February 1989** report.

Product	Overall score (out of 100)	Price	Size	Cost per use [2]	Fragrance	Comments
Finesse Regular	65	3.66	15	7	Herbal	—
Vidal Sasson Advanced Salon Formula For Normal Hair	65	3.68	12	8	Marzipan/almond	—
Ivory Dishwashing Liquid	65	1.54	22	2	Sweet	L
Jhirmack Gelàve Gel Normal Hair	65	4.24	12	10	Floral/herbal	K
White Rain Extra Body	65	1.65	18	2	Floral/faint herbal	—
Johnson's Baby	64	3.59	15	6	Sweet/floral	—
Avon Natural Brilliance For Dry/ Damaged Hair	64	2.49	16	4	Faint floral	—
Kroger Extra Balsam & Protein Treatment Normal To Dry Hair	64	1.37	15	2	Sweet/spicy/herbal	—
Vidal Sasson Advanced Extra Body For Fine or Limp Hair	64	3.68	12	8	Marzipan/almond	—
Nexxus Assure	63	6.92	16	12	Citrus	H,K
Helene Curtis Salon Selectives Level 5 Regular For Normal Hair	62	2.38	15	4	Fruity	—
Prell Normal To Dry Hair [bottle]	62	3.42	15	6	Herbal/spicy	K
Fabergé Organics With Extra Body Ingredients	62	1.68	15	3	Herbal	G
Fabergé Organics	62	1.68	15	3	Herbal	G
Redken Classic Amino Pon For Chemically Treated Hair	60	10.31	16.9	17	Fruity	F,H,I,K
Prell Concentrate Normal To Dry Hair [tube]	56	3.30	7 [1]	15	Herbal/spicy	F,H,I,J,K
Head & Shoulders Concentrate Normal To Dry [tube]	54	3.53	5.5 [1]	20	Sweet/slightly spicy	F,H,I,J,K

[1] *Ounces, not fluid ounces.* [2] *Based on a total of 1½ teaspoons per shampoo (lathering twice).*

Key to Comments
A–More generous lathering than most.
B–Faster, richer, more emollient, and longer-lasting lather than most.
C–Easier to rinse out than most.
D–Allowed easier wet combing than most.
E–Left dry hair silkier and easier to comb than most.
F–Lathered less than most.
G–Lathered slower than most.
H–Lathering was slower and suds were coarser than most.
I–Lather faded faster than most.
J–More difficult to rinse out than most.
K–Thicker than most tested shampoos.
L–Thinner than most tested shampoos.

Other ingredients. The predominant ingredient in most shampoos is water. Thickeners or thinners can be used to adjust the viscosity of the product. A shampoo's thickness affects the ease with which it can be worked into the hair.

Shampoos also contain coloring agents. They're purely cosmetic and make the product, not your hair, look better. Preservatives are usually added, too. They keep any exotic natural ingredient from spoiling.

Although many shampoos contain them, foam enhancers are used most often in shampoos for oily hair, because detergents lather less on oily hair. If nothing else, the suds may help you determine when you have done a good job of rinsing the shampoo out.

One of the most noticeable ingredients in shampoo is fragrance. According to the CU survey, a shampoo's fragrance was important to 34 percent of the respondents.

Recommendations

Just about any shampoo should clean your hair and leave it shiny and manageable. Even a dishwashing liquid can do a good job. In Consumers Union's tests, *Ivory Dishwashing Liquid* lathered and rinsed out well enough. It even left the hair shiny and manageable. But some people may be sensitive to its ingredients.

The most expensive shampoos are the concentrates and the salon formulas. That isn't to say that you shouldn't have fun and spend a little on a shampoo you like. It is, after all, a small luxury. If you find a brand that makes you and your hair feel good, that has a pleasing scent, or that offers a container to match your bathroom color scheme, enjoy it.

TOILET PAPER

In addition to judging a brand of toilet paper by how much it costs, you might use other clues to quality: How heavy is the roll? How dense is it? Is the paper one ply or two? Do the words on the package or in the brand's name connote softness? In fact, a heavy, dense roll of two-ply toilet paper is apt to be of a better overall quality than a light, squishy roll of one-ply paper. Claims of softness are another matter; a "soft" brand can be relatively scratchy.

As for absorbency, some papers lap a few drops of water in less than a second; the drops will remain on other brands for a minute or more. In the important characteristic of wet strength, there are large differences among the brands. Most brands tear cleanly at the perforations, but some are imperfectly perforated, leading to annoying ragged tears. Most brands do well with respect to the paper holding together in use without shredding, falling apart, or pilling up.

Among brands, there's a wide range of softness, from very soft to scratchy. That's because it's expensive to make soft yet strong paper. To make a soft toilet paper that won't disintegrate when you don't want it to, a company has to use either more paper or additional paper-making processes.

At first, soft toilet paper had to be made up of two plies—the only way to compensate for the inherent weakness of the paper was to double it up. Since two-ply paper costs more to produce than one-ply paper, a company that could make a soft yet strong one-ply paper could reduce its production costs, and that could help improve a company's profit picture.

In the early 1960s, a new paper-making process involved air drying the fibers, which fluffed the paper and provided single-ply softness without an unacceptable loss of strength. Later, other techniques were used. Adding hardwood fibers makes a softer paper than using pulpwood alone. To give soft paper strength it otherwise wouldn't have, a pattern can be impressed that helps hold the paper together. A binding substance can be printed onto the paper to do the same thing. A single-ply tissue can be built up as a sandwich, with a strong layer in the middle and soft layers on the outside.

Any of these processes, of course, add to the expense of paper making, costs that are passed along. You can't find a soft toilet paper among the cheapest brands. Despite the advances in paper making, most of the softest brands are still two-ply papers. Soft papers also tend to be more absorbent than scratchy papers and most soft papers are strong and durable.

A brand of toilet paper bought in one part of the country sometimes performs very differently from the same brand bought elsewhere. Presumably, different plants make the papers; that's a common practice in the industry, since paper is bulky, and therefore paper products are costly to ship.

Value

Toilet paper is priced to fall into certain price ranges, and often an apparently cheap (or expensive) brand is indeed cheaper (or more expensive) than others.

Making reliable cost comparisons in the supermarket is increasingly difficult, however. Toilet paper manufacturers have long disguised price rises in their products by paring the products' size. Once, a typical sheet of toilet paper was 4½ by 5 inches. Now, sheets 4½ inches square are the generous ones.

The number of sheets in a roll has also been declining. Once, 400 sheets per roll was the norm. If it seems you're using up toilet paper faster than you used to, you may be using one of several brands that have fewer sheets in a roll.

The number of rolls in a package also varies, from one to eight. As a consequence of all this juggling, the square feet per package, noted on all the labels, varies drastically. That makes in-store price comparisons difficult, unless your supermarket figures its unit prices on the basis of square footage.

Recommendations

To a large degree, you do have to pay more to get good toilet paper. Actually, buying the cheap brands may turn out to be a false economy. Depending on how you measure out the amount of toilet paper to use, you could use twice as much of these one-ply papers as you would of a more expensive two-ply paper.

You don't have to buy the best quality, however. Two-ply supermarket brands can be quite good, and have moderate prices.

A number of brands are scented, which you may or may not find attractive.

Stains and Spots

STAINS AND SPOTS ON FABRICS

Fabrics have become far more complex than in the past. In addition to finishes intended to help clothes resist wrinkling and soiling, there are an astonishingly large number of fabrics and fabric blends used in garments. Removing fabric stains has become more of a challenge than ever before. Simple laundering, even of fabrics that have been traditionally launderable, may no longer do a good job of stain removal. Some of the newer fabrics and finishes have an affinity for resistant spots and stains, despite detergent manufacturers' efforts to develop products that can keep up with textile technology.

As has always been the case, spotting (the term for stain removal) a colored item can be much more difficult than spotting a white fabric because of the concern about removing some color along with the stain. This can be a very real problem with dyes or prints whose color may become partially dissolved in water or in cleaning solvent, or when a dye or print has not been correctly applied by the fabric manufacturer. The proliferation of accidental spots that result from do-it-yourself projects involving paints, varnishes, adhesives, glues, and chemicals of all kinds further complicates stain removal. These materials can stain clothing, and manufacturers' formulations change frequently. That combination creates constantly changing problems for professional dry cleaners, let alone consumers who do not have the training or facilities of a professional dry-cleaning establishment.

If you want to plan ahead, you can prepare a stain-removal "first-aid kit." You may prefer not to take the time and trouble, and may want to depend instead on your laundry equipment or the local dry cleaner to handle spot and stain problems. In addition to providing a list of supplies, this chapter also presents the basic procedures for removing stains at home, focusing on general approaches that should prove helpful and practical. The material is intended to be helpful to consumers faced with emergency stains on fabrics, as well as with some stains that are not in the emergency class.

Stain-removal supplies

Most stain-removal products are common household items. But that does not mean they can be stored just anywhere. Most of the substances are hazardous and should be kept in a safe place, away from heat or open flame and well out of children's reach.

Acetone. Some nail polish removers are all or part acetone, a chemical that may be effective in dissolving stains caused by plastic-like substances used in formulating nail polish, household cements, and some paints and varnishes. Acetone can be purchased in paint and hardware stores, but it is poisonous and highly inflammable. Acetone should never be inhaled or allowed to be absorbed through the skin. Despite its potential effectiveness on tough stains, acetone is not a substance that should be routinely kept around the house. Furthermore, acetone should never be used on acetate fabrics because the chemical will seriously damage the fabric.

Alcohol. Rubbing alcohol (or unflavored vodka if rubbing alcohol isn't available) can be effective on certain kinds of stains, for example some ballpoint-pen ink stains. But be careful about using alcohol on dyed fabrics. Test an inside seam to be sure the alcohol won't cause the dye to run. Another caution: Any alcohol product that isn't 100 percent alcohol (200 proof) contains water. And water can be damaging to fabrics that are intended to be dry-cleaned only. For other, more tolerant fabrics, you may want to keep a mixture of rubbing alcohol and water in a handy place for use before laundering them. Wholly or partially removing stains before laundering eliminates the potential problem of having the discoloration become "set" in the wash.

Bleach. Chlorine bleach is a common laundry aid for removing stains, but it can permanently damage and stain silk, wool, or modern elastic fabrics such as those containing Spandex. Furthermore, some fabric finishes absorb chlorine, and are consequently weakened or discolored. Even if the care label states that the garment can be bleached, it's best to use chlorine bleach sparingly on any fabric that has any substantial color to it.

All-fabric bleach depends on oxygen as a bleaching agent. Oxygen is also the active ingredient in hydrogen peroxide, the mild antiseptic sold over-the-counter in drugstores (not to be confused with a stronger product sold for bleaching hair). Hydrogen peroxide acts faster and better at stain removal than an all-fabric, oxygen laundry bleach, but, like all bleaches, it must be rinsed out very thoroughly after it is used on fabric.

Oxygen-type bleaches are safe for just about any fabric that won't be damaged by water, but dyed fabrics should be tested for colorfastness before using any kind of bleach, unless the care label permits it.

Detergent. A solution of ordinary dishwashing liquid and cool water can be surprisingly effective at stain removal, providing the stained material won't be hurt by water. Avoid warm or hot water because heat has a tendency to set stains, making them difficult or impossible to remove.

Dry-cleaning solvent. In addition to being cautious about a spot remover's effects on fabrics, you should be aware of its effect on humans as well. Volatile dry-cleaning solvents are dangerous in either or both of two ways: Their fumes are hazardous to inhale and they may be highly inflammable. Many spot-removing fluids contain perchlorethylene, methylene chloride, or both, and these substances are known to cause cancer in animals. Always follow these precautions to ensure maximum safety:

• It is distinctly unhealthy to inhale fumes from dry-cleaning solvents. These solvents can also cause skin irritation and be absorbed into the body through the skin. Wear rubber gloves. Do not work on a garment while it is being worn.

• Work in a shady spot out-of-doors, if possible. If not, work near an open window, away from all flame, including pilot lights on a stove or gas water heater. If you are using a solvent-based cleaner or other material whose fumes should not be inhaled (read the container's warnings) and are cleaning something immovable, such as carpeting, or relatively immovable, such as heavy furniture, establish good cross ventilation with a window fan set to exhaust air.

• Do not smoke. Although nonflammable cleaning solvents do not ignite in contact with a flame or spark, they may decompose and produce toxic vapors.

• Use only a very small amount of fluid at a time. Do not pour the cleaner into an open dish; dampen the cleaning cloth directly from the container. Limit the use of a cleaning solvent to small areas of fabric at a time. Keep the bottle of fluid stoppered except when you are actually using it.

• Never use dry-cleaning solvent in a washing machine. Do not put articles that are damp with solvent in a clothes dryer.

• Don't buy spot remover in large quantities. Properly used, a little goes a long way, and storing large amounts means risking fire hazards, accidental ingestion, spills, and the accidental escape of vapors. Furthermore, large quantities could encourage using the spot remover too liberally and perhaps carelessly.

• Avoid containers that are likely to tip over or break easily.

Dry spotting solution. This substance is termed "dry," not because it feels or looks dry, but because it does not dissolve in water, and is therefore intended to be used on stains that are not soluble in water and on fabrics that should not be wet with water. Dry-cleaning solvent is one form of dry spotting liquid.

In most cases, use dry-cleaning solvent as purchased. In cases of very concentrated, dry stains, you can make your own solution by combining one part of mineral oil with eight parts of dry-cleaning solvent. (Observe all precautions above for using dry-cleaning solvent.) The oil helps to lubricate the fabric, thereby reducing the potential for damage as the spot is rubbed. Store the solution in an airtight container and label it clearly and indelibly. A dry spotter is most useful for greasy stains, because most grease does not dissolve in water.

Enzyme laundry products.   These come as presoaks or as boosters in regular laundry detergents. Protein stains such as blood and other body fluids, egg and egg-containing products, and milk or cream may yield quite well to soaking in an enzyme product, following package directions.

Wet spotting solution.   Unlike a dry spotting solution, a wet spotter is intended to be used for removing stains that are soluble in water on fabrics that can be safely laundered. Make up a batch with equal parts of glycerin (available in drugstores) and dishwashing liquid, diluted with eight parts of water. Store the mixture in a plastic squeeze bottle and label it clearly and indelibly. Shake the container well before using the wet spotter.

Guidelines for removing stains

Before trying to remove a stain from a garment, read the care label. Garments produced since 1972 are required by law to have a permanent label giving instructions for proper care. Labels for washable items carry information on washing method, water temperature, drying method, drying temperature, and whether bleach can be used. If the instructions on the care label say "professionally dry-clean only," do not attempt to remove a stain yourself. Take the garment to the cleaner and, if you know, tell the cleaner what caused the stain and when the spill happened. If the label indicates the garment should *not* be dry-cleaned, avoid using spot removers; their solvents may damage the color and possibly the fabric fibers. Items that cannot be washed or dry-cleaned may be labeled "Wipe with damp cloth only."

Stores that sell piece or yard goods must provide care information on the end of each bolt of fabric. The rule excludes remnants up to 10 yards long that are clearly marked of "undetermined origin." Labels that can be sewn into garments must be available on request; be sure to ask for them.

It is usually easier to remove fresh stains than old ones. That's because many substances that stain fabrics tend to set as they age, making the stain increasingly difficult to remove. But it is futile to try to remove a spot from a garment that needs laundering or dry-cleaning in the first place. The stain remover not only will remove the spot but will also make the area with which it came into contact cleaner than the rest of the garment. The result: Instead of having a soiled garment with a soiled spot, you end up with a soiled garment with a clean spot.

Where to work. Whether you attempt to remove garment stains indoors or outdoors, the working surface you use should be hard and made of a material that won't be affected by the spot remover.

A heavy glass pie pan turned upside down makes a good work surface. Other glass surfaces also work well. Spot removers can damage the finish of a table or countertop and transfer a new stain to the fabric on which you are working. Use aluminum foil to protect such a work surface from chemical drips or spills.

Before you begin. Before using a spot remover, test its effect on the fabric by using the substance on a sample of the material or on an inside seam, hem, the inside of a pocket, or the tail of a blouse or shirt. Silk, satin, velvet, crepe, rayon moiré, and gabardines may be spoiled by a spot remover. "Sized" fabrics, such as many taffetas and failles (which contain substances to stiffen the structure), and fabrics that are not colorfast are also very tricky to work with. With the former, spot removers containing water disturb the sizing, leaving permanent rings and white areas; with the latter, color may be removed, leaving an unsightly, faded spot.

Some soft woolens and cashmeres are sensitive to the water in cleaning fluids. The water may shrink the fabric's fibers, and the rubbing that accompanies spot removal may cause fabric fuzzing and pilling. Loosely woven materials are likely to be damaged if brushed or rubbed while they are wet.

A spot remover may cause loss of fabric luster. And it may also remove nonpermanent finishes, designs, or pigment prints.

If a stained garment is washable, check whether the care label permits bleaching, and whether chlorine or all-fabric (nonchlorine) bleach is the kind to use. All-fabric bleaches tend to be less effective than the chlorine type, but they are also less harsh on fabrics. Washing is by far the easiest way to deal with stains on clothes. In general, water-soluble stains (sugar, for example) usually yield to water alone, or to a water and detergent solution.

If you can't remove a stain with a solvent or a detergent, it's generally best to let a professional cleaner do the job. But be aware of the risk of having tried to do it yourself: You may have set the stain to the extent that the dry cleaner may not be able to remove it entirely. Unfortunately, stain removal—and particularly stain removal at home—is not a very exact science.

Some stains, especially paint and writing ink, may prove impossible for even a professional dry cleaner to remove if they are given time to set. Immediate action may prevent a permanent stain.

Stains that tend to dye the fabric sometimes yield either to water or to a dry-cleaning solvent, but sometimes neither will remove them. Lipstick, for example, can be extremely stubborn to remove, despite your best efforts.

Avoid ironing a stained garment. The iron's heat and pressure may make the stain impossible to remove.

How to proceed

The first thing to do about any stain is to remove as much of the substance of the stain as possible. Blot or scrape off the excess immediately, being as careful as possible not to rub the stain into the fabric. If the fabric can tolerate it and the stain is still wet, use plenty of water. That will dilute the stain and make later treatment easier and more effective. If the stain is dry, gently scrape off any excess with a spoon or coin. Here are some pointers for dealing with problem stains after the emergency first-aid measures have been taken. If in doubt, improvise, but only according to the care label, within the fabric's tolerance for dry-cleaning solvent, water (cold or hot), detergent, or detergent with bleach. And before you try in earnest to remove any stain, check for color-fastness using the spot-removing substance, again *within the guidelines recommended by the care label.*

Ballpoint-pen ink. A stationery store may have a product specifically intended for this. It's worth trying. Otherwise, and if the ink isn't indelible, try using alcohol with a clean rag or paper towel underneath the fabric. Follow the alcohol treatment with dishwashing liquid or wet spotter, and then launder. Make certain the wet spotter has dried completely before laundering. If the stain persists, relaunder with bleach, and hope for the best.

Grass stains. These stains are very persistent and often turn out to be permanent. Nevertheless, removal efforts are worth a try. Check for color fastness by trying some alcohol on an unexposed portion of the fabric. Wet the stain with alcohol. Blot up the excess and sponge with water, followed by a sponging with dishwashing liquid or wet spotter. Rinse the stain and then soak the garment in a solution of laundry enzyme product and water. Rinse again and launder with bleach, if the fabric can tolerate it.

Greasy or oily stains. These are probably the most common stains, usually caused by food. Here's how to proceed.

1. Place a clean white rag or some other absorbent material under the stain.
2. Moisten a cloth with the cleaning solution. Dry-cleaning solvent or dry spotter are most effective for oil and grease stains. (Observe all precautions on page 194.) If possible, the cleansing cloth should be of a fabric similar to that being cleaned. Otherwise, any clean, white, absorbent cloth should do.
3. Use light strokes, blot lightly, or combine these actions. Work from the center of the stain outward beyond its edge. Work as fast as possible, using only a small amount of cleaner at a time.

Keep rubbing outward from the center until there is no clear line between the moistened spot and the surrounding area.

4. Remove the last traces of cleaning solvent by blotting with a dry cloth. Hang up the garment, preferably in open air.

5. If your first attempt is not successful, go through the same procedure again, using a clean section of the blotting material, and a clean cloth. Following the dry-cleaning solvent, you may want to treat the stain with a solution of dishwashing liquid, if the fabric will tolerate water.

Sometimes this process removes the greasy portion of the stain, but leaves a water ring behind. Try lightly sponging the ring with a small amount of dry-cleaning solvent.

Alternatively, remove rings by using a mixture of a mild detergent and water, if the fabric can tolerate it, followed by rinsing with clear water.

Pet urine.   It is especially important to act as quickly as possible, before the stain has had a chance to dry out. Dried urine is very difficult to remove, and can lead to persistent odor problems. First blot up as much as possible. Then apply plenty of cool water, followed by a dishwashing detergent solution and a thorough rinse. Some pet owners attest to the powers of lots of soda water for pet stains. There may be more fancy than fact to any special effectiveness of soda water; a lot of plain water probably works just as well.

Protein stains.   Milk and cream, ice cream, butter, mayonnaise, egg, fruit stains, and blood and body discharges are common causes of protein stains. Avoid warm or hot water (to prevent setting the stain). Soak the stained fabric for about half an hour or longer in a laundry enzyme product. If bloodstains remain, check for colorfastness, then try bleaching with hydrogen peroxide antiseptic solution. Then launder in cool water.

Scorch.   Severe scorching permanently damages fabrics. Light scorch marks may be reduced by laundering with bleach.

Underarm deodorant.   One effective stain preventive is to let deodorant dry on your skin before getting dressed. Dried or old deodorant stains can be very difficult to remove, even with the most aggressive laundering. Unfortunately, a great many deodorant stains occur on garments that cannot be laundered safely.

Waxy stains.   Candle drippings, crayons, floor wax, and tar are common sources for waxy stains. Use the edge of a spoon or a very dull knife to scrape off as much of the staining material as possible. Working outside or in a well-ventilated area, place the stained fabric between layers of white paper towels or white rags, and apply dry-cleaning solvent liberally. Then launder the fabric, if it is launderable, after the dry-cleaning solvent has dried completely. Repeat the whole process if necessary. You might try an all-fabric bleach if any stain remains, or chlorine bleach on fabric that won't be ruined by such treatment.

Wine.   Blot up as much as possible as quickly as possible. Then use ample amounts of water, blotting all the while. Water should, of course, only be used on fabrics that can tolerate it. Otherwise, just stick to blotting until the garment can be taken to a professional dry cleaner.

If you want to tackle a difficult stain yourself, common sense combined with the outlined methods and materials may help. In general, unless a stain requires immediate action, a garment or other fabric should be cleaned at home in the normal way, following the care label recommendations and not trying any special techniques. If the garment would normally go to a professional dry cleaner, take it there as soon as is feasible. It is always helpful to the dry cleaner if you can identify the stain and its age.

TIPS ON HOW TO CLEAN PRACTICALLY ANYTHING

Acetate fabric. Dry-cleaning is safest for this delicate fabric even if there are laundering instructions on the care label. Laundering must be done very carefully. Avoid wringing or twisting garments. Dry acetate items by draping them over a clothesline.

Air. See page 51.

Air conditioners. Clean a window air conditioner's filter or change it frequently during the air-conditioning season to keep the machine's efficiency as high as possible. When cleaning or changing the filter, vacuum clean any visible cooling coils. (Be careful not to cut yourself on sharp edges.)

Plastic foam filters can be washed at the kitchen sink, using dishwashing liquid and water. Condenser coils facing outside need cleaning too, but the unit may have to be removed from the window to do the job. In very sooty areas, or when the air conditioner is in a window over a heavily trafficked street, you may need to hire a professional firm that does steam cleaning.

All-purpose cleaners. See page 59.

Aluminum cookware. Aluminum is a soft metal. Fine scratch marks on aluminum, unavoidable in the course of regular cleaning with a soapy scrubbing pad, will be less noticeable if the utensil is scrubbed with straight, back-and-forth motions, rather than in a circular pattern.

Antique silver.   Light and dark color gradations lend old or intricately decorated pieces their charm and good looks—and add to their value. Never use a dip-type cleaner or electrolysis on antique silver. Both tend to eliminate the contrasting colors in the metal. (See page 144.)

Appliance exteriors.   The baked enamel surface on many kitchen and laundry appliances scratches quite easily, unlike the glass-hard porcelain enamel finish that is common on kitchen ranges and on some washing machine or other appliance tops. Never use an abrasive cleaner on baked enamel. Soap and water should do the job. If it doesn't, a liquid all-purpose cleaner can help, but check the label instructions to be sure the manufacturer states it's safe to use on painted surfaces. Otherwise, use a product made especially for baked enamel finishes, one that combines cleaning and waxing in one operation.

Asphalt tile.   Damp mop for day-to-day cleaning. Don't use solvent-based wax; the solvent can soften the tile.

Attic ventilation.   *See* Fan.

Auto carpeting, upholstery, and mats.   A plug-in, light-weight, hand-held vacuum cleaner works best. A cordless model is less powerful, but may work well enough on loose surface litter.

Auto finish.   It's possible to tell whether a car needs repolishing with a simple test. Splash some water on the finish: If the water forms into beads, the polish is still intact. If the water runs off in sheets, new polish is needed. (See page 150.)

Barbecue grills.   If you run a gas barbecue for about 15 minutes at the highest heat setting—after cooking is done—most grills will look reasonably clean but will still need some brushing to get rid of heavy residue. Leave the grill on a charcoal barbecue for about 20 minutes after cooking to get similar results. Any remaining baked-on dirt should yield to an abrasive powdered cleaner.

Bathroom.   See page 62.

Bathroom fixtures.   Bathroom cleaners can discolor aluminum and brass—especially brass. Rinse off excess cleaner immediately to prevent or minimize the problem.

Bleach. See page 110.

Blenders. A glass container stays better looking longer than plastic because it resists scratching and staining. A glass container should also be dishwasher safe; a plastic container probably should not go into a dishwasher. It might soften or melt if placed too close to the machine's heating element.

Brass and copper. Although a soapy steel-wool pad will do the job, copper and brass are soft metals, and steel wool will leave tiny but visible scratch marks. There are special copper and brass cleaners that should be used before steel wool if the corrosion layer isn't too thick, or after rubbing with fine steel wool reduces the visibility of any scratches. After polishing, wash the metal thoroughly to prevent polish residue from staining the metal.

Butcher block. *See* Wood work surface.

Carpet. See pages 17 and 30.

Carpet grit. Use a full-size upright vacuum cleaner or canister model with a power nozzle. (See page 30.)

Cat litter box. There may be enough residual ammonia remaining in a litter box after it has been emptied to create a hazard if the box is cleaned with chlorine bleach. That's because noxious fumes are created when ammonia and chlorine bleach are mixed together.

China dishware. It's best to wash fine china by hand with dishwashing liquid. Harsh dishwasher detergents can wear away the overglaze and metallic decorations on some fine china, and fine china can be easily chipped and broken by forceful water or jostling with pots and pans. Everyday china can be washed in the dishwasher. (See page 1.)

Chromium plate. This mirrorlike metal finish protects the base metal, keeping it from corroding. Unfortunately, chrome plate is easily worn away. Use the mildest cleaners, avoiding abrasive ones as much as possible. Protect chrome plate on an automobile with an application of auto wax.

Citrus juicer. The easiest-to-clean juicers have the cone, strainer, and juice container as a single unit. Models with several pieces have to be taken apart, washed, dried, and put back together. It's helpful if the pieces can be put into a dishwasher; check the manufacturer's instructions.

Clothes dryer. Clean a dryer's lint screen frequently, preferably after every load. That will maintain high drying efficiency and will help to prevent excessive heat buildup. Vacuum clean any visible lint collection in other parts of the machine, but leave any disassembly to a service technician. (See page 95.)

Clothes steamer. See page 129.

Coffee maker. The carafe and brew basket of a drip-type coffee maker should be cleaned after every use, because dried coffee oils can ruin the taste of even the best blend. Coffee taste may also be improved by using a special coffee-maker cleaner sold in supermarkets and hardware stores. Because minerals accumulate in the tank and tubes of automatic-drip units, it's important to clean them now and then, especially if they are used with hard water. Try running white vinegar diluted with water through the machine. It's a chore, but worth the trouble.

Compact discs. See page 147.

Continuous-cleaning oven. The porous finish of a continuous-cleaning oven is supposed to dissipate light dirt gradually at normal cooking temperatures. But major spills won't go away. You have to wipe them up right after they happen. Minor spills are slowly eliminated, partly because they spread out on the finish, which is mottled, thereby helping to disguise patches of dirt.

Do not scrub the oven or use conventional oven cleaners—either would ruin the special finish. You can protect the most exposed surface from becoming soiled in the first place. Cover the oven bottom with aluminum foil, but be careful to avoid blocking any vents in a gas oven or short-circuiting an electric element.

Copper. *See* Brass and copper.

Copper-bottomed cookware. Steel wool works for cleaning blackened pot bottoms, but bronze wool causes fewer scratch marks. Finish the job with a copper polish.

Countertop. Never use an abrasive cleanser on a plastic-laminate surface. Clean these easy-to-scratch areas with the gentlest possible product. Hot utensils can cause hard-to-remove marks and, even worse, loosen the bond between the countertop surface and the base material. In the bathroom, liquid cleaners should be rinsed off to prevent damage to the countertop finish.

Curtains. Vacuum clean thin fabrics at a reduced suction setting to prevent the fabric from being drawn into the cleaner's nozzle.

Dehumidifier. Vacuum the coils at least once a year, more often in a dusty environment. That will help maintain the appliance's performance.

Delicate fabrics. The less time some delicate fabrics spend in water, even cold water, the better. You may find that a liquid dishwashing detergent is as effective as a special-purpose product. (See page 106.)

Dish sanitizing. Some dishwashers have a final rinse cycle that uses extra-hot water, and their makers may refer to protection against colds and flus. In fact, once you put "sanitized" dishes into the cupboard, household microbes quickly settle on them, the same microbes that are on everything else in the house.

Dishwasher. See page 9.

Dishwasher detergents. See pages 1 and 4.

Dishwashing liquids. See page 4.

Disinfecting. It's really not possible to prevent the spread of germs in the house by using a disinfectant. When a medical problem requires using a germicide, ask a doctor for advice on how to proceed.

Drains. Most chemical drain cleaners are dangerous to use. It's better to keep drains open in the first place by using a sieve in the drain opening to keep hair and lint out, and by flushing drains with very hot water once a week.

Dust. A little bit of furniture spray polish on a rag makes the rag tacky enough to pick up more dust than a dry cloth. (See page 51.)

Electric blanket. Follow the manufacturer's instructions for laundering (usually a cold or warm wash and low-heat machine drying or, even better, line drying). Never have an electric blanket or pad dry-cleaned; dry-cleaning chemicals can damage the wiring.

Electric range tops. Electric elements are all self-cleaning since spills burn off quickly. If you soak an electric element in water, it may be damaged.

Clean the panel under control knobs by pulling them off. Use care scrubbing around the control panel: The markings can often be rubbed off with steel wool or an abrasive powdered cleanser.

You can raise or remove the cooktop to clean beneath it. But some electric ranges have a fixed cooktop; you have to poke your hand through the burner holes. Clean drip pans and reflector bowls with the least abrasive cleanser that will keep them looking up to par. A new spare set of drip pans or reflectors is handy for making the cooktop presentable on a moment's notice.

Electrostatic precipitator. See page 53.

Enzyme laundry products. Laundry boosters and some regular laundry detergents contain enzymes that help to dissolve stains such as the protein in egg, blood, and other body fluids, and the carbohydrate in chocolate and gravy stains.

Fabric pilling. See page 102.

Fan. Dirty fan blades impair air-moving efficiency and detract from the appliance's appearance as well. Clean metal blades cautiously to prevent bending them, which can cause unwanted vibration when the fan is turned on. A whole-house or attic fan's louvers and screening should be brushed and vacuumed at least once a season to keep air flow at the maximum possible rate.

Fine china and glassware. Harsh machine dishwasher detergents and possible jostling by jets of water inside the machine could cause damage or even breakage. You may want to play it safe and wash such items by hand.

Floor cleaning. A lightweight upright vacuum cleaner works well for picking up loose dirt from bare floors. For stains and adherent soil, however, use a damp (not wet) sponge mop or its equivalent. Try to keep water away from the seams and edges of hard-surface floor coverings, thereby minimizing the possibility that the cement will deteriorate and the floor will loosen and curl up.

Floor wax buildup. Use half a cup of powdered floor cleaner and two cups of ammonia in a gallon of cool water and fine steel wool for stubborn spots. Alternatively, try a wax remover.

Food processor. Simple, clean lines make for easy cleaning. Use a damp sponge for gaps around switches and trim.

Freezer. Self-defrosting is best. You can skip the chore and just swab down inside surfaces with a cleaning solution of baking soda (bicarbonate of soda) and water.

A chest freezer has a smooth interior and removable wire baskets or dividers instead of shelves. Use a windshield ice scraper to remove frost and hasten defrosting. An upright freezer requires more patience because you must wait for the ice to melt around the cooling coils in the shelves. If you use a tool to scrape and pry ice away to speed the process, the result could be damage to the refrigeration system that is expensive to repair.

Defrost when the food supply is low. Transfer remaining food to the refrigerator's freezer or cooling compartment. Or wrap food in layers of newspaper for insulation while you defrost.

Furniture.   The original oil or lacquer finish on a piece of furniture provides the best protection. Clean up spills quickly, before they have a chance to attack the finish. Use the softest possible cloth for dusting.

If you apply polish each time you dust, excessive wax buildup can result, with loss of the wood's natural beauty, plus difficulty in getting the kind of luster you really want. Don't wipe against the grain. Use soft insulating pads under hot, heavy, or sharp objects or containers. Treat dents or burns with steam from a steam iron, applied through several thicknesses of dampened brown wrapping paper. Consecutive applications can swell the wood sufficiently to bring it up to the surrounding level. (See pages 43–46.)

Furniture nicks and scratches.   Some polishes are colored to match the furniture wood, and thereby "fill" the marred area, but the color match must be accurate for coverup to work well.

Garbage bags.   See page 68.

Garbage disposer.   Most manufacturers suggest letting a disposer run—or at least letting the water run—for thirty to sixty seconds after grinding is finished. Some also suggest purging the disposer by filling the sink halfway with water, removing the drain stopper, and turning the machine on for a few seconds.

Garden trash disposal.   See page 164.

Glass-fiber fabric.   This material tends to shed fine particles, but it is resistant to soiling and can be very decorative. It is very fragile and should be carefully hand laundered and line dried.

Glass surfaces. Use as little glass cleaner as possible, and thereby avoid streaking. Plain water streaks the least. Try a homemade cleaner: half a cup of sudsy household ammonia, a pint of rubbing alcohol (70 percent isopropanol), a teaspoonful of liquid dishwashing detergent, and enough water to make a gallon. (See page 73.)

Glassware. It is best to wash crystal glassware by hand; there's a possibility of chipping and breakage if you wash such items in a machine. (See page 9.)

Greasy dirt on hard surfaces. Pine oil in some all-purpose cleaners helps penetrate and loosen greasy dirt.

Hair. Some people find that ordinary dishwashing liquid does fine as a shampoo, providing they aren't sensitive to its ingredients. (See page 180.)

Hair conditioners.   See page 174.

Hard-surface floor stains.   See page 28.

Harsh-feeling fabrics.   Modern detergents clean fabrics very effectively and rinse out so completely that clothes may be left feeling scratchy. A clothes dryer's tumbling action adds to the scratchiness by making thin fabrics stick together and also creating static electricity. Fabric softeners take care of both problems. (See page 103.)

Heater.   Many space heaters have shiny reflecting surfaces to help direct the heat where you want it. If the shiny area becomes dulled, the heater will become less effective. After unplugging the appliance, vacuum clean any surfaces you can reach.

Heating pad.   Never use a heating pad without its fabric cover. That will help prevent skin burns as well as damage to a pad's waterproof exterior. Wash the cover when necessary. Throw away any pad that has frayed wiring, cracks in any portion of the waterproof cover or line cord, or holes in the cover.

Heating system.   Vacuum clean radiators and fins regularly during the heating season to keep their operating efficiency at a maximum. Change or wash any filters in a warm-air heating system at least once during the heating season, as well as during the summer if the air ducts also serve as part of a central air-conditioning system.

Heavily soiled laundry.   Even though laundry detergents usually contain "antiredeposition agents" to keep dirt suspended in the wash water until it's spun from the tub, even the best agents can't cope with a great deal of dirt. That's why detergent makers advise washing heavily soiled items separately.

Hot plate.   Unplug before cleaning. If food spills, it should be possible to raise a unit's nonremovable heating elements to clean the drip pans beneath them. You may also need to clean beneath the drip pan, an area that may not be accessible without some disassembly.

Humidifier.   Molds and bacteria from humidifiers and vaporizers can trigger allergic symptoms. Although ultrasonic models do not emit live microorganisms, they have been implicated in spraying fragments of bacteria and molds into the air. Therefore, like cool-mist and evaporative humidifiers, an ultrasonic humidifier should be scrupulously cleaned daily.

After unplugging and emptying the humidifier, clean it as directed by the manufacturer or, if there are no directions, rinse the tank with a solution of one tablespoon of chlorine bleach in a pint of water; for large units, use a cup of bleach in a gallon of water. Then rinse the tank with fresh water.

A steam vaporizer, the kind that boils water and produces moisture in the form of steam, doesn't present problems of molds and bacteria. But a steam vaporizer must still be cleaned to keep it working properly. Rust accumulations in a steam vaporizer are harmless, but should be rinsed out periodically, particularly before storing the unit.

Humidifier dust.   If you use a humidifier, you may be forever wiping up white dust that settles on furniture and other surfaces, even beyond the room in which the cool-mist or ultrasonic humidifier is located. The dust is from minerals, and the particles are quite small, so they're easily inhaled into the deepest part of the lungs. The minerals from water are nontoxic, but exposure to similar particles can aggravate respiratory diseases. And toxic substances in the water, such as lead or asbestos, could pose increased health risk if inhaled. Therefore, controlling dust output is more than a matter of mere housekeeping. Use only distilled water or demineralized water in cool-mist or ultrasonic humidifiers.

Insect killers.   First unplug the appliance. It's usually difficult to poke through the outer screen or blow through it with a vacuum cleaner's exhaust. It's much easier to take the unit apart, at least to the extent of taking off the sides so that the grid can be properly brushed off.

Jewelry. Ultrasonic cleaning devices are widely used for industrial purposes, but a few such products are available for home use. They are supposed to be able to clean jewelry as well as dentures, watchbands, and other small, intricately shaped objects that can be immersed in liquid.

The home ultrasonic cleaner is plugged into an ordinary electric outlet and filled with water containing a special cleaning agent. When the cleaner is turned on, electronic circuitry creates ultrasonic waves in the solution. The agitation loosens soil on the object to be cleaned, even in inaccessible areas.

Lawn debris. See page 164.

Linen. This is a durable fabric whose appearance and "feel" improve with laundering. Linen that has been chemically treated for wrinkle resistance may not be able to withstand hot water washing.

Lint on garments. A washing machine's lint filter helps, but tumbling in a clothes dryer may be even more effective. Line drying leaves items linty, although it prolongs life, particularly of delicate items.

Litter on carpeting and hard-surface floors. Use a lightweight suction vacuum cleaner. Reserve uprights and power brushes for cleaning deep in a carpet's pile.

Metal cleaning. See page 141.

Microwave cookware. Except for the browning dishes and the crevices on some trivets, cleaning microwave cookware should be easy with just plain soap and water. Some plastic utensils have a nonstick finish. That's usually unnecessary, since sticking food is seldom a problem in microwave cooking. The nonstick finishes are probably a drawback because they scratch easily and look worn quickly. Browning dishes sear food and accumulate a fair amount of burnt-on soil that requires some cleaning effort to remove.

Microwave oven. Wipe the inside with just plain water, or water with a bit of dishwashing liquid. Spills and spatters are generally easy to wipe up with a damp (not wet) sponge. Keep the oven clean to prevent odors from developing. Pay particularly close attention to the door and the door seal. They should be kept scrupulously clean to help maintain the seal's tightness, thereby keeping any microwave leakage to the lowest possible level.

Mildew around the house. Mildew has an unpleasant odor and appearance. It's a common household mold that thrives in dark, damp, poorly ventilated places—and it can be easier to prevent than to eliminate. Chlorine bleach, diluted four parts of bleach to one part water, is a good mildewcide for general use around the house. The chemicals in moth flakes and pellets are hazardous to humans, but used judiciously in enclosed spaces, they can help to keep mildew under control.

Mildew can also be controlled by lowering the humidity in a closed-in space such as a closet. During the spring and summer, when mildew growth is greatest, use a continuously burning 60-watt bulb in a large closet to raise the temperature slightly (and thereby lower the humidity). A smaller bulb should do in a smaller enclosure. Be certain that the bulb is well away from any stored articles. The electricity cost is about $2.50 a month, at national average rates, plus the price of a bulb once a month, assuming a bulb life of 750 hours.

Mildew in bathrooms. Specialty bathroom cleaners contain chlorine bleach, an effective mildew fighter. But undiluted chlorine bleach is the best and cheapest mildew fighter. Thoroughly rinse any mildewed surface washed with bleach. Never mix bleach with other cleaning products. Bleach reacts with many acidic and alkaline household cleaners and can produce very hazardous gases. (See pages 62–64.)

No-wax floors. Damp mop once a week and use a self-cleaning cleaner-wax combination product occasionally.

Nylon. White nylon items should be washed separately because of nylon's tendency to pick up colors from other items in a laundry load. Oily substances can stick to nylon; treat these stains quickly, before they have a chance to set.

Oven. *See* Continuous-cleaning oven and Self-cleaning oven.

Oven cleaners. See page 80.

Painted surfaces. All-purpose cleaners should be tried on an inconspicuous area first. Cleaners containing pine oil can be very damaging to paint.

Paper towels. See page 83.

Phonograph records. See page 148.

Pilling on fabrics. See page 102.

Polyester. Fabrics containing polyester fibers have a strong affinity for oily substances. Treat oily stains as soon as possible after you notice them. Unfortunately, even quick attention may not result in satisfactory stain removal.

Porcelain enamel bathroom fixtures. Sinks, bathtubs, toilets, and other plumbing fixtures are generally made of metal with a heavy outside layer of glasslike porcelain. Porcelain can tolerate abrasive cleansers without wearing off, but the shiny finish will be gradually destroyed, making the fixture less resistant to staining and therefore more difficult to clean. Stick to nonabrasive cleansers on new or nearly new fixtures.

Porcelain enamel kitchen fixtures and cookware. Treat these items as gently as possible to avoid unsightly scratches that can attract dirt and make future cleaning increasingly difficult. A somewhat abrasive cleanser is usually necessary, however, to remove aluminum pot scrapes. Leave moistened cleanser on scrapes for about fifteen minutes before scrubbing.

Portable food mixers. Crevices and grooves trap food and dirt. A dampened old toothbrush can help. A plastic housing can hide dirt better than a chrome-finished one, which shows every fingerprint and smear.

Protein stains. For stains made by egg, milk, blood, and other body fluids, a laundry booster can help.

Pump sprays. Cleaners in aerosol cans don't give you as much control over where you want to spray as products that come in pump-spray containers. And you get a bonus with a pump spray by not having to pay for aerosol propellant.

Refrigerator/freezer. The condenser coil, which helps disperse heat, is outside the cabinet, where it tends to collect dust. Dust lowers the appliance's efficiency and raises the cost of running it. The condenser should be cleaned once or twice a year, particularly before hot weather sets in, because high outside temperatures impose special demands on a refrigerating system.

It's easy enough to clean a back-mounted condenser once you

pull out the refrigerator. But in many models, the coil is mounted in a compartment underneath the cabinet. Clean that area by using a condenser-coil cleaning brush (available in hardware and appliance stores) and a vacuum cleaner's crevice tool. Most manufacturers tell you to clean from the front. That's difficult if the coil is under a shield and toward the refrigerator's back. Cleaning the coil from the back after you remove the cardboard "service access" cover is a bit easier.

The drip pan under a refrigerator can develop odors from food spills that drip into it from inside the refrigerator. Check it from time to time, and rinse the pan with water.

Cleaning inside the refrigerator is best done with the mildest possible detergent or with just a damp sponge. Try to avoid scratching soft plastic surfaces. A solution of baking soda and water is probably enough to do the job if water alone doesn't work. It's particularly important to keep the door seal (gasket) clean: dirt buildup impairs the gasket's ability to keep cold air in.

Rust stains on kitchen and bathroom fixtures.   See page 90.

Self-cleaning oven.   Use the self-cleaning cycle as often as necessary. The energy cost (using national average rates) is about the same per cleaning as an application of a chemical cleaner in an oven without the self-cleaning feature.

The self-cleaning cycle turns the most stubborn spills into a powdery gray ash residue. At the end of the cycle you simply wipe off the residue. A wiping solution of vinegar and water works well.

The self-cleaning cycle produces smoke and fumes, which exit through a vent on the backguard of gas models or under a rear element of electrics. If there's a loose duct from the oven to the rear element, hard-to-clean dirt may be deposited under the cooktop during the cleaning cycle. Ventilate the kitchen during the self-cleaning cycle to prevent smoke and fume particles from becoming deposited on the kitchen's walls and ceiling.

A self-cleaning oven's door and frame usually need some scrubbing outside the door seal, where vaporized soil can leak through. Use the mildest, nonabrasive cleanser that will do the job. Avoid scrubbing the gasket itself, except very gently with a wet, slightly soapy sponge.

Shaver.   Men's electric shavers need daily cleaning. Unclip the blade cover and shake or brush clippings from the cutters and the underside of the head. Once every week or two, the shaver should be cleaned thoroughly to help maintain its ability to operate satisfactorily. That job usually involves removing, disassembling, brushing, and refitting the cutters and the head.

In time, a shaver's head may break (particularly if it's of the very thin, foil type). Shop for a replacement head. There's usually no need to junk the shaver unless there's something wrong with it or unless you want to get a better one.

Silk. Garments made of silk usually require dry cleaning because water and silk are often not compatible. However, there are some silk garments that can tolerate washing in water. Be guided by care labels.

Silver. Ordinary silver polishes usually contain a very fine abrasive, and some silver is taken off with the tarnish. The finer the polish, and the less rubbing, the smaller the amount of silver removed.

Slow cooker. Avoid an abrasive cleaner or steel wool in favor of a sponge, cloth, or plastic scrubber. Washup is easiest with an appliance that has a removable liner that can be immersed. If the liner is not removable, take care not to wet any electrical parts of the cooker.

Smoke detector. To keep detectors operating properly, vacuum them yearly, cleaning with the vacuum wand from a full-powered canister cleaner, if possible. If a detector has a fixed cover, pass the wand across the cover's openings. If a detector's cover is removable, *gently* vacuum the sensor chambers.

Spots on carpeting. See page 21.

Spots on glassware and dishes. This is a particularly annoying problem in areas of the country that have hard water. Try switching to a name-brand detergent (rather than a store brand), and if you are already using a name-brand detergent, try adding a rinse agent. These products help to reduce spotting. Many dishwashers have dispensers for such additives.

Stainless-steel cookware. Heat stains may respond to a stainless-steel polish, but a soapy steel wool pad may be necessary. (See page 143.)

Stainless steel flatware. Scratches or surface imperfections tend to affect the stain resistance of stainless steel tableware adversely. Consequently, flatware should not be cleaned with scouring powder or steel wool. It is advisable to wash stainless steel soon after using it to minimize any possible staining.

Steam iron.   If an iron's soleplate has a nonstick finish, any adherent starch or dirt should come off easily enough by wiping with a damp sponge. For an iron without a nonstick finish, clean with soap and water or a fine metal polish. Avoid any abrasive that causes scratching. When the soleplate is clean, run it over a piece of wax paper (at a low heat setting) to coat a scratched soleplate. That should make the iron easier to push. (See page 127.)

Tea stains.   Try chlorine bleach (or a cleanser containing it) on kitchen utensils and appliances.

Television set.   A television's screen attracts fingerprints, but even more of a nuisance is its tendency to accumulate dust and grime as a result of static electricity. With the set turned off, use glass cleaner sparingly. Avoid getting cleaner on the cabinet.

Toaster, toaster oven, toaster oven–broiler.   Clean the crumbs from these appliances often enough to prevent an accumulation that will smolder. Too many crumbs may also impede the operation of door-opening mechanisms.

A "continuous-clean" interior is supposed to rid itself of grease and grime at normal cooking temperatures. That doesn't seem to work very well, although a continuous-clean finish's dull, usually mottled appearance may present a cleaner appearance for a longer time than an ordinary finish. In the long run, a continuous-clean finish may be something of a disadvantage since its rough, soft surface eventually makes cleaning very difficult.

Toilet cleaning.   Stubborn stains are largely due to mineral buildup from hard water. Brush-on cleaners are best, especially if used frequently.

Travel irons.   See page 129.

Vacuum cleaners.   Clumps of dust or other debris can clog a vacuum cleaner's hose. One way to dislodge them is with a broom or mop handle inserted into the hose, or else with a straightened garment hanger used *very carefully* to prevent puncturing the hose cover. Change the paper bag or clean a cloth one as soon as the cleaner's suction drops noticeably, even if the bag doesn't seem full. Small quantities of fine, dense dirt can reduce a bag's efficiency and consequently a cleaner's suction.

Vaporizers. *See* Humidifiers.

Vinyl and vinyl asbestos floor. Damp mop for day-to-day cleaning. Self-polishing water-based wax is best for providing luster (depending on whether or not the floor has a "permanent" glossy finish). Asbestos dust is hazardous, but the asbestos in vinyl asbestos flooring is bound in, providing the floor isn't sand-papered or abraded in any other way that would cause dust to be released.

Waffle maker. The bits of food that stick to nonstick grids should be easy to dust away with a pastry brush when the grids are still slightly warm from cooking. When you want to wash away excess oil, dunk removable grids in a sinkful of warm, sudsy water. (Never dunk the appliance itself.) Flat grids for grilling usually require thorough cleaning—sometimes soaking—to remove hamburger grease or sticky cheese. Most manufacturers recommend washing the grids by hand rather than in a dishwasher.

Washing machine. Follow the manufacturer's instructions for cleaning underneath the agitator or for cleaning a lint filter. Sponge away detergent accumulations from around the top of the machine.

Reserve the hot water setting for very dirty laundry loads. Warm or cold water should do well for most clothes loads—it saves energy (hot water) and it helps to maintain the permanent-press finish. Slow agitation and spin speeds help to minimize wrinkling, and are musts for delicate items.

Water heater. To lengthen tank life, drain off some hot water periodically to keep sediment from accumulating at the bottom of the tank. In areas with hard water, draining is best done every month. Where the water is soft, every three or four months should be all right.

Wood floors. Hard urethane finishes shouldn't require more than dry mopping to stay lustrous. When waxing is necessary or desirable, spread liquid or paste solvent-based wax with an appropriate applicator. The wax acts as a cleaner as well as a finish. (Avoid using water, including water-based wax, on a wood floor except when refinishing, or if the floor has a well-sealed urethane finish.) You can buff by hand, but that's the hard way. A waxing machine makes short work of polishing and buffing. (See pages 22–27.) Stains from friction between footwear and the floor can be removed by rubbing lightly with a cloth barely dampened with turpentine or paint thinner.

Wood work surface.   Butcher blocks and other wood work surfaces used for food preparation should be cleaned thoroughly after each use to minimize bacterial growth. It's a good idea to get into the habit of using one side of a wooden cutting board for vegetables and fruits, and other side for meats, thereby avoiding excessive bacterial contamination of both sides.

Wool.   Dry cleaning is the safest method, unless the item has a care label stating that it is machine washable. If it's all right to launder wool, *use only cool or cold water*, and minimum agitation and spinning to prevent shrinkage and matting of the wool fibers. Do not use bleach.

Index